Ultimate ITIL® 4 ITSM for AI-Powered Service Management

Practical Strategies for Integrating AI with ITIL® 4 ITSM Practices to Automate Service Delivery and Drive Enterprise-Wide Transformation

Sankarsan Biswas

www.orangeava.com

First Published: November 2025

Published By: Orange Education Pvt Ltd, AVA®

Address: 9, Daryaganj, Delhi, 110002, India

275 New North Road Islington Suite 1314 London,
N1 7AA, United Kingdom

ISBN (PBK): 978-93-49888-36-4
ISBN (E-BOOK): 978-93-49888-68-5

Scan the QR code to explore our entire catalogue

www.orangeava.com

Dedicated To

My Beloved Parents:

Late Shri Santosh Kumar Biswas,
Late Mrs. Swapna Biswas.

And

My Dearest Wife, Nandita as well as my Daughter,
Sudarshana.

About the Author

Sankarsan Biswas is a distinguished IT Service Management (ITSM) professional, thought leader, and author with over three decades of experience in global IT industry. A PeopleCert Ambassador and accredited ITIL trainer, he holds the elite credentials of ITIL Master, ITIL 4 Managing Professional, ITIL 4 Strategic Leader, and ITIL V3 Expert. His career is dedicated to helping enterprises achieve service excellence, resilience, and governance maturity through ITIL, COBIT, and ISO frameworks.

As an author, Sankarsan has written *Ultimate Guide to ITIL4 Foundation Certification Guide* and *Ultimate ITIL 4 for Scaling ITSM in Enterprises*. The first serves as a practical handbook for ITIL learners, while the second offers deep insights, case studies, automation strategies, and enterprise-scale adoption techniques–reflecting his commitment to advancing ITSM practices with actionable, real-world guidance.

He has led ITSM consulting assignments across aviation, transportation, telecom, banking, and energy sectors in the Middle East and India–designing and implementing ITIL-aligned processes, governance models, RFPs, and service management transformations. Previously, he held senior leadership roles at IBM, HCL, and ANZ Grindlays Bank (now Standard Chartered), overseeing global service delivery across UK, Ireland, Poland, the Middle East, and India. His expertise spans ITSM, information security, data center operations, DR/BCP, transition management, and vendor governance.

A passionate mentor, he has trained hundreds in ITIL and ITSM, served as Academic Head for Cloud and IT Infrastructure programs at iNurture Education Solutions, and designed curricula bridging academia and industry.

Sankarsan embodies the ITIL spirit of continual improvement–combining global exposure, deep expertise, and visionary guidance to help organizations thrive in a rapidly evolving digital landscape!

About the Technical Reviewer

Michael Imhoff Nielsen is an Expert Director for Imhoff Consult, specializing in ITSM. With 40 years of experience in the IT industry, he has worked as a developer, consultant, assessor, instructor, and mentor. He holds certifications in ITIL, COBIT, SIAM, PRINCE2, and Prosci Change Management, and is an accredited instructor and assessor for ITIL and SIAM. As an ITSM consultant, he has been part of short-term engagements and long-term projects, ranging from a few days to several years, across various organizations.

Michael's passion for sharing knowledge and driving improvement has led him to engage in volunteer work. He served on the board of the IT Service Management Forum Denmark for a decade and contributed to several local and global sub-committees and working groups. He also spent three years on the IT Service Management Forum International Executive Board, and five years as a SIAM network facilitator at the Danish IT Society. In addition, he has reviewed several publications, including ITIL V3 *Service Operation*, *Service Design*, and ITIL4 *Drive Stakeholder Value*, and was part of the translation team for the ITIL V3 *Glossary* and the ITIL *Foundation Handbook* into Danish.

In 2013, Michael was awarded the title of Fellow in Service Management by the PRISM Institute, recognizing his extensive experience, and contributions to the field.

Acknowledgments

I would like to express my heartfelt gratitude to all those who supported and encouraged me throughout the journey of writing this book, ***Ultimate ITIL® 4 ITSM for AI-Powered Service Management.***

First and foremost, I am deeply thankful to the readers of my earlier books, *Ultimate ITIL4 Foundation Certification Guide*, and *Ultimate ITIL4 for Scaling ITSM in Enterprise*, whose trust, feedback, and success stories inspired me to take on this next challenge. Their continued encouragement fueled my determination to write a book that goes beyond the foundation, aiming to demystify AI in ITSM practices.

My deepest appreciation goes to my dearest wife and beloved daughter, whose unwavering encouragement and belief in me instilled the confidence needed to embark on, and complete this book. Without their support, this endeavor would not have been possible.

I am sincerely grateful to the enterprises I had the privilege to work with, which provided me with invaluable exposure to AI in IT Service Management practices. The hands-on experience of understanding the impact of AI in processes, procedures, and real-world implementations played a crucial role in shaping the insights shared in this book.

I would also like to extend my gratitude to Mr. Michael Imhoff for his technical review and meticulous scrutiny. His insights and suggestions helped to ensure the relevance, accuracy, and authenticity of the content.

Finally, I appreciate the tremendous support from my professional colleagues and friends, including the editorial team at Orange Education Pvt. Ltd., who gave me the time, space, and encouragement to complete this work. Given the vastness and dynamism of AI as a concept, it was a challenge to explain without making the book overly voluminous. Their understanding made this ambitious project of mine achievable.

Thank you all for being an indispensable part of this incredible journey!

Preface

The world of IT Service Management (ITSM) is at the edge of a profound transformation. For decades, ITIL and related frameworks have guided organizations in structuring, stabilizing, and improving service delivery. But today, Artificial Intelligence (AI) is no longer just an emerging trend – it is reshaping the very foundations of how IT services are designed, delivered, and experienced.

This book, ***Ultimate ITIL® 4 ITSM for AI-Powered Service Management*** was born from my conviction that ITSM professionals must not only understand AI, but also harness it to unlock new dimensions of value. Traditional approaches to incidents, problems, changes, and requests are giving way to intelligent workflows, predictive analytics, and conversational experiences. We are moving from reactive service desks to proactive, self-healing ecosystems.

As an ITIL Master and practitioner with decades of experience, I have seen organizations succeed and struggle with ITSM transformations. The difference often lies in whether they adapt their practices to emerging realities, or remain bound to legacy ways of working. AI represents both an opportunity and a challenge – it promises speed, accuracy, and insight, but demands responsibility, governance, and trust!

This book aims to provide a roadmap for IT leaders, practitioners, and students who want to scale ITSM in the AI era. It blends the rigor of ITIL4 with the possibilities of AI, machine learning, and automation. Each chapter combines theory, practical workflows, and real-world examples so that you can apply the concepts immediately within your organization.

Ultimately, this is not just a book about tools or frameworks. It is about rethinking service management for a future where humans and AI collaborate to co-create value. I invite you to read with an open mind, reflect on your own service challenges, and experiment boldly with AI-driven practices.

Welcome to the journey of ITSM transformed – intelligent, adaptive, and future-ready.

This book is organized into 14 chapters, covering how Artificial Intelligence is transforming IT Service Management by enhancing traditional ITIL4 practices with automation, machine learning, and predictive insights. It covers practical strategies, workflows, and real-world examples to help organizations scale ITSM with AI, while ensuring governance, trust, and continual improvement. Designed for IT leaders, practitioners, and learners, it serves as a roadmap for building intelligent, adaptive, and future-ready service management.

Chapter 1: This chapter sets the stage by demystifying what AI truly means in the context of IT operations. It introduces foundational concepts such as Machine Learning (ML), Natural Language Processing (NLP), and Deep Learning (DL), while clarifying the distinctions between automation and intelligence. Readers will gain a clear view of how AI has evolved, and why it matters now more than ever in service management.

Chapter 2: This chapter revisits the core principles of ITSM, and explains how ITIL4 redefines service management through flexibility, value co-creation, and an integrated Service Value System. Readers will understand how ITSM is structured, what makes ITIL4 more adaptable, and where traditional models need AI-powered enhancements.

Chapter 3: This chapter identifies the key operational challenges in ITSM such as repetitive tasks, delayed responses, and information overload—that are ideal candidates for AI intervention. It offers a balanced view of achievable short-term wins, and the potential for long-term strategic transformation through intelligent service automation.

Chapter 4: This chapter introduces the key types of AI such as machine learning, deep learning, and natural language processing in a service management context. It explains how these technologies work in simple terms, and how they power everyday ITSM functions like classification, sentiment detection, and automation.

Chapter 5: This chapter explores how popular ITSM platforms such as ServiceNow, ManageEngine, and Jira are already embedding AI into their ecosystems. It demystifies vendor claims, and gives readers a realistic view of what AI features are practical, and how they can enhance day-to-day service desk as well as operations work.

Chapter 6: This chapter dives into AIOps—Artificial Intelligence for IT Operations—and its impact on proactive monitoring, root cause analysis, and incident prevention. It maps AIOps capabilities to ITIL4 practices, and outlines how intelligent operations can reduce noise and improve service resilience.

Chapter 7: This chapter provides use cases showing how AI assists with incident triage, auto-classification, and root cause prediction. It emphasizes how AI can improve response times, reduce escalations, and shift service operations from reactive to proactive modes.

Chapter 8: This chapter explains how AI helps to assess change risk, streamline service requests, and build intelligent knowledge bases. Readers will learn how AI supports seamless fulfillment workflows, deflection strategies, and self-service experiences.

Chapter 9: This chapter maps AI's contributions across ITIL4's guiding principles and value chain activities. It shows how AI supports value co-creation, enhances governance, and fits into continual improvement initiatives.

Chapter 10: This chapter outlines how organizations can assess their readiness for AI, from data maturity and process standardization to cultural adoption. It includes a practical checklist and phased approach to starting small, and scaling with confidence.

Chapter 11: This chapter discusses how to manage AI responsibly by addressing data privacy, algorithmic bias, and compliance concerns. It connects AI practices with ITIL4 governance and organizational risk management frameworks.

Chapter 12: This chapter provides a strategic and tactical framework for adopting AI across ITSM. It includes AI maturity models, success metrics, and tips for integrating AI into continual improvement and service value realization.

Chapter 13: This chapter explores how AI will reshape roles within ITSM—from service desk agents to process owners. It highlights the importance of upskilling, adapting mindsets, and embracing a hybrid human-AI service model.

Chapter 14: This chapter looks ahead to the next wave of innovation, including generative AI, conversational bots, and design thinking in service delivery. It offers predictions and preparation steps for futureproofing ITSM capabilities.

Get a Free eBook

We hope you are enjoying your recently purchased book! Your feedback is incredibly valuable to us, and to all other readers looking for great books.

If you found this book helpful or enjoyable, we would truly appreciate it, if you could take a moment to leave a short review with a 5 star rating on Amazon. It helps us grow, and lets other readers discover our books.

As a thank you, we would love to send you a free digital copy of this book, and a **30%** discount code on your next cart value on our official websites:

www.orangeava.com

www.orangeava.in (For Indian Subcontinent)

☑ **Here's how:**

Leave a review for the book on Amazon.

Take a screenshot of your review, and send an email to **info@orangeava.com** (it can be just the confirmation screen).

Once, we receive your screenshot, we will send you the digital file, within 24 hours.

Thank you so much for your support – it means a lot to us!

Colored Images

Please follow the links or scan the QR codes to download the ***Images*** of the book:

You can find code bundles of our books on our official Github Repository. Go to the following link to and QR code to explore the further:

https://github.com/orgs/ava-orange-education/repositories

Please follow the link to download the Colored Images of the book:
https://rebrand.ly/qcvajvy

In case there's an update to the code, it will be updated on the existing GitHub repository.

Errata

We take immense pride in our work at **Orange Education Pvt Ltd,** and follow best practices to ensure the accuracy of our content to provide an indulging reading experience to our subscribers. Our readers are our mirrors, and we use their inputs to reflect and improve upon human errors, if any, that may have occurred during the publishing processes involved. To let us maintain the quality and help us reach out to any readers who might be having difficulties due to any unforeseen errors, please write to us at :

errata@orangeava.com

Your support, suggestions, and feedback are highly appreciated.

DID YOU KNOW

Did you know that Orange Education Pvt Ltd offers eBook versions of every book published, with PDF and ePub files available? You can upgrade to the eBook version at **www.orangeava.com** and as a print book customer, you are entitled to a discount on the eBook copy. Get in touch with us at: **info@orangeava.com** for more details.

At **www.orangeava.com**, you can also read a collection of free technical articles, sign up for a range of free newsletters, and receive exclusive discounts and offers on Print Books and eBooks.

PIRACY

If you come across any illegal copies of our works in any form on the internet, we would be grateful if you would provide us with the location address or website name. Please contact us at **info@orangeava.com** with a link to the material.

ARE YOU INTERESTED IN AUTHORING WITH US?

If there is a topic that you have expertise in, and you are interested in either writing or contributing to a book, please write to us at **business@orangeava.com**. We are on a journey to help developers and tech professionals to gain insights on the present technological advancements and innovations happening across the globe and build a community that believes Knowledge is best acquired by sharing and learning with others. Please reach out to us to learn what our audience demands and how you can be part of this educational reform. We also welcome ideas from tech experts and help them build learning and development content for their domains.

REVIEWS

Please leave a review. Once you have read and used this book, why not leave a review on the site that you purchased it from? Potential readers can then see and use your unbiased opinion to make purchase decisions. We at Orange Education would love to know what you think about our products, and our authors can learn from your feedback. Thank you!

For more information about Orange Education, please visit **www.orangeava.com**.

Table of Contents

1. **Introduction to AI in the Modern IT Landscape** 1
   - Introduction 1
   - Structure 1
   - Understanding What AI is and What it is Not 2
     - *Understanding What AI is Not* 6
   - The Evolution of AI in IT Operations 9
   - From Automation to Intelligence: Key Terminologies 11
     - *Machine Learning* 12
     - *Natural Language Processing* 13
     - *Deep Learning* 15
     - *Artificial Intelligence for IT Operations* 17
   - Conclusion 19
   - Multiple Choice Questions 20
   - Answers 21
   - Questions 21
   - Key Terms 22
2. **Understanding the Core of IT Service Management** 24
   - Introduction 24
   - Structure 24
   - Understanding ITSM and Reshaping It through ITIL4 25
     - *Introduction to ITSM* 25
     - *Traditional ITSM: Process-Centric and Reactive* 26
     - *The Road Travelled by ITIL4 for Reshaping ITSM* 27
   - Service Value System and Service Value Chain 28
     - *Understanding the Service Value System* 29
     - *Governance* 31
     - *Understanding the Service Value Chain* 31
     - *Practices* 33
     - *Continual Improvement* 33

More about Service Value Chain ... 34
Value Streams: Beyond the Lifecycle ... 35
ITSM Needs Intelligence to Stay Relevant ... 37
Gaps in Decision-Making Without Intelligence ... 38
The Case for Intelligent ITSM ... 39
The Need for Intelligent ITSM ... 39
Conclusion ... 40
Multiple Choice Questions ... 40
Answers ... 41
Questions ... 41
Key Terms ... 42
3. Indispensibility of AI in Modern ITSM ... 44
Introduction ... 44
Structure ... 44
Key Pain Points in ITSM Ripe for AI ... 44
Repetition: The Invisible Drain on IT Resources ... 45
Delays: Reactive Models Compromise SLAs ... 46
Data Overload: Too Much Noise, Too Few Insights ... 46
Inconsistent Decision-Making and Prioritization ... 47
Skill Mismatch and Reassignment Loops ... 48
Underused Knowledge Bases ... 49
Lack of Real-Time Operational Intelligence ... 49
AI's Potential for Boosting Efficiency, Accuracy, and Proactivity ... 50
Boosting Efficiency: Doing More with Less ... 51
Improving Accuracy: Getting It Right the First Time ... 52
Driving Proactivity: From Reactive to Preventive ITSM ... 53
Quick Wins versus Long-Term Transformation ... 54
Quick Wins: Small Steps, Big Impact ... 54
Long-Term Transformation: Building a Cognitive ITSM Ecosystem ... 55
Balancing Both: A Phased, Scalable Strategy ... 56
Conclusion ... 57

Multiple Choice Questions....58
Answers....59
Questions....59
Key Terms....60
4. Understanding AI for Service Teams....61
Introduction....61
Structure....62
Machine Learning, Deep Learning, Natural Language Processing....62
Why AI Concepts Matter for Service Management....62
Understanding Machine Learning: Learning from Experience....62
Understanding Deep Learning: Going Deeper with DATA....64
Understanding Natural Language Processing: Making Sense of Human Language....65
Supervised versus Unsupervised Learning....67
Understanding Supervised Learning....68
Use Cases in ITSM....68
Understanding Unsupervised Learning....68
Use Cases in ITSM....68
Comparison: Supervised versus Unsupervised Learning....69
Pros and Cons....69
Unsupervised Learning....69
Real-Life Examples of Supervised Learning in ITSM....70
Real-Life Examples of Unsupervised Learning in ITSM....70
Application of These Concepts in a Service Environment....70
Supervised Learning in Service Environments....71
Unsupervised Learning in Service Environments....71
Application in Real-World Environment....72
Machine Learning (ML)....73
Deep Learning (DL)....73
Natural Language Processing (NLP)....73

Supervised Learning 73

Unsupervised Learning 74

Selecting the Right AI Technique Based on Problem, Type, and Context 74

Conclusion.... 74

Multiple Choice Questions.... 75

Answers.... 76

Questions.... 76

Key Terms....77

5. AI-Powered Tools Already in Use....79

Introduction.... 79

Structure....80

Introduction to Generative AI....80

Understanding Generative AI....80

Understanding The Building Blocks.... 81

Real-World Applications in ITSM....81

Limitations and Ethical Considerations.... 82

Getting Started: How to Explore GenAI in ITSM Safely.... 83

The Road Ahead: Strategic Implications.... 83

Summary.... 83

Exploring the Capabilities of ChatGPT and Similar TOOLs in a Service Context.... 84

From Conversational Curiosity to Service Desk Powerhouse.... 84

Key Capabilities of ChatGPT-Like Tools for ITSM.... 84

Real-World Scenarios.... 85

Scenario 1: End-User Support via Chat.... 85

Scenario 2: Agent Sidekick.... 86

Scenario 3: Knowledge Base Drafting.... 86

Challenges and Considerations.... 86

Accuracy and Hallucination.... 86

Security and Data Privacy.... 87

Auditability and Governance 87
Training on Organization-Specific Context 87
Integrating These Tools Within Organizations 87
Future Potential 87
Summary 88
Using AI features in ServiceNow, ManageEngine, Jira, and Other Platforms 88
ServiceNow: The Front-Runner in AI-Powered ITSM 88
ManageEngine ServiceDesk Plus: Practical AI for Mid-Market 89
Jira Service Management: Agile + AI 90
Other Emerging Platforms with AI Capabilities 91
Challenges in Evaluating AI Features 91
Strategic Takeaways for Service Leaders 92
Summary 92
Examples: Ticket Classification, Sentiment Analysis, Auto-Remediation 92
Ticket Classification: From Chaos to Clarity 93
How AI Enhances Ticket Classification 93
Sentiment Analysis: Listening between the Lines 93
Auto-Remediation: Closing the Loop Without Human Intervention 94
Bringing It Together: The Intelligent Service Desk 96
Summary and Next Steps 96
Vendor-Neutral Perspective on Capabilities 96
Principles of a Vendor-Neutral Evaluation 97
AI Maturity Checklist: Applied across Platforms 98
Vendor-Neutral Best Practices for AI Adoption 98
Real-World Comparison Scenario 99
Summary: AI Without the Logo 99
Conclusion 99
Multiple Choice Questions 100
Answers 101

Questions ... 101
Key Terms ... 102
Appendices ... 103
Appendix A ... 103
Suggestive AI Capability Maturity Levels in ITSM Platforms ... 103
Appendix B ... 104
AI Scope and Feature Breadth ... 104
Appendix C ... 104
Data Learning and Model Adaptability ... 104
Appendix D ... 104
Workflow Integration ... 104
Appendix E ... 105
Privacy, Security, and Governance ... 105
Appendix F ... 105
User Experience and Adoption ... 105
Appendix G ... 106
Scoring and Maturity Levels based on the Scores from the Preceding Five Appendices ... 106
6. AIOps and Intelligent Operations ... 107
Introduction ... 107
Structure ... 107
Understanding AIOps ... 108
Defining AIOps: More Than Just a Buzzword ... 108
The Key Pillars of AIOps ... 109
Requirement for AIOps ... 109
Real-Life Example 1: A Bank's Nighttime Outage ... 109
Real-Life Example 2: E-Commerce Platform Outage Prevention ... 110
Real-Life Example 3: Financial Institution's Login Issue ... 111
Debunking AIOps Misconceptions ... 111
AIOps and the Human Element ... 111
The Bottom Line ... 112

How AI Supports Event Correlation, Anomaly Detection, Root Cause Analysis 113

Event Correlation: From Chaos to Context 113

Anomaly Detection: Spotting the Unusual Before It Breaks 114

Root Cause Analysis (RCA): Finding the "Why" Behind the Incident 114

Combined Impact in a Service Environment 115

Final Thoughts 115

Mapping AIOps to ITIL4's Monitoring and Event Management, Incident, and Problem Management 115

Monitoring and Event Management: Moving from Alert Overload to Intelligent Insight 116

Real-Life Example 116

Incident Management: Detecting and Resolving Faster, Smarter 117

Real-Life Example 117

Problem Management: From Guesswork to Data-Driven Prevention 117

Real-Life Example 118

Final Thoughts 118

Role of GenAI in Synthesizing Operational Data and Recommendations 119

Understanding the Shift: From Data to Understanding 119

Real-Life Use Case 1: Incident Summary and Action Suggestion 120

Real-Life Use Case 2: Conversational RCA and Knowledge Capture 120

Real-Life Use Case 3: Enhancing Problem Management with Recommendations 121

Where GenAI Fits in the ITIL4 Service Lifecycle 121

Challenges and Considerations 122

The Human-AI Partnership 122

Final Thoughts 122

Conclusion.....123

Multiple Choice Questions.....123

Answers.....124

Questions.....124

Key Terms.....125

7. Revolutionizing Incident and Problem Management with AI..... 127

Introduction.....127

Structure.....128

Auto-Routing, Ticket Triaging, Root Cause Prediction.....128

Auto-Routing: Precision Assignment at Machine Speed.....128

Real-Life Example.....128

Ticket Triaging: Smarter Classification and Prioritization.....128

Real-Life Example.....129

Automated Incident Summaries: Reducing Manual Burden.....129

Real-Life Example.....129

Root Cause Prediction: Pattern Learning from Historical Data.....129

Real-Life Example.....129

Root Cause Analysis (RCA): Augmented by AI, Not Replaced.....129

Real-Life Example.....130

Noise Reduction and Pattern Detection.....130

AI-Powered Noise Reduction: Precision at Scale.....131

Real-Life Example.....131

Pattern Detection: Discovering the Undiscovered.....132

Real-Life Example.....132

Combined Power: Correlation with Context.....132

Real-Life Example.....133

Case studies of AI Enhancing Operational Excellence.....133

Telecom Giant Cuts Alert Fatigue by 90% Using AIOps.....133

Healthcare Group Automates Ticket Triage for Clinical Systems.....134

Insurance Firm Uses ChatGPT Integration for Automated Summaries......134
Retail Chain Detects Weekly Pattern in POS Incidents......135
Banking Institution Predicts Root Cause of API Failures......135
Manufacturing Firm Reduces Ticket Volume via Self-Healing Scripts......135
University IT Helpdesk Improves FCR with AI-Based Auto-Routing......136
Government IT Agency Detects Anomalies in Change Management......136
Logistics Company Prevents Downtime via Predictive Maintenance......136
Energy Utility Improves User Sentiment Monitoring......137
Conclusion......138
Multiple Choice Questions......139
Answers......140
Questions......140
Key Terms......141
8. AI-Enhanced Change Enablement, Request, and Knowledge Management......143
Introduction......143
Structure......144
Change Risk Analysis and Automation......144
Components of AI-Driven Risk Analysis......144
Use Case: Real-Life Example – Telecom Enterprise......145
Automation Opportunities in Change Enablement......146
Challenges and Best Practices......147
Strategic Takeaways......147
Virtual Assistants and Smart Knowledge Bases......148
Virtual Assistants in ITSM......148
Real-Life Example: Virtual Assistant (VA) in a University IT Helpdesk......149
Smart Knowledge Bases......149

From Static to Smart 150

Real-Life Example: Smart Knowledge Base in a Managed Services Firm 151

Virtual Assistants + Smart KBs = Self-service Synergy 151

Implementation Considerations 152

Predicting Ticket Volumes and Request Fulfillment 153

Core Components of AI-Powered Forecasting 154

Predicting Request Fulfillment Patterns 154

Real-Life Example 1: Predicting Ticket Volume in a Retail Company 155

Real-Life Example 2: Request Fulfillment Optimization in an Insurance Company 155

Operationalizing Predictions in ITSM Tools 156

Conclusion 157

Multiple Choice Questions 158

Answers 159

Questions 159

Key Terms 160

9. AI and the ITIL4 Service Value System 161

Introduction 161

Structure 161

How AI Supports Guiding Principles: Focus on Value, Optimize, and Automate 162

Focus on Value 162

Start Where You Are 162

Progress Iteratively with Feedback 163

Collaborate and Promote Visibility 163

Think and Work Holistically 164

Keep It Simple and Practical 164

Optimize and Automate 165

AI in Governance, Service Design, and Continual Improvement 166

AI in Governance 166

AI in Service Design 167

AI Improving Continually 167

Step 1: What is the Vision? 169

Step 2: Where are we now? 169

Step 3: Where do we want to be? 170

Step 4: How do we get there? 170

Step 5: Take Action 170

Step 6: Did we get there? 171

Step 7: How do we keep the Momentum going? 171

Building AI into the Service Value Chain Activities 172

Plan 172

Improve 173

Engage 173

Design and Transition 174

Obtain/Build 174

Deliver and Support 175

Engage 176

Plan 177

Design and Transition 177

Obtain/Build 177

Deliver and Support 178

Improve 178

Conclusion 179

Multiple Choice Questions 180

Answers 182

Questions 182

Key Terms 183

10. Preparing ITSM Environments for AI Adoption 184

Introduction 184

Structure 184

AI-Readiness Assessment 185

The Importance of Conducting an AI-Readiness Assessment 185

Core Dimensions of AI Readiness 185

Sample AI-Readiness Maturity Model 187

Real-Life Examples 187

Conducting the Assessment: Step-by-Step 188

Skills, Data, Culture, and Tooling Checklist 189

Skills: Building a Future-Ready Workforce 190

Data: The Fuel That Powers AI 191

Culture: The Soil Where AI Takes Root 192

Tooling: The AI-Ready ITSM Ecosystem 193

How to Start Small and Scale Responsibly 194

Starting Small is a Strategic Approach, not a Cautious One 194

Choosing the Right "First Use Case" 195

Real-Life Example: Mid-Sized Financial Institution (ServiceNow) 196

Framework for Responsible Scaling 196

Guardrails for Responsible AI Scaling 197

Building Trust through Incremental Wins 198

Conclusion 199

Multiple Choice Questions 200

Answers 201

Questions 201

Key Terms 202

11. Governance, Risk, and Ethics in AI-powered ITSM 203

Introduction 203

Structure 204

Ensuring Transparency, Explainability, and Fairness 204

How These Principles Define Responsible AI Implementation in ITSM 204

How These Principles Matter in ITSM 205

The GenAI Challenge: Managing Hallucinations and Inaccuracy 205

Use Case: Transparent Auto-Triage System 206

Frameworks and Best Practices 207
Technology Enablers 207
Data Privacy and Compliance (GDPR, ISO 42001, and more) 208
Understanding GDPR: It is More Than Consent 208
ISO/IEC 42001: The First International AI Management Standard 209
Addressing Personally Identifiable Information (PII) in AI Workflows 210
Cross-Border Data Processing: Navigating Jurisdictional Complexity 210
Transparency, Consent, and User Communication 211
Governance Integration with ITIL4 211
Future Outlook: Evolving Laws and Adaptive AI Governance 211
AI-Powered ITSM Data Privacy and Compliance Checklist 212
Aligning with Organizational Risk Frameworks 213
Understanding Organizational Risk Frameworks 213
Mapping AI Risks in ITSM to Enterprise Risk Domains 215
Embedding AI Risk into Existing Risk Registers 216
Aligning Roles and Responsibilities 216
Implementing Controls and Mitigations 217
Aligning with ITIL4 Governance Practices 218
Reporting and Escalation 219
Future Outlook: Toward Dynamic and Adaptive Risk Management 220
Conclusion 220
Multiple Choice Questions 221
Answers 222
Questions 222
Key Terms 223
12. Building a Smarter ITSM Roadmap 225
Introduction 225
Structure 225
Strategic and Tactical Adoption Models 226

Strategic Adoption Model: Setting the North Star ... 226
Tactical Adoption Model: Translating Vision into Action ... 227
Strategic versus Tactical: Complementary Forces ... 228
Common Pitfalls and How to Avoid Them ... 229
Integrating with Continual Improvement ... 230
Maturity Models and Continual Improvement Loops ... 231
Understanding Maturity Models in AI-Driven ITSM ... 231
Using Maturity Models to Drive Planning and Prioritization ... 232
The Role of Continual Improvement Loops ... 233
Combining the Models for Maximum Impact ... 233
Common Mistakes to Avoid ... 235
Metrics to Measure Impact and Value Realization ... 236
The Importance of Measurement in AI-Driven ITSM ... 236
Categories of AI-Driven Metrics in ITSM ... 236
Operational Efficiency Metrics ... 237
Service Quality and Accuracy Metrics ... 238
User Experience Metrics ... 238
Business Value Metrics ... 239
Establishing Baselines and Benchmarks ... 240
Real-Life Scenario: Measuring Impact in a Telecom Service Desk ... 240
Linking Metrics to Business Objectives ... 241
Dashboards and Reporting Tools ... 242
Common Pitfalls in Measuring AI Impact ... 242
Embedding Metrics into the Continual Improvement Cycle ... 243
Conclusion ... 244
Multiple Choice Questions ... 245
Answers ... 246
Questions ... 246
Key Terms ... 247
13. The Evolving Role of The ITSM Professional ... 249
Introduction ... 249

Structure....250
Augmenting – Not Replacing – Service Professionals with AI....250
Real-Life Example: Service Desk at a Global Bank....252
Upskilling and Mindset Shifts....255
The Skills of the Past versus The Skills of the Future....257
From Task Execution → to Strategic Orchestration....257
From Static Knowledge → to Continuous Learning....257
Mindset Shifts: Beyond Tools, Towards Transformation....258
Use Case: Upskilling at a Managed Services Provider (MSP)....258
The Human Side of Intelligent Service Delivery....260
Real-World Use Case: AI and Empathy in Action....260
Key Human Qualities That Elevate AI-Augmented Service....261
Human-AI Collaboration: Not Replacement, but Augmentation....262
Service Design Thinking: Embedding Humanity in Journeys....262
Practical Recommendations....262
Real-Life Story: The Executive That Called Back....263
Final Deduction: The Soul of Service....263
Conclusion....263
Multiple Choice Questions....264
Answers....266
Questions....266
Key Terms....267
14. What is Next? GenAI, ChatGPT, and Beyond....268
Introduction....268
Structure....268
The Role of Generative AI in ITSM....269
Understanding Generative AI in the ITSM Context....269
Understanding the Difference Between GenAI and Traditional AI in ITSM....269
Final Deduction: Shaping the Future, Responsibly....271

AI in Service Experience, Design Thinking, and Proactive Services 272

Understanding Service Experience in ITSM 272

How AI Enhances Service Experience 272

Applying Design Thinking to ITSM with AI 272

Final Deduction: AI with Empathy, Design with Intent 274

Long-Term Trends Shaping AI in Service Management 275

Convergence of AI and ITSM Platforms 275

Embedded AI Capabilities Become Native 275

Unified Data Lakes and Intelligence Layers 275

Rise of Autonomous ITSM 276

From Automation to Autonomy 276

Event-Driven, Self-Healing Systems 276

AI-Powered Experience Personalization 276

Role-Aware and Context-Aware Services 277

Predictive Engagement Models 277

Democratization of AI in ITSM 277

No-Code AI Builders for Service Teams 277

Prompt Engineering as a Core Skill 277

Regulation, Ethics, and Trust as Pillars 277

Rise of AI Governance Frameworks 278

Transparent and Traceable AI 278

Integration of Emotional and Conversational AI 278

Sentiment-Aware Service Delivery 279

Multimodal Interfaces 279

AI for Sustainable and Green ITSM 279

Energy-Aware Optimization 279

Sustainability Dashboards 279

Continual Learning and Adaptive AI Models 279

Feedback-Driven Improvement 280

Federated and Privacy-Preserving Learning 280

Final Deduction: Designing for Tomorrow, Acting Today 280

Conclusion.. 280
Multiple Choice Questions..281
Answers...282
Questions...283
Key Terms...283
Index..285

CHAPTER 1
Introduction to AI in the Modern IT Landscape

Introduction

In today's hyper-connected, cloud-driven world, IT environments are more complex than ever before. Traditional tools and reactive methods are struggling to keep pace with the scale, speed, and expectations of modern service delivery. Enter **Artificial Intelligence (AI)** – not as a buzzword, but as a transformative force reshaping how we manage, support, and improve IT services.

But what exactly is AI? What does it mean in the practical sense for IT professionals, service managers, or support teams? This chapter cuts through the hype to provide a clear, grounded understanding of AI – and sets the foundation for how it fits within the ITSM ecosystem.

Hence, whether you are hearing these concepts for the first time, or looking to sharpen your strategic understanding, this chapter will help you grasp not just what AI is, but why it matters now more than ever in service management.

Structure

In this chapter, we will discuss the following topics:

- Understanding What AI is and What it is Not
- The Evolution of AI in IT Operations
- From Automation to Intelligence: Key Terminologies

Understanding What AI is and What it is Not

To understand how AI can enhance IT Service Management (ITSM), we must first understand what AI truly is—and what it is not. Misconceptions around AI are common, often shaped by science fiction or exaggerated marketing. Before diving into machine learning, natural language processing, or AIOps, we need to build a clear, realistic foundation.

So, let us begin by answering a fundamental question: **What is Artificial Intelligence—and what is it not?**

At its core, Artificial Intelligence (AI) is about enabling machines to perform tasks that typically require human intelligence such as learning from data, recognizing patterns, understanding language, or making decisions. It is not about building robots with feelings or replacing humans with digital clones. Instead, AI in ITSM is about helping systems make sense of large volumes of data, identify issues faster, and support smarter decisions.

However, many people still confuse AI with automation, analytics, or even science fiction. The truth is: AI is not magic, and it is not human. It does not "think" or "understand" in the way we do. What it does do—very well—is *detect patterns, make predictions, and trigger actions, based on training from the past data.*

To separate the myth from reality, we will explore not just what AI is, but also what it is not—so that we can move forward with clarity, not confusion.

The word, "Artificial" means something that is made or produced by humans rather than occurring naturally.

In simple terms, we can say that Artificial is man-made, not natural.

Examples:

- Artificial light = light from a bulb, not the sun
- Artificial flavor = man-made chemicals mimicking natural taste

Artificial Intelligence means teaching machines to think and act like humans, so that they can solve problems, make decisions, or understand things, just like we do.

AI is when computers or machines are able to do tasks that normally need human intelligence.

Everyday examples of AI:

- Mobile phone voice assistant (such as Siri or Google Assistant).
- Chatbots that answer your questions on websites.

- Netflix recommending shows you might like to watch.
- Google Maps predicting traffic, and giving the fastest routes.
- Face recognition, when unlocking your phone.

It is not natural like human thinking – it is created by people using computer programs that let machines learn from data and past experiences. Artificial Intelligence is the ability of machines to "learn, decide, and act smartly"–just like humans, but using data and algorithms.

In the context of Artificial Intelligence:

- "Artificial" refers to intelligence that is created by humans, not something that naturally exists, such as human or animal intelligence.
- It is a simulation of human-like thinking, decision-making, or learning – but done by machines or software.

After understanding the term artificial, let us explore intelligence in the context of IT Service Management (ITSM) and the DIKW model, with a clear focus on how it translates into smarter decision-making and value co-creation.

In ITSM, intelligence refers to the capability to make informed, timely, and effective decisions using data, information, and knowledge. It enables organizations to:

- Detect issues proactively.
- Automate responses based on context.
- Optimize resources dynamically.
- Adapt services to changing business needs.

AI, analytics, and continual improvement initiatives are ways to embed intelligence into the service value system.

The DIKW hierarchy is a widely used model that explains how raw data is transformed into actionable intelligence and wisdom.

The following figure is a pictorial description of the DIKW model:

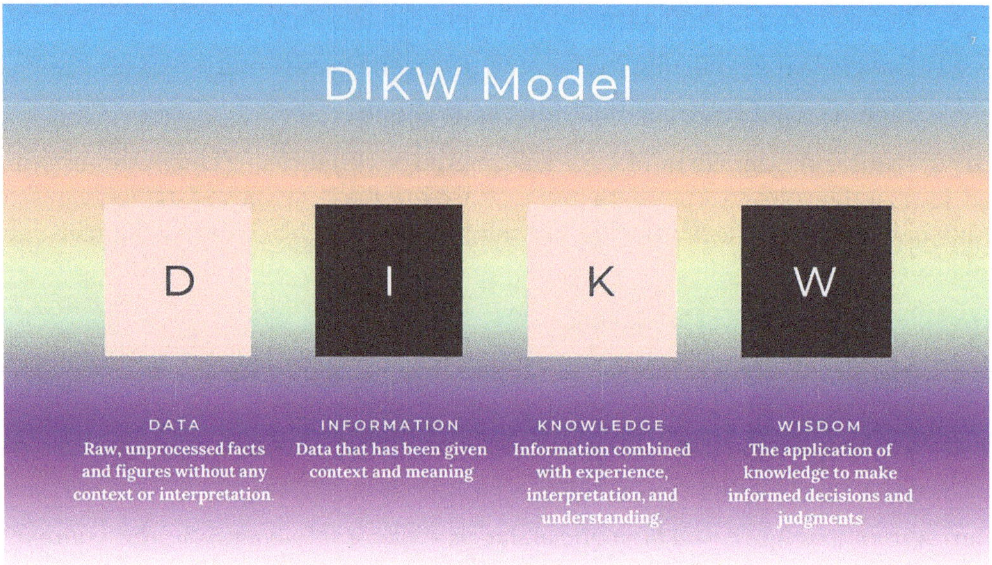

Figure 1.1: *DIKW Model*

To enhance our understanding, let us break it down with examples in ITSM:

Data consists of raw and unprocessed facts. Data can be defined as uninterpreted signals or values collected from systems, users, or environments.

Examples in ITSM:

- 10,000 event logs from a server.
- Timestamped error codes from an application.
- User-submitted incident: "My screen is frozen."

We must take note that "On its own, data has no meaning–it just exists".

Information can be regarded when Data is given context and structure. Information can be defined as organized data that answers basic questions such as who, what, where, and when.

Examples:

- "Server X generated 500 error logs between 3:00–4:00 AM."
- "25 users reported application slowness after the latest update."
- "Network latency has doubled on VPN connections since the firewall patch."

We must take note here that Information provides situational awareness, but does not yet explain why or how.

Knowledge is interpreted information with experience and rules. Knowledge can be defined as Information processed, analyzed, and understood–often including heuristics, patterns, and relationships.

Examples:

- "These errors indicate a known memory leak issue in version 3.2 of the app."
- "High latency is commonly observed when firewall Rule B is active with Policy C."
- "This incident matches a previous major outage from last quarter."

The important point is that Knowledge enables effective action. It informs "what should be done."

Wisdom (or Intelligence) is Judgment and contextual application together. Wisdom can be defined (in ITSM terms) as the ability to use knowledge to make strategic or predictive decisions, often factoring in uncertainty, impact, and long-term consequences.

Examples:

- "Since this pattern led to a critical incident last month, we should initiate change control and roll back."
- "If this alert cluster repeats three times in an hour, escalate to L2 and notify the service owner automatically."
- "This customer segment is at risk of SLA breach; trigger proactive support."

This is where automation, machine learning, and decision-support tools can play a big role by virtue of turning operational knowledge into real-time intelligence.

AI tools help accelerate the DIKW journey by:

- Collecting data at scale (logs, tickets, telemetry)
- Organizing it into meaningful information (alerts, trends)
- Learning from it to build knowledge (incident correlations, root cause suggestions)
- Acting on it with intelligence (auto-routing, chatbot responses, anomaly prediction)

The following table lists the summary of levels, meaning, each with an example and its role:

DIKW Level	Meaning	Example in ITSM	Role in Smart ITSM
Data	Raw facts	500 alerts, user complaint logs	Monitoring

Information	Contextualized data	Alert spike between 2-3 AM	Situational awareness
Knowledge	Patterns and interpretation	Alerts linked to patch deployment	Problem-solving, KEDB, analytics
Intelligence/Wisdom	Strategic decisions	Pre-emptively roll back risky change	AI/ML automation, predictive action

Table 1.1: *Summary of Levels and Meanings with Examples and Roles*

Understanding What AI is Not

AI is often misunderstood due to hype and sci-fi portrayals. Let us demystify it.

- AI is not magic:
  - It does not "think" or "feel" like humans.
  - It follows mathematical models and patterns learned from data.

  Example:

  AI can suggest a solution to a known error, but it does not "understand" your frustration like a human would.

- AI is not human-like general intelligence:
  - AI does not have consciousness, common sense, or emotions.
  - It performs specific tasks it is trained for–this is called Narrow AI.

  Example:

  A chatbot can answer FAQs but will not understand sarcasm or emotional context, unless explicitly programmed and trained.

- AI is not 100% accurate or unbiased:
  - AI learns from historical data. If that data is biased or flawed, AI's decisions will be too.
  - It requires supervision, tuning, and governance.

  Example:

  An AI-based resume screener might reject candidates unfairly, if the training data favored one profile type.

- AI is not fully autonomous:
  - Most AI systems still rely on human input, monitoring, and control.

  - "Autonomous" AI (like self-driving cars) still needs real-world validation, and human oversight.

  Example:

  AI can propose a change in an IT environment, but a Change Manager still needs to approve it (as per ITIL governance).

- AI is not automation.
- Automation follows predefined rules.
- AI learns patterns, and makes predictions or decisions based on data.

  Example:

  - Automation: "If disk space < 20%, then raise an alert."
  - AI: "Predict server crash risk, based on past trends of disk, memory, and CPU usage combined."

In continuation of the preceding understanding, the following table lists What AI Cannot Do (Yet):

AI cannot...	**Why**	**Example**
Understand emotions deeply.	Lacks empathy	AI can detect "anger" in text, but cannot comfort a user like a human.
Make ethical decisions independently.	Needs human values and governance	AI may suggest terminating a service for cost reasons, ignoring the social impact.
Replace complex, multi-layered human judgment.	Cannot grasp business context or human nuance	AI can prioritize incidents by severity, but not understand internal politics or customer sensitivity.
Work without good quality data.	Garbage in = garbage out	Poor data leads to bad recommendations in incident trends.
Learn new tasks without retraining.	Needs task-specific data	AI trained on ticket routing cannot suddenly start doing capacity forecasting.

Table 1.2: *Lists What AI Cannot Do (Yet)*

To summarize, it can be stated that AI is a powerful tool, but not a human brain.

It helps us make smarter decisions, but it does not "think," "feel," or "understand" like we do. ***It learns from data, not from life.***

The following table is a comparison of "Myths and Reality":

Myth	Reality
AI is like a human brain.	AI mimics specific human tasks, but it does not think, feel, or understand.
AI can work without any data.	AI needs large amounts of quality data to learn and perform well.
AI makes perfect, unbiased decisions.	AI reflects the bias of its training data, unless carefully monitored.
AI can do everything on its own.	AI usually supports humans–most systems require human oversight or approval.
AI = Automation.	Automation follows fixed rules. AI learns patterns and adapts dynamically.
AI can understand context like a human.	AI interprets patterns, but lacks emotional or cultural understanding.
AI will replace all ITSM roles.	AI will **augment** ITSM professionals, not replace them.

Table 1.3: *Myth versus Reality*

So, based on the preceding table, it is quite apparent that AI cannot do a lot of things. We will consider in the following table what AI cannot (yet) do in IT Service Management (ITSM).

The following table lists a few important limitations with explanations:

Limitations	Explanations
Understand emotions or empathy	NLP can detect tone, but AI lacks genuine human understanding.
Make ethical or governance-based decisions	It needs human-defined boundaries (change approvals, escalations, and so on).
Learn new tasks on its own	Each task (for example, routing versus sentiment analysis) needs separate training models.
Fix bad data or poor service design	AI amplifies what it learns. Poor data = poor results.
Replace complex, human stakeholder judgment	It can be suggested based on data, but not weigh political, strategic, or legal context.

Table 1.4: *Limitations with Explanations*

The Evolution of AI in IT Operations

AI did not enter IT operations overnight. Its journey has been gradual, and shaped by decades of innovation, growing data complexity, and the relentless demand for faster, more reliable service delivery. What began as basic automation and rule-based systems has evolved into intelligent platforms capable of learning, predicting, and even acting autonomously.

In this section, we trace the path of AI in IT operations–from its early beginnings in static scripts and monitoring tools, to today's dynamic, real-time AIOps platforms that help organizations prevent outages, reduce noise, and drive smarter decision-making at scale.

Understanding this evolution is key to appreciating what AI can offer ITSM today–and where it is headed next.

The following is a timeline-based breakdown of its evolution, followed by its application-specific growth in IT operations and ITSM:

Era	Key Developments
1950s–1960s	Birth of AI – Alan Turing proposes "Can machines think?" (Turing Test). Early symbolic AI (logic/rules). ELIZA – designed to simulate a conversation.
1970s–1980s	Expert systems emerge (for example, MYCIN for medical diagnosis). Knowledge-driven, rule-based reasoning systems.
1990s	Rise of machine learning – focus shifts from rule-writing to training on data. Algorithms mature.
Late 1990s–2000s	The Big Data era begins. AI starts to improve with more data availability. IBM's Deep Blue beats chess champion.
2010–2015	Deep Learning boom. Neural networks outperform traditional models in image, speech, and language tasks.
2016–2019	AI becomes mainstream: Virtual assistants, AIOps, language models (like GPT), and predictive analytics in ITSM.
2020s	Rise of **Generative AI**, autonomous systems, and **AI ethics**. AI is embedded in business and IT processes too.

Table 1.5: *Timeline of AI Evolution*

After discovering the Evolution path, now it is the turn of the evolution of AI in IT Operations and ITSM.

AI in IT operations (AIOps) has grown through three major phases:

1. Rule-Based Automation (Pre-AI)
   - Scripts, cron jobs, and threshold-based alerts
   - Example: "If CPU > 90%, send an alert"
   - Limitation: No learning or pattern recognition
2. AI-Enabled Automation (Machine Learning and Analytics)
   - AI systems begin learning from historical data
   - Use cases:
     - Incident trend prediction
     - Ticket auto-routing
     - Root cause analysis suggestions

   Example: "If this pattern of alerts happened before a crash, predict it again"
3. AIOps and Cognitive Automation (Current Phase)
   - Real-time learning and decision-making
   - Uses Natural Language Processing (NLP), Deep Learning, and Event Correlation
   - Use cases:
     - AI-assisted Chatbots.
     - Predictive service degradation.
     - Automated service remediation.
     - Sentiment analysis from tickets.
   - Platforms: Moogsoft, BigPanda, Dynatrace, and ServiceNow AI modules.

It is important to discover What Drives the Evolution. The following table lists the important drivers, and their impact on AI adoption in ITSM:

Driver	Impact on AI Adoption in ITSM
Increased computing power	Enables deep learning and real-time decisioning.
Explosion of data	AI learns better with vast, diverse datasets.
Cloud-native environments	Increased complexity drives the need for smarter, scalable operations.

Demand for agility	Businesses want predictive and proactive service management.
Toolchain maturity	Platforms now integrate AI as a core capability, not an add-on.

Table 1.6: *Drivers for the Evolution*

If AI Evolution is to be described in One Sentence, then it should be that AI has evolved from rule-following systems to self-learning agents that enhance human decision-making in complex IT environments.

The following table is a side-by-side comparison table for "Old AI versus Modern AI versus AIOps".

Aspect	**Old AI (Pre-2000s)**	**Modern AI (2000s-2020)**	**AIOps / Cognitive ITSM (2020s)**
Approach	Rule-based (IF-THEN)	Data-driven Machine Learning	Context-aware, real-time learning
Learning Method	No learning, manual updates	Learns from historical data	Learns + adapts in real-time from live data
Examples	Expert systems, search bots	Ticket routing, predictive analytics	Root cause prediction, auto-remediation
Tools	Prolog, Lisp, CLIPS	Python ML libs, Scikit-learn	Moogsoft, BigPanda, ServiceNow AI
Use in ITSM	Diagnostic scripts	Chatbots, anomaly detection	Proactive ops, AIOps platform integration
Human Involvement	Full control	Partial control	Shared control with AI assistance

Table 1.7: *Old AI versus Modern AI versus AIOps*

From Automation to Intelligence: Key Terminologies

As IT operations evolve, so does the language we use to describe how work gets done. What began as simple automation–executing repetitive tasks through scripts–has now progressed to intelligent systems that can learn, understand, predict, and act with minimal human input.

To truly grasp the power of AI in ITSM, it is essential to understand the key building blocks behind this transformation. Terms such as **Machine Learning (ML)**, **Natural**

Language Processing (NLP), **Deep Learning (DL)**, and **Artificial Intelligence for IT Operations (AIOps)** are often used interchangeably, but each plays a distinct role in the shift from rule-based automation to adaptive intelligence.

This section breaks down these terms in plain language, and explains how each one contributes to smarter, faster, and more reliable IT service management.

Machine Learning

Machine Learning (ML) is a type of artificial intelligence that allows computers to learn from data, and improve over time, without being explicitly programmed.

In simple terms, instead of telling the computer exactly what to do, we give it lots of examples, and let it figure out the patterns on its own.

Analogy to Understand It:

Think of how a child learns to recognize animals:

- You show the child many pictures of cats and say, "This is a cat."
- Over time, the child starts recognizing other cats, even if they look slightly different.
- That is learning from examples, just like ML.

Let us understand the method of Machine Learning Working in a more simplified manner.

- We give the computer data → (for example, thousands of past incident tickets)
- We tell it what the correct outcomes are → (for example, which team resolved each type of issue)
- The system finds patterns in the data → (for example, tickets with "VPN" often go to the Network Team)
- It starts making predictions on new data → (for example, routing new VPN-related incidents to the correct team automatically)

There are multiple Types of Machine Learning. The following table lists the same with ITSM examples:

Type of ML	**How it Works**	**ITSM Example**
Supervised Learning	Learns from labeled data	Predict the ticket category, based on past tickets.

Unsupervised Learning	Finds patterns in unlabeled data	Group similar incidents to identify problem clusters.
Reinforcement Learning	Learns through trial and error	AI-based self-healing systems optimizing actions over time.

Table 1.8: *Types of Machine Learning*

A few of the real-life examples of ML (In and Outside ITSM) are as follows:

In ITSM:

- Auto-routing incidents, based on keywords and history.
- Predicting major incidents by analyzing alert trends.
- Classifying tickets into categories (for example, hardware and software)
- Detecting anomalies in system behavior (for example, sudden CPU spikes)

In Everyday Life:

- Netflix recommending movies you will like.
- Spam filters that move junk emails to your spam folder.
- Google Maps predicting traffic based on historical patterns.
- E-commerce sites suggesting products you may want to buy.

Now, we also need to understand what ML is not, and a few important of them are as follows:

- ML is not magic – it needs lots of good data to work.
- ML does not think like humans – it finds patterns, not reasons.
- ML makes mistakes, especially if trained on bad data.

In summary, Machine Learning is teaching a machine using data, not instructions.

It learns patterns, makes predictions, and improves over time.

Now, let us proceed to understand Natural Language Processing (NLP).

Natural Language Processing

Natural Language Processing (NLP) is a branch of AI that helps computers understand, interpret, and respond to human language – the way we speak or write.

In simple terms, NLP allows computers to read, hear, and "make sense" of words, just like humans do.

It is what powers chatbots, voice assistants, and even automatic ticket categorization in ITSM systems.

In our day-to-day life, we can think of NLP like giving a computer the ability to read and understand a book, listen to a conversation, or summarize a message – something humans do naturally, but machines need special models to do.

Now, let us understand the steps for achieving these objectives, and the steps are as follows:

1. Text Input (or Speech converted to text) → "My email is not working."
2. Break into parts → ["My", "email", "is not", "working"].
3. Analyze Meaning → It is about email not functioning – a likely incident.
4. Take Action → Assign to the Email Support Group or suggest a known solution.

The following table lists a few important NLP capabilities with ITSM examples:

NLP Capability	Description	ITSM Example
Text Classification	Assign categories to the text.	Auto-categorize a ticket as "Network" or "Software".
Entity Recognition	Find important terms (names, dates, and so on.)	Detect "printer" or "VPN" in user-submitted issues.
Sentiment Analysis	Detect emotions in the text.	Escalate frustrated user tickets for faster attention.
Intent Detection	Identify what the user wants.	"Reset password" → Route to self-service.
Summarization	Shorten long texts, while keeping the meaning intact	Summarize change request descriptions.
Text Generation	Generate human-like replies.	Chatbot responding with a helpful troubleshooting step.

Table 1.9: *NLP Capabilities*

Here are a few examples, we generally come across in our lives every day, including ITSM.

In ITSM:

- Chatbots answering user queries
- Auto-filling ticket categories, based on user input
- Voice-based virtual agents
- Translating technical KB articles for end users

In Daily Life:

- Google Translate
- Siri, Alexa, and Google Assistant

- Autocorrect and predictive text
- Email spam detection
- Smart search (for example, Google "weather tomorrow")

Same as for machine learning, we need to understand what NLP cannot do (Yet):

- It does not understand language like a human being; it interprets patterns, not feelings.
- It may misinterpret slang, sarcasm, or local phrases.
- It needs lots of training data to be accurate and relevant.

Natural Language Processing (NLP) is how AI reads, listens, and responds to human language.

It is what powers smarter chatbots, better ticket handling, and more human-like interaction in ITSM tools.

Next in the queue is Deep Learning (DL).

Deep Learning

Deep Learning is a special kind of Machine Learning that uses structures called neural networks to learn from very large and complex sets of data, often in ways that mimic how the human brain works.

To make it easier to understand, we can simply state that Deep Learning is what allows AI to understand things such as images, speech, and complex patterns, even better than traditional machine learning in some cases.

To understand the analogy, let us think of a brain with layers of neurons. Deep Learning models work similarly, using layers of processing to extract and understand features step-by-step.

For example:

- First layer sees pixels,
- The next layer sees edges,
- Then shapes,
- Then the whole object (for example, the "laptop").

Without being highly technical, and to the benefit of the vast majority of the readers, let us understand how Deep Learning Works in a Simplified manner. Deep Learning uses Artificial Neural Network (ANN) models inspired by how the brain works to learn from data.

Here is the step-by-step approach for the situation "for a computer recognizing an ITSM email):

1. Input Data: Raw email: "My laptop will not connect to Wi-Fi."
2. Neural Layers: The deep learning model processes the text through multiple layers:
    - Layer 1: Recognize words
    - Layer 2: Identify key phrases
    - Layer 3: Understand the intent (Connectivity Issue)
    - Layer 4: Predict category (Network Issue)
3. Output: Auto-route to Network Support Team, or suggest a known fix.

After reading so far, it is quite obvious that the question which is cropping up in your mind is "Why Deep"?

The answer to that is because the model has many layers of learning, each building on the previous one – hence, "deep" learning.

It becomes imperative for us to be aware of where Deep Learning Shines.

The following table lists a few important ones with an Example in ITSM to relate:

Area	**Example in ITSM**
Speech Recognition	Voice-based ticket creation ("Create ticket for Wi-Fi")
Image Analysis	Reading error screenshots or scanned handwritten forms
Advanced NLP	Understanding long emails, summarizing them accurately
Anomaly Detection	Finding subtle, complex patterns in logs or metrics
Predictive Maintenance	Identifying hardware failures before they happen

Table 1.10: *ITSM Examples of the Situation Where DL Shines*

Let us consider a few more examples we come across daily.

In ITSM:

- AI assistants that understand voice or long text.
- Advanced log analysis tools using anomaly detection.
- Chatbots that hold human-like conversations.
- Automatic escalation of VIP or emotionally charged tickets.

In Real Life:

- Self-driving cars identifying objects.
- Face recognition in smartphones.

- YouTube recommending videos.
- Google Translator's voice and image translation.

It is also important to be aware of what Deep Learning Cannot Do (Yet), and they are as follows:

- It requires huge amounts of data to perform well.
- It is often a "black box" – hard to understand how it made a decision.
- It can be easily biased, if trained on bad data.
- It is resource-intensive – needs high computing power (like GPUs).

Deep Learning is a powerful form of machine learning that helps AI see, hear, and understand the complex data, especially useful for voice, images, and nuanced text in ITSM.

It is behind smart assistants, advanced chatbots, and predictive tools in modern service management.

Next, we are going to understand what AIOps is.

Artificial Intelligence for IT Operations

Artificial Intelligence for IT Operations (AIOps) is the application of AI and Machine Learning (ML) to enhance and automate IT operations. It helps IT teams manage complex systems faster, smarter, and with fewer human errors.

For a beginner, we can state that AIOps uses AI to detect, diagnose, and fix IT issues – often before anyone even notices.

Think of AIOps as a super-smart monitoring system that not only notices a problem but also tells you why it is happening, and suggests or takes action to fix it.

It is like moving from a basic thermometer to a smart health assistant that detects symptoms, diagnoses the issue, and even applies treatment.

As a consequence of the same, we need to understand why AIOps matters in ITSM.

The reasons for the same are as follows:

Modern IT environments are:

- Hybrid (on-prem + cloud)
- Highly distributed (apps, APIs, and containers)
- High volume (thousands of events per minute)

Human teams cannot keep up. AIOps helps by:

- Reducing noise

- Correlating events
- Spotting anomalies early
- Automating resolution

Let us put this performance in simple five steps:

1. Ingests data - From logs, metrics, events, tickets, APIs, and so on.
2. Cleans and normalizes - Filters irrelevant noise, and formats everything.
3. Analyses - Uses AI/ML to find patterns, anomalies, and correlations.
4. Diagnoses - Identifies probable root causes or dependencies.
5. Acts - Recommends next steps or automates remediation.

The following table lists the required capabilities of AIOps:

Capability	Description	ITSM Use Case Example
Noise Reduction	Suppress redundant alerts	5,000 similar alerts → 1 actionable incident
Event Correlation	Link multiple events to a single root cause.	VPN, server, and DB errors linked to the outage.
Anomaly Detection	Find behavior that is "not normal".	Detect a CPU spike that normally never occurs.
Root Cause Analysis	Suggest the probable cause of an issue.	Pinpoint failing microservice in seconds.
Predictive Alerting	Warn about the future issues.	Forecast disk failure, two days in advance.
Automated Remediation	Automatically fix the known issues.	Restart the service or roll back the config change.

Table 1.11: *AIOps Capabilities*

In order to strengthen our understanding of AIOps, let us consider a few real-life examples of AIOps in action as follows:

In ITSM:

- Predicting outages before users raise incidents.
- Auto-closing duplicate alerts or low-impact events.

- Guiding L1 teams with suggested resolutions.
- Prioritizing incidents, based on impact patterns.

In Everyday Enterprise Ops:

- E-commerce sites avoiding downtime during sales.
- Banks preemptively resolving latency in payment gateways.
- Telecoms fixing core network issues, before mass complaints.

It is also important that we understand what AIOps cannot do (Yet):

- Replace IT teams completely – it augments, not replaces.
- Guarantee 100% accuracy – wrong or biased data can lead to false positives/negatives.
- Work instantly – needs training, tuning, and integration with ITSM tools.
- Fully replace human decision-making in complex or ethical choices.

To summarize the understanding, let us state that AIOps brings together data, AI, and automation to make IT operations faster, smarter, and more proactive.

It reduces alert and fatigue, improves service reliability, and supports ITIL4's goal of co-creating value through intelligent service delivery.

Conclusion

In this chapter, we laid the essential groundwork for understanding Artificial Intelligence in the context of IT Service Management. We began by demystifying what AI truly is–and what it is not–cutting through common myths to establish a clear, practical foundation. We explored how intelligence, as viewed through the DIKW model, empowers service management to evolve from reactive support to predictive, value-driven operations.

Through a guided journey of core concepts–Machine Learning, Natural Language Processing, Deep Learning, and AIOps–we saw how AI technologies are reshaping, and how IT services are delivered, supported, and continually improved. From automating ticket routing to anticipating outages, and from understanding customer sentiment to enabling autonomous resolution, **AI is not replacing ITSM but augmenting it**, **helping humans make smarter and faster decisions**.

But with all its promise, AI is still a tool, not a replacement for human judgment, empathy, or governance. It is most powerful when applied thoughtfully, ethically, and in alignment with organizational strategies.

This foundational understanding sets the stage for the rest of the book. In the chapters ahead, we will delve deeper into **real-world applications**, **governance**

models, **tool integrations**, and **strategies** for scaling AI within ITSM. With each step, the goal remains clear: To build a smarter, more resilient, and truly intelligent service management landscape.

In the next chapter, we are going to discuss the DNA of IT Service Management (ITSM).

Multiple Choice Questions

1. What does Artificial Intelligence primarily enable machines to do in the context of ITSM?
    a. Replace human IT staff entirely.
    b. Execute fixed commands only.
    c. Learn from data, and support smarter decisions.
    d. Understand human emotions such as empathy.
2. According to the DIKW model, which level represents the ability to make strategic or predictive decisions?
    a. Data
    b. Information
    c. Knowledge
    d. Intelligence (Wisdom)
3. What is the key difference between AI and traditional automation?
    a. AI works only with hardware, and automation works with software.
    b. Automation reacts to data, while AI ignores it.
    c. AI learns from patterns in data, while automation follows predefined rules.
    d. AI replaces human governance, but automation does not.
4. Which of the following best describes the role of Natural Language Processing (NLP) in ITSM?
    a. It allows machines to install patches on remote systems.
    b. It enables systems to understand and interpret human language.
    c. It replaces all ticketing systems with voice bots.
    d. It prevents phishing attacks automatically.

5. What is the main benefit of AIOps in modern IT operations?
    a. Replacing service desk agents with chatbots.
    b. Fully automating all business decisions.
    c. Enabling predictive, real-time IT operations with reduced noise and faster resolution.
    d. Eliminating the need for monitoring tools.

Answers

1. c
2. d
3. c
4. b
5. c

Questions

1. Define Artificial Intelligence in your own words, and explain how it differs from automation in ITSM.
2. Using the DIKW model, describe how raw data transforms into actionable intelligence within IT Service Management.
3. List and briefly explain three misconceptions about AI that are commonly encountered in the IT industry.
4. What are some key limitations of AI in the context of ITSM, and why is human oversight still necessary?
5. Trace the historical evolution of AI from the 1950s to the present, and highlight the key milestones relevant to IT operations.
6. Describe the role of Machine Learning in ITSM, and provide examples of how it enhances service management tasks.
7. How does Natural Language Processing (NLP) support smarter interaction and automation in service desk operations?
8. Explain how Deep Learning(DL) differs from traditional Machine Learning, and mention specific ITSM use cases where DL is most effective.

9. What is AIOps, and how does it combine data, AI, and automation to improve IT operations in complex environments?
10. Summarize the key drivers that have accelerated the adoption of AI in ITSM over the last decade.

Key Terms

- **Artificial Intelligence (AI):** Artificial Intelligence refers to the simulation of human intelligence in machines that are programmed to learn, reason, and act, based on data. In ITSM, AI helps systems to make decisions, automate responses, and enhance service efficiency.
- **DIKW Model:** The Data, Information, Knowledge, Wisdom (DIKW) model describes how raw data evolves into actionable intelligence. It provides a structured framework for understanding how insights are derived and applied in service management.
- **Machine Learning (ML):** Machine Learning is a branch of AI where systems learn from historical data, without being explicitly programmed. In ITSM, ML is used for tasks such as ticket classification, trend prediction, and anomaly detection.
- **Natural Language Processing (NLP):** NLP enables computers to understand, interpret, and respond to human language. It is widely used in ITSM for chatbots, auto-categorizing tickets, and analyzing sentiment in user communications.
- **Deep Learning (DL):** Deep Learning is a subset of ML that uses neural networks with many layers to process the complex data. It excels in tasks such as voice recognition, advanced log analysis, and intelligent virtual assistants in ITSM.
- **Artificial Intelligence for IT Operations (AIOps):** AIOps applies AI and ML to enhance and automate IT operations, improving speed and accuracy. It correlates events, predicts issues, and enables proactive remediation in complex IT environments.
- **Automation:** Automation refers to the execution of predefined tasks, without human intervention, typically using scripts or workflows. Unlike AI, it does not learn or adapt, but is essential for repeatable service tasks.
- **Sentiment Analysis:** Sentiment Analysis is an NLP technique that detects emotions and tone in user communications. It helps ITSM teams prioritize responses to frustrated or high-risk users.

- **Event Correlation:** Event Correlation links multiple alerts or system events to a single root cause. This AIOps capability reduces noise, and helps IT teams focus on meaningful incidents.
- **Predictive Analytics:** Predictive Analytics uses historical data and machine learning to forecast future outcomes. In ITSM, it helps to identify the potential outages, capacity issues, or SLA breaches, before they occur.

Chapter 2
Understanding the Core of IT Service Management

Introduction

In today's digital-first economy, organizations rely more than ever on seamless, scalable, and reliable IT services. But what defines the structure and philosophy of effective IT service delivery? This is where IT Service Management (ITSM) comes into play—providing the foundational framework for designing, delivering, managing, and improving IT services that truly align with business needs.

Yet, ITSM is not static. Over the years, it has evolved from rigid process-centric models to more adaptive, value-focused systems. **ITIL4**, the most recent evolution of the ITIL framework, represents a paradigm shift, placing **value co-creation**, **agility**, and **end-to-end thinking** at its core. It encourages organizations to view ITSM not as a set of siloed processes, but as a dynamic ecosystem.

In this chapter, we will explore what truly makes up the DNA of ITSM. We will start by understanding its core definition and how ITIL4 reshapes ITSM for the modern era. We will then decode the **Service Value System (SVS)** and **Service Value Chain (SVC)**—the heart of ITIL4's architecture. Finally, we will identify the pain points of traditional ITSM that often fall short in the absence of intelligence, setting the stage for AI-powered transformation.

Let us dive deeper into what makes ITSM tick—and what makes it future-ready.

Structure

In this chapter, we will discuss the following topics:

- Understanding ITSM and Reshaping it through ITIL4

- Service Value System and Service Value Chain
- ITSM Needs Intelligence to Stay Relevant

Understanding ITSM and Reshaping It through ITIL4

Behind every seamless digital experience—whether it is a mobile banking app, a cloud-hosted learning platform, or a remote work environment—lies a disciplined approach to managing IT services. This is the essence of IT Service Management (ITSM). It is not just about fixing incidents or running helpdesks; ITSM governs how organizations plan, deliver, support, and continually improve IT services that underpin business success.

However, as digital demands grow more complex and real-time, traditional ITSM models have begun to show their age. Siloed processes, rigid workflows, and reactive mindsets are no longer enough. Enter **ITIL4**—a modern, flexible, and value-centric framework that reshapes ITSM for agility, co-creation, and continuous improvement in a digital world.

In this section, we will define ITSM, explore its foundational goals, and then dive into how ITIL4 transforms ITSM from a process-heavy discipline to a dynamic enabler of business value.

Introduction to ITSM

IT Service Management (ITSM) is a comprehensive and structured approach that governs the end-to-end lifecycle of IT services within an organization. It encompasses the **planning, design, delivery, operation, and continual improvement** of IT services to ensure they consistently meet both **business objectives** and **customer expectations**. ITSM focuses on aligning IT operations with strategic business goals by implementing **well-defined processes**, clear roles and responsibilities, and performance measurement systems.

At its core, ITSM is about transforming IT from a support function into a **value-creating partner**. It ensures that IT services are not just available, but reliable, cost-effective, user-friendly, and capable of adapting to changing business demands. Important practices to begin the journey under ITSM include **Incident Management, Change Enablement, Problem Management, Service Request Management, and Service Level Management**.

By emphasizing **process standardization**, **service quality**, **governance**, and **continual improvement**, ITSM helps organizations improve efficiency, reduce operational risks, enhance user satisfaction, and foster innovation in a structured and controlled manner.

IT Service Management (ITSM) refers to a strategic and operational approach for designing, delivering, managing, and improving IT services in alignment with business needs. It emphasizes process standardization, service quality, and continual improvement.

The key characteristics of ITSM are as follows:

- Focus on process standardization
- Emphasis on service lifecycle
- Governed by frameworks such as ITIL, COBIT, ISO/IEC 20000

Example:

A university's IT department uses ITSM to handle everything from onboarding new students into digital learning platforms to managing Wi-Fi outages during exams.

Core goals of ITSM include:

- Delivering value to customers through services
- Ensuring service quality and reliability
- Minimizing service disruption and downtime
- Improving efficiency and customer satisfaction

Example: A retail chain uses ITSM to ensure all its Point-of-Sale (POS) systems across stores run efficiently. When a POS device fails, the support team follows a standardized incident resolution process to restore service as quickly as possible, minimizing business disruption.

Traditional ITSM: Process-Centric and Reactive

Earlier ITSM models, including ITIL V3, focused on service lifecycle stages such as Service Strategy, Service Design, Service Transition, Service Operation, and Continual Service Improvement. While effective in stable environments, they struggled with agility, speed, and adaptability.

The most important and critical issues encountered are as follows:

- Siloed processes (incident, change, problem) treated independently
- Focused more on process compliance than business outcomes
- Reactive rather than proactive service delivery

Example:

An insurance company experiences delays in resolving customer login issues. Tickets are passed between the ServiceDesk, network, and application teams with no shared visibility or ownership, resulting in long downtimes and poor customer satisfaction.

As a consequence of the encountered key issues, the key challenges of traditional ITSM are derived as follows:

- Siloed functions leading to fragmented service delivery
- Reactive processes triggered after incidents occur
- Difficulty adapting to Agile or DevOps-driven models
- Limited emphasis on user experience and business outcomes

Example: An insurance company handles IT incidents through separate tiers (L1, L2, L3) without shared visibility. As a result, tickets are bounced between teams, causing delays and user dissatisfaction.

The Road Travelled by ITIL4 for Reshaping ITSM

ITIL4 redefines ITSM by moving away from a rigid, process-heavy approach to a holistic, flexible, and value-focused model. It introduces the concept of the **Service Value System (SVS)**, where all organizational components work together to enable value co-creation.

Key shifts introduced by ITIL4 include:

- **From processes to value streams:** Emphasis on outcomes and experience
- **From silos to integration:** End-to-end service thinking
- **From reactive to proactive:** Embracing automation, AI, and continual improvement
- **From fixed roles to flexibility:** Supporting Agile, DevOps, and cloud-native environments

The following table lists the comparisons between traditional ITSM and Modern ITSM:

Aspect	Traditional ITSM	ITIL4 Modern ITSM
Focus	Process compliance	Value co-creation
Approach	Siloed processes	Integrated value streams
Tools	IT-centric	Technology + People + Value Streams
Governance	Static controls	Dynamic governance
Innovation Support	Limited	Supports Agile, DevOps, and AI

Table 2.1: *List of Comparisons*

Example: A fintech company adopts ITIL4 to integrate DevOps with ITSM. Using the guiding principle "*Progress Iteratively with Feedback*," they release frequent app updates, while continuously improving incident management processes based on real-time monitoring and customer feedback.

New Emphases in ITIL4:

- Service Value System (SVS)
- Four Dimensions of Service Management
- Guiding Principles
- Continual Improvement
- Service Value Chain
- Value Streams
- Practices

Example: A fintech startup adopts ITIL4 practices to align its DevOps pipeline with incident and change management. They use the principle "*Progress Iteratively with Feedback*" to rapidly deploy features while improving stability.

In the next section, we will explore the heart of ITIL4–the Service Value System and the Service Value Chain, which form the structural backbone of intelligent, adaptive, and value-driven IT service delivery.

Service Value System and Service Value Chain

Traditional ITSM models often viewed service management as a linear journey: define a service, deliver it, and support it. But in today's fast-paced, interconnected IT environments, service delivery is far from linear. Services evolve continuously, shaped by shifting customer expectations, emerging technologies, and business priorities.

To respond to this complexity, **ITIL4 introduces the Service Value System (SVS)**–a holistic framework that unifies organizational components and activities to co-create value. At the heart of the SVS lies the **Service Value Chain (SVC)**, a flexible operating model that enables adaptable value streams, rather than rigid processes.

This section will unpack the SVS and SVC in detail, illustrating how they empower organizations to navigate uncertainty, integrate Agile and DevOps, and build service delivery models that are resilient, scalable, and customer-centric.

Understanding the Service Value System

The Service Value System (SVS) is a core concept in ITIL4, representing a comprehensive approach for the development, provision, and ongoing enhancement of services, aimed at offering a comprehensive perspective on the interplay of all organizational elements and activities in fostering value generation through IT-enabled services. Effective service management necessitates systematic operation. The ITIL Service Value System (SVS) identifies the crucial inputs that are necessary for this system's effective functioning. These key inputs include 'opportunity' and 'demand.' 'Opportunity' refers to the potential paths an organization can take to either increase stakeholder value or enhance overall organizational performance. Conversely, 'demand' relates to the needs or desires for products and services from both internal and external customers.

The primary result of implementing the SVS is the creation of 'value,' which encompasses the perceived benefits, utility, and importance of different elements. Within ITIL4, the SVS framework is adept at generating a variety of values, serving a wide array of stakeholders effectively. For effective service management, IT must operate systematically. The ITIL Service Value System (SVS) outlines the essential inputs required for this system to function efficiently. These primary inputs are opportunity and demand. Here, 'opportunity' refers to the potential avenues through which the organization can enhance value for its stakeholders or achieve overall improvement. On the other hand, 'demand' signifies the requirement or aspiration for products and services among both internal and external customers. The ultimate output of the SVS is the generation of 'value,' which is the perceived benefits, usefulness, and importance of various aspects. The SVS model within ITIL4 is designed to facilitate the creation of diverse forms of value, catering to a broad spectrum of stakeholders.

For a successful organization, it is crucial to develop both organizational agility and resilience. Organizational agility refers to the capacity to quickly and effectively adapt to internal changes. This can involve adjustments in the organization's scope, dealing with mergers or acquisitions, altering organizational practices, adapting to new technologies, or evolving relationships with partners and suppliers.

On the other hand, organizational resilience is about the ability to foresee, prepare for, respond to, and adapt to both gradual and sudden external changes. These external factors may include political, economic, social, technological, legal, or environmental aspects. Achieving resilience requires a shared understanding of the organization's priorities and goals to maintain direction and alignment despite external changes.

Furthermore, the organization should be viewed as part of a broader ecosystem, including consumer organizations and both internal and external service providers, that work together to deliver and consume products and services.

The ITIL Service Value System (SVS) plays a key role in fostering organizational agility and resilience. It aids in adopting a unified direction focused on value, which is understood by all members of the organization, and promotes continual improvement across the organization.

The SVS represents how all the components and activities of an organization work together to create value through IT-enabled services.

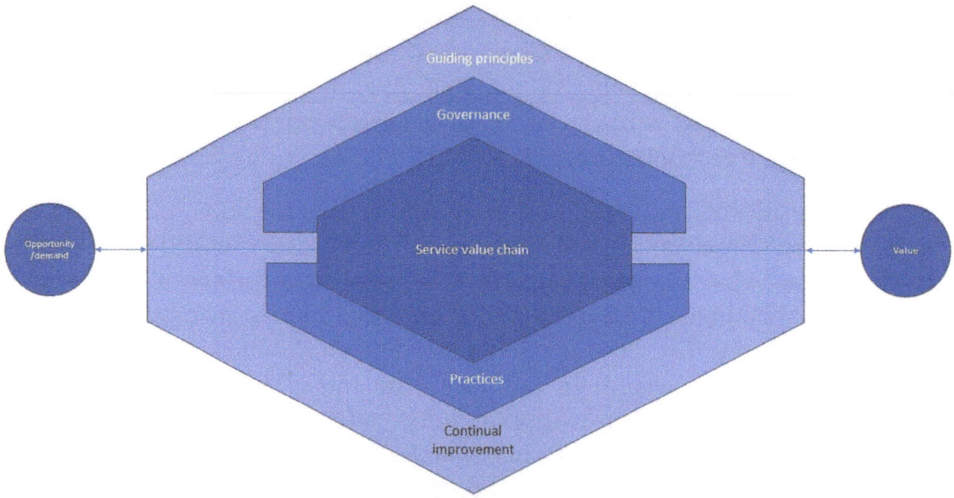

Figure 2.1: *Service Value System (SVS)*

Here is a breakdown of the key elements of the ITIL4 Service Value System:

Guiding Principles

These recommendations serve as a constant guide for an organization, unaffected by shifts in its objectives, strategies, work nature, or organizational framework.

They include principles such as:

- **Focus on value:** An organization's activities should always, directly, or indirectly, contribute to generating value for itself, its customers, and other stakeholders.
- **Start where you are**: When striving to replace outdated, ineffective methods or services with improved ones, there is often a strong inclination to discard previous efforts and start anew.
- **Progress iteratively with feedback**: Avoid the urge to tackle everything simultaneously. Even large-scale projects need to be approached iteratively. Divide the work into smaller, more easily handled segments that can be

executed and completed efficiently, enhancing focus and manageability for each task.

- **Collaborate and promote visibility:** When initiatives engage the right individuals in appropriate roles, the efforts gain from stronger commitment, enhanced relevance due to better-informed decision-making, and a higher chance of sustained success.
- **Think and work holistically:** No service, practice, process, department, or supplier operates independently.
- **Keep it simple and practical:** ITIL4 strives to achieve objectives using the fewest possible steps. Employ outcome-oriented thinking to devise practical solutions that yield valuable results. Remove any process, service, action, or metric that fails to add value or generate a positive result.
- **Optimize and automate**: When implementing this principle, it is crucial to focus on value creation, simplify processes, guarantee the efficiency of each step, value the time of all participants, generate quick wins to motivate usage, and eliminate any steps or processes that do not add value.

Governance

Every organization is steered by a governing body, comprising either an individual or a group accountable for the organization's overall performance and adherence to regulations. This body exists in all sizes and types of organizations and may consist of a board of directors or executive managers who assume a distinct governance role during such activities. They bear the responsibility for ensuring the organization's compliance with internal policies and external legal requirements.

Governance in the SVS sets the direction and limits for the system, ensuring that the organization's management activities are aligned and consistent with its vision, mission, and values.

Governance involves evaluating, directing, and monitoring the organization's operational activities.

Understanding the Service Value Chain

The service value chain, a pivotal element of the Service Value System (SVS), is an operational model defining essential activities for addressing demand and enabling value realization through the development and management of products and services.

The ITIL framework illustrates the six activities of the service value chain, each leading to the creation of products, services, and subsequent value.

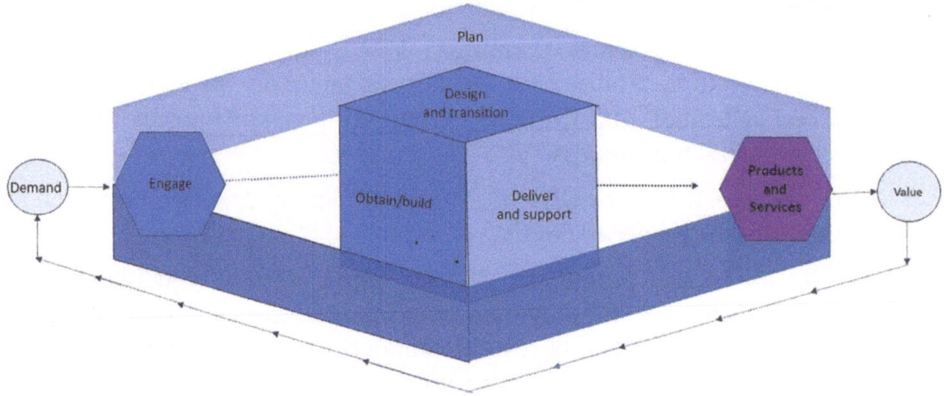

Figure 2.2: *Service Value Chain (SVC)*

The Service Value Chain consists of a series of linked actions that an organization undertakes to provide valuable products and services to its customers and other stakeholders.

The six key activities in the service value chain are as follows:

- **Plan:** The 'Plan' activity within the service value chain aims to establish a unified understanding of the organization's vision, present state, and direction for improvement, encompassing all four dimensions and the complete range of products and services.
- **Improve:** The 'Improve' activity in the service value chain focuses on the continuous enhancement of products, services, and practices throughout all value chain activities and the four dimensions of service management.
- **Engage:** The purpose of the Engage value chain activity in the ITIL4 Service Value Chain is to ensure effective communication and a solid relationship with stakeholders. This activity is crucial for understanding the needs and demands of both internal and external stakeholders, including customers, users, and partners.
- **Design and Transition:** The 'Design and Transition' activity within the service value chain is focused on ensuring that products and services consistently meet stakeholder expectations in terms of quality, cost-efficiency, and time-to-market.
- **Obtain/Build**: The 'Obtain/Build' activity in the service value chain aims to ensure the availability of service components as needed, aligning with agreed specifications and requirements.
- **Deliver and Support**: The 'Deliver and Support' activity within the service value chain is dedicated to ensuring that services are provided and

maintained in line with agreed-upon specifications and the expectations of stakeholders.

Practices

Practices are defined as *"sets or collections of organizational resources designed for performing work or accomplishing an objective"*. ITIL4 defines 34 practices, which are categorized into three types: General Management Practices (14), Service Management Practices (17), and Technical Management Practices (3).

The following figure lists the categorized practices:

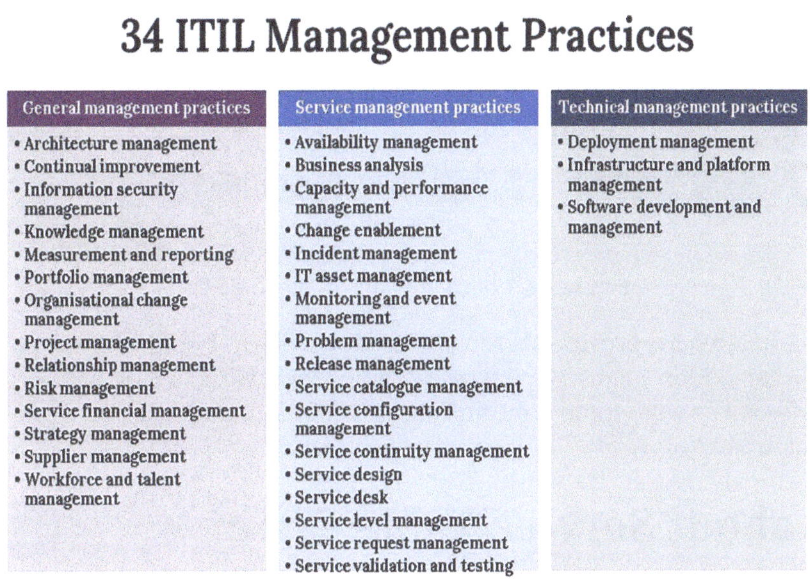

Figure 2.3: *34 ITIL Management Practices*

Continual Improvement

This component emphasizes the need for organizations to continually evolve and improve their products, services, practices, and processes in response to the changing business needs or technological advancements.

It incorporates the continual improvement model, offering a systematic method for organizations to evaluate their present condition, identify improvement opportunities, and implement changes.

The following table breaks down the improvement process into manageable segments with distinct objectives that can be attained step by step:

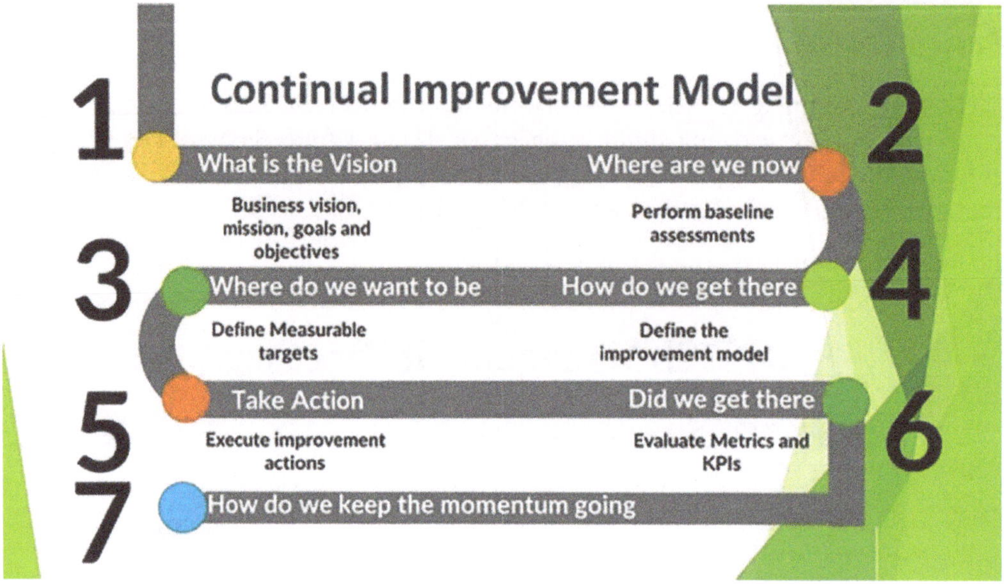

***Figure 2.4**: Continual Improvement Model*

Example: A healthcare provider revamps its appointment booking system. Using the SVS, the organization aligns governance (compliance with health data regulations), principles (focus on value), and continual improvement to deliver a secure and patient-friendly solution.

More about Service Value Chain

The SVC is the core of the SVS and acts as a flexible, non-linear operating model that defines six key activities along with relevant ITIL4 management practices:

- **Plan**: Strategy, governance, and planning
- **Improve**: Continual service improvement
- **Engage**: Interactions with stakeholders
- **Design and Transition**: Building and deploying new services
- **Obtain/Build**: Creating or sourcing service components
- **Deliver and Support**: Operating live services

Example: A telecom company launches a self-service portal:

- **Plan:** Research shows customer demand for digital self-service
- **Design and Transition:** Portal design with user journey mapping

- **Obtain/Build:** APIs sourced to integrate with the billing system
- **Engage:** Beta rollout to early adopters
- **Deliver and Support:** Support teams handle live queries
- **Improve:** Feedback leads to UI enhancements

Value Streams: Beyond the Lifecycle

Unlike the linear stages in ITIL V3, ITIL4 promotes **value streams** and end-to-end workflows that cut across various SVC activities to deliver outcomes.

The traditional ITIL V3 lifecycle can be described as a sequential process: Service Strategy → Service Design → Service Transition → Service Operation → Continual Service Improvement.

In contrast, **ITIL4 introduces Value Streams** as flexible, outcome-focused workflows that operate across the value chain.

In ITIL4, a **value stream** is the complete journey of how an organization delivers value to its customers, from initial demand to final outcome. It connects people, processes, tools, and practices to create seamless, end-to-end workflows. By focusing on **value streams**, ITIL4 shifts attention from siloed processes to holistic service delivery, ensuring that every step adds value and supports business goals. For example, a value stream for resolving an incident might include logging the issue, analyzing it, resolving it, and then capturing feedback–all working together to restore service and improve user satisfaction.

Example:

A bank uses a **value stream** to onboard a customer:

- Capture demand → Validate → Approve → Provision service → Notify customer → Follow-up

This stream can cut across multiple SVC activities combined with several practices in a dynamic, non-linear way.

Value Stream Example: Employee onboarding in an enterprise:

- HR requests account creation (Engage).
- IT provisions hardware and software (Obtain/Build).
- Support team provides orientation (Deliver and Support).
- Feedback is collected for future onboarding improvement (Improve).

Why This Matters:

- Encourages collaboration across functions

- Improves visibility and accountability
- Enables faster and more flexible delivery

The overall concepts can be summarized as follows:

- The SVS provides an end-to-end view, illustrating how every component and activity should synergize as a system to facilitate the creation of value.
- It is adaptable to various organizational structures and strategies, allowing flexibility in how different elements are applied in different contexts.
- The SVS also highlights the importance of external factors and how they impact the service value system, including regulatory requirements, market trends, and emerging technologies.

Also, it will be beneficial to understand the interconnected nature of the SVS as follows:

- The SVS is designed to be adaptable and flexible, allowing organizations to apply its components in various configurations depending on their unique challenges, opportunities, and needs.
- The SVS demonstrates how various sections of an organization need to operate in a synchronized manner to facilitate value creation. It emphasizes the importance of a systemic view, where changes in one area can impact others.
- External factors and stakeholders' needs also influence the SVS, making it essential for organizations to remain agile and responsive to changing environments and requirements.
- The SVS in ITIL4 reflects the complexity and interconnectedness of modern IT service management, where traditional silos are broken down in favor of a more holistic, integrated approach.
- The SVS aligns IT and service management activities with the broader business strategy, ensuring that they contribute effectively to achieving organizational goals.

In essence, the Service Value System in ITIL4 provides a comprehensive framework for organizations to create, manage, and continuously improve their IT services. It integrates principles, governance, practices, and continual improvement to ensure that IT services consistently create and deliver value.

In summary, the Service Value System in ITIL4 is a comprehensive model that integrates various elements crucial for effective service management. It emphasizes a holistic approach, ensuring that organizations can adapt to change and continually deliver value through services powered by IT.

In the next section, we will examine where traditional ITSM falls short–especially in the absence of intelligence–and how modern ITSM must evolve to meet today's business demands.

ITSM Needs Intelligence to Stay Relevant

While traditional ITSM has served organizations well for decades, it was largely designed for an era where stability mattered more than speed. Today, that equation has flipped. Digital services must be fast, adaptive, and intelligent. Unfortunately, **traditional ITSM often lacks the situational awareness, contextual insights, and learning capabilities** required to meet modern expectations.

To elaborate more, we can state that while traditional ITSM frameworks established much-needed structure and control, they often lack the speed, insight, and adaptability demanded by today's digital enterprises. In the absence of intelligence, ITSM can quickly become reactive, inefficient, and disconnected from real business value.

Without intelligence–be it in the form of data-driven decision-making, automation, or predictive analytics–ITSM remains reactive, fragmented, and inefficient. Alert fatigue, ticket overload, and missed opportunities for improvement are just a few symptoms of this gap.

In this section, we will explore the inherent limitations of non-intelligent ITSM, demonstrate where it fails in real-world scenarios, and set the stage for why embedding AI into the fabric of ITSM is no longer optional–it is essential.

The following table lists the limitations of traditional ITSM:

Challenge	**Description**
Reactive Approach	Problems are solved after they impact users Incidents are addressed after disruption, not proactively prevented
Process Silos	Teams operate independently, causing delays and misalignment Lack of cross-functional collaboration hinders problem resolution
Lack of Contextual Insight	Metrics do not reflect end-to-end customer experience
Alert Fatigue	Thousands of alerts, no prioritization or correlation
Rigid Workflows	Inability to adapt quickly to change
Information Overload	High alert volumes without correlation overwhelm support teams
Static Workflows	Rigid rules make it hard to adapt to business or technology changes
Poor User Experience	Delayed responses and a lack of personalization frustrate end users

Table 2.2: *Limitations of Traditional ITSM*

Example: A bank's IT team receives thousands of alerts during an online banking outage. Without intelligent filtering, it takes hours to find the root cause–a failed microservice in the backend.

Gaps in Decision-Making Without Intelligence

Without AI, analytics, or automation, ITSM systems rely heavily on human analysis and manual intervention. This causes delays, inconsistencies, and missed opportunities to optimize services.

Key Issues:

- **Inability to predict recurring issues or failures**

  Example:

  - A retail organization experiences frequent outages in its Point of Sale (POS) system every Friday evening. Since there is no AI or predictive analytics in place, the IT support team treats each outage as an isolated incident. This leads to reactive firefighting rather than identifying a pattern (for example, system overload due to weekly data syncs), and the issue recurs without a long-term fix.

- **Lack of contextual understanding for prioritization**

  Example:

  - An airline's IT helpdesk receives two incidents simultaneously–one from a pilot reporting a navigation software glitch, and another from a back-office employee facing email login issues. Without AI-driven context, both tickets are assigned equal priority in the system queue. As a result, the critical flight issue is delayed, impacting safety and causing operational delays.

- **No early warnings to prevent SLA breaches**

  Example:

  - A telecom company has an SLA to resolve high-priority incidents within 1 hour. Without automation or intelligence, there is no mechanism to alert managers that a ticket has remained untouched for 45 minutes. By the time it is noticed manually, the SLA is breached, affecting customer satisfaction and incurring penalties.

- **Overreliance on historical data and subjective decision-making**

  Example:

  - A bank's service desk team continues to allocate more resources to branch printer issues because, historically, it has received many such tickets. However, recent trends show a sharp decline in printer-related calls and a rise in mobile banking app issues. Without real-time analytics, the team sticks to outdated assumptions, misallocates resources and fails to address emerging priorities.

The Case for Intelligent ITSM

Modern ITSM must go beyond workflows. It should integrate real-time analytics, automation, and AI capabilities that:

- Detect anomalies and patterns proactively
- Correlate events across systems
- Suggest next actions or resolutions
- Optimize resource allocation

Example: A managed service provider implements AIOps to handle client infrastructure. The AI engine predicts potential service degradation by analyzing log trends and initiates automated remediation before the client is affected.

Why intelligence matters - Without AI or data-driven insight, traditional ITSM:

- Misses patterns (for example, repeated incident spikes)
- Cannot forecast issues (no predictive analytics)
- Lacks personalization (same SLAs for all customers)

Example: An e-commerce company has thousands of user complaints during flash sales. Without intelligent trend analysis, they fail to identify that database CPU usage was peaking under load every Friday evening.

The Need for Intelligent ITSM

In today's fast-paced digital environment, traditional ITSM approaches–driven by manual processes and static data–are no longer sufficient to meet evolving business demands. Organizations require intelligent ITSM systems that leverage AI, machine learning, and automation to enhance decision-making, predict incidents, personalize user experiences, and ensure proactive service delivery. By embedding intelligence, ITSM transforms from a reactive support function into a strategic enabler of business resilience, agility, and continual improvement.

Transition Focus:

- From process execution → to value orchestration
- From manual triage → to AI-driven prioritization

- From static dashboards → to predictive and prescriptive analytics

Example: A managed service provider integrates AIOps with its ITSM tool:

- AI clusters alerts based on context
- Suggests probable root causes
- Auto-routes tickets to the right team
- Prevents SLA breaches through early warnings

Conclusion

In this chapter, we unpacked the very foundation–the "DNA"–of modern ITSM. We saw how ITIL4 reimagines service management through an adaptable, value-driven model built on the Service Value System. We also examined how traditional ITSM, though process-rich, struggles to deliver agility and foresight without intelligence.

This sets the stage for the upcoming chapters, where we will explore how Artificial Intelligence becomes the catalyst that fills these gaps, enabling smarter decisions, faster responses, and a truly adaptive ITSM ecosystem.

In the next chapter, we will explore how Artificial Intelligence fills these gaps, enabling smarter, faster, and more resilient ITSM practices that align with ITIL4's vision for value-driven service management.

Multiple Choice Questions

1. What is the primary purpose of the Service Value System (SVS) in ITIL4?

   a. To automate service desk operations

   b. To ensure technical compliance across all IT services

   c. To coordinate all components and activities of an organization to create value

   d. To replace the need for service lifecycle stages

2. Which of the following is NOT one of the six Service Value Chain (SVC) activities in ITIL4?

   a. Engage

   b. Execute

   c. Plan

   d. Improve

3. How does ITIL4 differ from traditional ITSM in its approach to service management?
    a. It focuses more on incident closure rates.
    b. It encourages strict adherence to process documentation.
    c. It emphasizes value co-creation and agility.
    d. It eliminates the need for governance.
4. What is a key drawback of traditional ITSM without intelligence?
    a. It encourages value stream integration.
    b. It relies on manual decision-making, causing delays and inefficiencies.
    c. It automatically adapts to the changing business needs.
    d. It uses AI to predict service issues.
5. According to ITIL4, what is the benefit of shifting from process execution to value orchestration?
    a. More rigid workflows
    b. Better alignment of IT services with business outcomes
    c. Increased service costs
    d. Reduced stakeholder involvement

Answers

1. c
2. b
3. c
4. b
5. b

Questions

1. Explain how ITIL4 reshapes traditional ITSM and why this shift is necessary in a digital-first economy.
2. Describe the core components and purpose of the ITIL4 Service Value System (SVS). How does it support value co-creation?

3. What are the six activities of the ITIL4 Service Value Chain, and how do they interact to deliver value?
4. Discuss the limitations of traditional ITSM in today's fast-paced business environment. Provide examples.
5. How does ITIL4 encourage integration across organizational silos, and what benefits does this offer?
6. What role do value streams play in ITIL4? How do they differ from the lifecycle approach in ITIL V3?
7. Define organizational agility and resilience in the context of ITSM. Why are these capabilities essential?
8. What are the guiding principles in ITIL4, and how do they contribute to intelligent and adaptive service management?
9. Identify the key issues that arise when decision-making in ITSM is not supported by intelligence. Provide real-world examples.
10. Discuss how the shift from manual triage to AI-driven prioritization enhances ITSM effectiveness and customer satisfaction.

Key Terms

- **IT Service Management (ITSM):** A strategic approach to designing, delivering, managing, and improving IT services to align with the business objectives.
- **ITIL4:** The latest evolution of the ITIL framework, emphasizing value co-creation, agility, and adaptability in ITSM.
- **Service Value System (SVS):** An ITIL4 framework that illustrates how all organizational components work together to co-create value through IT services.
- **Service Value Chain (SVC):** The core of the SVS, consisting of six interlinked activities that transform demand into value.
- **Value Stream:** An end-to-end workflow that cuts across various SVC activities to deliver specific outcomes for stakeholders.
- **Guiding Principles:** Universal ITIL4 recommendations that guide organizations in decision-making and service improvement, regardless of changes.
- **Governance:** The mechanism in ITIL4 that ensures policies, compliance, and strategic alignment across all IT activities.

- **Continual Improvement:** A core ITIL4 component focused on ongoing enhancements to services, processes, and practices to deliver greater value.
- **Organizational Agility:** The ability of an organization to adapt quickly to internal changes, such as new technologies or evolving business needs.
- **Intelligent ITSM:** The integration of AI, automation, and analytics into ITSM to enable proactive, data-driven decision-making and service delivery.

CHAPTER 3
Indispensibility of AI in Modern ITSM

Introduction

IT Service Management (ITSM) is under growing pressure to deliver faster, smarter, and more scalable services in an increasingly digital and complex environment. Yet many ITSM teams still struggle with outdated workflows, manual interventions, and reactive firefighting. These inefficiencies are not just operational inconveniences–they represent lost value, compromised user experiences, and missed opportunities for innovation. This is precisely where Artificial Intelligence (AI) steps in, not as a futuristic luxury, but as a practical enabler of transformation.

In this chapter, we will explore the core pain points that plague traditional ITSM–repetition, delays, and data overload–and examine how AI is uniquely positioned to address them. From automating routine tickets to predicting incidents before they occur, AI holds the key to unlocking a more intelligent, proactive, and efficient IT service landscape. So, whether you are aiming for quick wins or planning a long-term strategic shift, the case for AI in ITSM has never been stronger–or more urgent.

Structure

In this chapter, we will discuss the following topics:

- Key Pain Points in ITSM Ripe for AI
- AI's Potential for Boosting Efficiency, Accuracy, and Proactivity
- Quick Wins versus Long-Term Transformation

Key Pain Points in ITSM Ripe for AI

Despite decades of process optimization, modern IT Service Management (ITSM) still suffers from persistent pain points that hamper efficiency, responsiveness, and user satisfaction. Among these, three critical issues stand out as prime candidates for AI-driven transformation: **repetitive tasks, delayed responses, and data overload**. These challenges not only drain resources but also restrict the agility and value delivery of IT operations.

In today's digital enterprise, IT Service Management (ITSM) is expected to be fast, consistent, and business-aligned. Yet in reality, IT teams often find themselves stuck in a cycle of manual tasks, siloed information, and reactive firefighting. While ITIL4 and modern frameworks offer more agile and flexible models, the operational execution still relies heavily on human intervention. The result? Service delivery that is slower than expected, less accurate than needed, and harder to scale than desired.

Artificial Intelligence (AI) offers a new frontier—not to replace humans but to enhance how ITSM functions by targeting specific pain points that traditional approaches struggle to resolve. These are not futuristic ambitions; these are current-state inefficiencies that AI is uniquely equipped to solve.

Repetition: The Invisible Drain on IT Resources

A significant portion of ITSM work is repetitive by nature—password resets, access requests, software installations, status updates, and basic troubleshooting make up a large share of tickets handled daily. These tasks are time-consuming, error-prone, and unfulfilling for human agents, who could instead focus on more complex or value-adding activities.

- The Problem: Routine, repeatable tasks consume a disproportionate amount of service desk resources. Common examples include password resets, status updates, software installations, and basic troubleshooting—activities that add minimal strategic value but demand significant agent time.
- Real Life Example: At a healthcare organization, nearly 40% of the IT support tickets were password reset requests. Agents spent an average of 4 minutes per ticket, translating to over 200 hours per month in just one task.
- AI Solution: Intelligent virtual agents (chatbots) and Robotic Process Automation (RPA) tools can handle these tasks autonomously. When integrated with identity management systems, users can reset their passwords securely via conversational interfaces—zero human intervention needed.
- **Outcome:**
    - Higher first-contact resolution
    - Reduced ticket backlog
    - Happier agents focused on high-value work

Delays: Reactive Models Compromise SLAs

ITSM teams often operate in a reactive mode, addressing issues only after users report them. Delays are introduced at every stage–incident detection, triage, assignment, escalation, and resolution. These delays increase Mean Time to Resolution (MTTR), impact SLAs, and frustrate users.

- **Example:** Traditional ITSM relies heavily on users to report issues, often after significant disruption. Once a ticket is logged, delays compound during triage, categorization, and assignment. This leads to SLA breaches, frustrated users, and missed business commitments.
- **Real-Life Example:** In a logistics firm, users experienced slow response times during peak hours. By the time the helpdesk was aware of degraded network performance, the productivity of multiple departments had already been impacted.
- **AI Solution:** AI-powered anomaly detection and event correlation (via AIOps) can flag potential incidents early, even before users are aware. Combined with historical patterns, AI can prioritize and route incidents to the right teams instantly.
- **Outcome:**
  - Reduced Mean Time to Acknowledge (MTTA) and Mean Time to Resolve (MTTR)
  - Improved SLA compliance
  - Proactive incident prevention

Data Overload: Too Much Noise, Too Few Insights

ITSM platforms collect massive volumes of data from multiple channels–logs, alerts, tickets, configurations, user feedback, and monitoring systems. However, human agents often struggle to interpret this data in real time, leading to missed patterns, poor prioritization, and suboptimal decisions.

- **Example:** Modern IT environments produce a flood of data–monitoring logs, alerts, user feedback, asset configurations, and so on. The challenge is not collecting data; it is filtering the noise and surfacing actionable insights in real time.
- **Real-Life Example:** A financial services provider experienced a major outage that was preceded by 700+ system alerts in 48 hours. Due to alert fatigue, the real issue went unnoticed until it was too late.

- **AI Solution:** AI can ingest and analyze high-volume telemetry data, apply contextual filters, and identify critical patterns. Tools such as AIOps use unsupervised learning to correlate events, eliminate false positives, and escalate only meaningful alerts.
- **Outcome:**
    - Reduced alert fatigue
    - Increased situational awareness
    - Timely decision-making

The following table lists the summary of key pain points and AI interventions:

Pain Point	Operational Impact	AI-Driven Solution	Business Benefit
Repetition	Wasted effort on routine tasks	Chatbots, virtual agents, and intelligent RPA	Reduced workload, faster resolution, higher efficiency
Delays	SLA breaches, reactive firefighting	Predictive analytics, smart routing	Improved MTTR, proactive service
Data Overload	Inability to derive actionable insights	AIOps, event correlation, anomaly detection	Better decision-making, early risk mitigation

Table 3.1: *Summary of Key Pain Points and AI Interventions*

While **repetition, delays, and data overload** are among the most prominent and AI-ready pain points in ITSM, several **additional challenges** also make a strong case for AI intervention. The following are the **four more pain points** worth including in the discussion.

Inconsistent Decision-Making and Prioritization

Human agents often prioritize tickets based on subjective judgment, incomplete information, or "gut feeling," leading to inconsistencies in incident handling and SLA violations.

- **Example:** Without AI, ticket prioritization and categorization often depend on the individual agent's judgment, which varies widely. This inconsistency can result in important tickets being delayed or low-impact issues being escalated.
- **Real-Life Example:**

  In a global bank, service requests from executives were occasionally assigned lower priority due to a lack of contextual data on user roles, resulting in reputational damage.

- **AI Solution:**

  Natural Language Processing (NLP) and Machine Learning (ML) algorithms can scan ticket content, correlate it with user profiles, and suggest intelligent prioritization based on business impact and urgency.

- **Outcome:**
  - More consistent and objective prioritization
  - Reduced escalations
  - Better alignment with business priorities

Manual ticket prioritization often relies on human judgment, which can vary significantly based on experience, interpretation, or incomplete data, leading to inconsistent service quality and SLA breaches. A real-world case from a global bank showed how a lack of contextual understanding caused executive tickets to be mis prioritized, resulting in reputational impact. AI addresses this by using NLP and ML to analyze ticket content and user profiles, enabling more consistent, impact-driven prioritization. The result is reduced escalations and stronger alignment between IT operations and business priorities.

Skill Mismatch and Reassignment Loops

Assigning tickets to the wrong team or agent leads to prolonged resolution times and repeated reassignments.

- **Example:** Tickets are frequently misrouted to the wrong teams due to manual categorization or unclear ticket descriptions, causing repeated handoffs and delays in resolution.
- **Real-Life Example:** In a managed services provider, nearly 25% of tickets were reassigned at least once, adding an average of 8 hours to each case.
- **AI Solution:** AI can recommend the most suitable team or technician based on previous resolution patterns, ticket history, and expertise mapping.
- **Outcome:**
  - Faster first-time resolution
  - Lower ticket handling time
  - Improved agent utilization

Manual ticket assignment often results in mismatches between the issue and the team's expertise, leading to repeated reassignments and extended resolution times. For example, a managed services provider observed that 25% of tickets were reassigned at least once, adding significant delays. AI resolves this challenge by analyzing past ticket data, resolution history, and skill maps to recommend the most appropriate team or technician from the outset. This leads to faster first-time resolution, reduced handling time, and better utilization of support resources.

Underused Knowledge Bases

ITSM often suffers from underused or poorly structured knowledge bases. Agents reinvent solutions for recurring issues or fail to leverage existing documentation.

- **Example:** Even when knowledge bases exist, they are often underutilized due to poor structure or lack of discovery tools. Agents end up reinventing solutions for problems that have already been solved.
- **Real-Life Example:** A software company had over 1,500 Knowledge Base articles, but fewer than 5% were accessed regularly by agents during incident resolution.
- **AI Solution:** NLP-driven search and contextual recommendation engines can suggest the most relevant KB articles based on ticket content in real time.
- **Outcome:**
    - Increased First Contact Resolution (FCR)
    - Reduced ticket volume
    - Enhanced user self-service

Despite having extensive documentation, many organizations struggle with underutilized knowledge bases due to poor structure or lack of intelligent search capabilities. Agents often bypass existing solutions and resolve issues manually, leading to inefficiencies. In one software company, less than 5% of 1,500+ KB articles were accessed regularly. AI addresses this by using NLP-driven search and contextual recommendations to surface the most relevant articles in real time. This boosts First Contact Resolution (FCR), reduces ticket volume, and encourages both agent efficiency and user self-service.

Lack of Real-Time Operational Intelligence

IT managers and leadership often lack a live, consolidated view of operational health, leading to delayed strategic decisions and firefighting mode operations.

- **Example:** ITSM leaders often lack a live, consolidated view of what is happening across the service landscape, making it hard to make informed decisions or forecast issues.
- **Real-Life Example:** A CIO preparing for a quarterly review struggled to produce reports on incident trends and SLA breaches across business units due to fragmented tools and manual reporting.

- **AI Solution:** AI dashboards and analytics platforms can provide real-time, predictive insights into ITSM metrics, trends, and anomalies, offering both granular and strategic visibility.
- **Outcome:**
    - o Data-driven service improvement
    - o Early warning systems for major incidents
    - o Executive-level transparency

The following table lists the optional summary of additional Key pain points and AI interventions:

Additional Pain Point	AI-Driven Remedy	Benefit
Inconsistent prioritization	Context-aware triage using ML/NLP	SLA adherence, consistent user experience
Skill mismatch	AI-based technician and team assignment	Faster resolution, fewer ticket reassignments
Poor knowledge utilization	NLP-driven knowledge article suggestions	Improved First Contact Resolution (FCR), lower workload
Lack of real-time visibility	AI dashboards and predictive trend analysis	Data-driven decisions, proactive service improvement

Table 3.2: *Optional Summary of Additional Key Pain Points and AI Interventions*

These pain points are not theoretical–they are daily realities in organizations of every size and sector. AI offers practical, proven ways to eliminate friction, optimize performance, and create space for IT teams to innovate rather than react. By identifying where these problems lie and applying the right AI capabilities, organizations take the first step toward smarter, more service-oriented operations.

AI is not here to replace humans in ITSM, but to augment their capabilities–removing the repetitive, anticipating the inevitable, and clarifying the complex. By targeting these high-friction areas, organizations can take a strategic first step toward intelligent service management.

AI's Potential for Boosting Efficiency, Accuracy, and Proactivity

AI is not just a productivity booster–it is a strategic enabler. In the context of ITSM, where agility, consistency, and foresight are crucial, AI offers the capability to go beyond traditional automation. While automation reduces human effort, **AI enhances decision-making, scales operations intelligently, and introduces foresight into service delivery**. In this section, we explore how AI boosts **efficiency**, ensures

accuracy, and drives **proactivity** in ITSM environments–the three pillars that can redefine operational excellence.

Boosting Efficiency: Doing More with Less

In today's high-pressure IT environments, efficiency is no longer a luxury–it is a necessity. AI enables ITSM teams to "do more with less" by automating time-consuming, low-value tasks such as ticket categorization, password resets, and incident routing. This frees up human agents to focus on complex problem-solving and customer experience. With intelligent automation and AI-driven decision support, organizations can streamline workflows, reduce manual intervention, and optimize resource utilization. The result: faster response times, reduced operational costs, and more agile service delivery–without necessarily expanding the workforce or infrastructure.

- **The Challenge:** IT teams are often expected to support growing digital ecosystems without a proportional increase in headcount or budget. Manual effort, slow workflows, and fragmented tools lower throughput and overload support staff.
- **AI as the Solution:** AI improves operational efficiency by **automating complex multi-step tasks**, intelligently routing tickets, predicting workload peaks, and optimizing resource allocation.
- **Examples:**
    - **Intelligent Ticket Categorization and Routing:** AI models trained on historical data can automatically categorize and assign tickets to the appropriate support team. For instance, an NLP engine identifies keywords and sentiment from the user's input and instantly routes the ticket to the best-fit queue, reducing triage time from minutes to seconds.
    - **Dynamic Workload Balancing:** AI can monitor team performance in real time and recommend optimal workload distribution, ensuring no agent is overloaded.
- **Benefits:**
    - Faster service desk throughput
    - Lower handling times
    - Reduced escalations and reassignment cycles

Modern ITSM teams face growing demands without proportional increases in resources. Routine tasks such as ticket categorization, password resets, and incident routing consume valuable time and reduce service desk throughput. AI helps alleviate this by automating repetitive, low-value activities and intelligently distributing workload across teams. With tools such as NLP-based ticket routing and dynamic workload balancing, organizations can streamline operations, reduce manual effort, and improve service agility–ultimately delivering more value without scaling headcount or infrastructure.

Improving Accuracy: Getting It Right the First Time

In today's fast-paced digital environments, the cost of inaccuracy in IT service management is high, both in terms of operational inefficiency and user dissatisfaction. Whether it is misdiagnosing an incident, misclassifying a ticket, or applying the wrong resolution, even small errors can cascade into recurring disruptions and eroded trust. This is where AI becomes a game-changer. By minimizing human error and enhancing decision-making with data-driven insights, AI enables service teams to get it right the first time, ensuring that incidents are resolved accurately, consistently, and with lasting impact.

The Challenge: Human error in diagnosis, prioritization, or resolution often leads to repeat incidents, user dissatisfaction, and avoidable escalations. Inconsistent decisions, incorrect categorization, and misdiagnosis are common, even among experienced agents.

AI as the Solution: AI enhances accuracy by leveraging pattern recognition, contextual analysis, and real-time data correlation to reduce errors in judgment and execution.

- **Examples:**
  - **Predictive Root Cause Analysis:** AI analyzes incident trends, logs, and infrastructure metrics to pinpoint the most probable root cause of recurring issues, enabling precise and lasting resolution.
  - **Context-Aware Recommendations:** AI agents surface relevant KB articles, known error records, or historical solutions at the point of need, improving decision accuracy during incident resolution.
- **Benefits:**
  - Increased first-contact resolution
  - Reduced recurrence of known issues
  - Higher consistency in service delivery

Human error in ticket categorization, diagnosis, or prioritization can lead to repeat incidents, escalations, and inconsistent service. AI enhances accuracy by analyzing contextual data, recognizing patterns, and offering real-time decision support. With capabilities including predictive root cause analysis and context-aware knowledge recommendations, AI ensures that the right solutions are applied quickly and consistently. This results in higher first-contact resolution rates, fewer recurring issues, and a more reliable service experience for users.

Driving Proactivity: From Reactive to Preventive ITSM

Traditional ITSM has largely been reactive, responding to incidents only after users report them. AI shifts this paradigm by enabling predictive insights and early detection of anomalies before they escalate into full-blown issues. With capabilities such as pattern recognition, trend analysis, and anomaly detection, AI empowers service teams to anticipate outages, proactively schedule maintenance, and prevent SLA breaches. Instead of firefighting, IT teams become strategic enablers, minimizing downtime, enhancing service reliability, and delivering a smoother experience to users and stakeholders, alike.

The Challenge: Traditional ITSM operates in reactive mode–acting only after users report issues. This leads to lost time, service disruptions, and user dissatisfaction. IT leaders often lack early warnings or actionable foresight.

AI as the Solution: AI enables predictive and preventive service management by identifying the potential problems before they escalate, automating early interventions, and generating real-time insights.

- **Examples:**
    - **Anomaly Detection and Alerting:** AIOps platforms use machine learning to detect subtle deviations in system behavior (for example, CPU spikes, latency, abnormal log patterns) and alert the support team before thresholds are breached.
    - **User Behavior Analysis:** AI monitors usage patterns and predicts when a service might be nearing capacity, degrading in quality, or triggering shadow IT usage–empowering IT to act early.
- **Benefits:**
    - Reduced major incidents and SLA breaches.
    - Higher system uptime and service availability.
    - IT is seen as a proactive business enabler, not just a support function.

Traditional ITSM is reactive by nature–addressing issues only after they impact users. AI changes this by enabling predictive insights and early anomaly detection, allowing IT teams to act before problems escalate. Tools such as AIOps detect subtle behavioral changes, while user behavior analytics forecast demand surges or potential failures.

This shift from firefighting to foresight reduces major incidents, boosts uptime, and repositions IT as a proactive business enabler rather than a reactive support function.

The following table lists the comparison between traditional ITSM and AI-Augmented ITSM:

Capability	**Traditional ITSM**	**AI-Augmented ITSM**
Ticket Handling	Manual triage and assignment	Automated categorization and routing
Resolution Accuracy	Depends on the agent's knowledge	Contextual recommendations and past resolution mapping
Incident Management	Reactive and user-reported	Predictive insights and early anomaly detection
Knowledge Access	Search-based, keyword-dependent	AI-suggested articles based on ticket context
Performance Monitoring	Static dashboards and reports	Real-time analytics with intelligent alerting

Table 3.3: *Comparison between Traditional ITSM and AI-Augmented ITSM*

AI's true promise lies in **amplifying human capabilities**–not just replacing tasks, but enabling faster decisions, better judgment, and timely actions. For ITSM teams striving to meet the growing demands of digital business, AI offers a reliable partner in achieving operational excellence. It transforms the service desk into a smart, scalable, and proactive engine of business value.

Quick Wins versus Long-Term Transformation

For many organizations, adopting AI in ITSM can seem like a daunting, large-scale transformation initiative. However, AI implementation does not have to be "all or nothing." The journey to intelligent ITSM can begin with **quick, low-risk wins** that deliver immediate value while simultaneously building the foundation for **long-term, strategic transformation**. In this section, we explore both dimensions and how organizations can balance short-term ROI with a future-ready vision.

Quick Wins: Small Steps, Big Impact

Quick wins are **tactical, low-complexity applications of AI** that can be deployed with minimal disruption, using existing tools and data. These initiatives typically focus on **reducing workload, speeding up responses, and improving user experience** in well-defined, repeatable areas of ITSM.

The following is the list of common quick wins:

- **AI-Powered Virtual Agents (Chatbots):** Enable users to interact with the service desk 24/7 for common requests such as password resets, status updates, or FAQs.
    - *Example:* A university deployed an AI chatbot for IT helpdesk queries and saw a 30% drop in call volume within two months.
- **Auto-Categorization and Ticket Routing:** Use NLP and machine learning to assign the right priority, category, and team based on historical ticket data.
    - *Example:* A retail company reduced triage time by 70% by implementing ML-based routing.
- **Knowledge Article Recommendations:** Automatically suggest relevant KB articles based on ticket content.
    - *Example:* A telecom provider increased first-contact resolution by 18% by deploying an AI-powered knowledge suggestion engine.

The following table lists a few characteristics of quick wins:

Attribute	**Description**
Time to Implement	Days
Technical Complexity	Low to medium
Change Management	Minimal disruption; localized changes
Return on Investment	Immediate to short-term (~1-3 months)
Ideal Use Cases	Service desk, self-service, routing, knowledge access

Table 3.4: *Characteristics of Quick Wins*

Long-Term Transformation: Building a Cognitive ITSM Ecosystem

Long-term transformation involves embedding AI into the **core fabric of ITSM operations**, workflows, and governance. This requires changes to culture, architecture, processes, and capabilities—but it also unlocks transformative benefits such as **predictive service management, self-healing systems, and autonomous operations**.

Strategic Areas for Long-Term Transformation:

- **AIOps and Predictive Incident Management:** Leverage AI to detect anomalies, correlate events, and predict incidents before users are affected.

  - *Example:* A financial institution reduced P1 incidents by 40% using AI-driven predictive analytics and real-time event correlation.
- **Dynamic CMDB and AI-Augmented Asset Management:** Automatically update the configuration management database based on system behaviors and usage patterns.
  - *Example:* An insurance firm improved audit readiness and compliance accuracy with an AI-augmented CMDB.
- **AI-Driven Continual Improvement:** Use data mining, sentiment analysis, and trend detection to identify process improvement opportunities dynamically.
  - *Example:* A managed services provider used AI insights from ticket metadata to redesign its change enablement process, improving implementation success rates.
- **Intelligent Automation Orchestration:** Coordinate AI, RPA, and workflow engines to execute end-to-end service requests, incident responses, and recovery procedures autonomously.

The following table lists a few characteristics of long-term quick wins:

Attribute	Description
Time to Implement	Several months to years
Technical Complexity	High (integration with tools, data architecture needed)
Change Management	High organizational impact and stakeholder alignment
Return on Investment	Medium to long-term (~6–24 months)
Ideal Use Cases	Predictive maintenance, AIOps, cognitive workflows

Table 3.5: *Characteristics of Long-Term Wins*

Balancing Both: A Phased, Scalable Strategy

Organizations don't have to choose between short-term gains and long-term vision. The most successful ITSM leaders approach AI adoption through **a phased strategy**–starting with quick wins that build confidence, generate momentum, and lay the groundwork for strategic transformation.

Maturity Pathway:

- Use AI both for collecting and analyzing data
- **Start with foundational AI use cases** (chatbots, smart routing, KB suggestions)

- **Establish governance and change readiness** for AI expansion.
- **Scale into integrated solutions** such as AIOps and predictive analytics.
- **Continuously review outcomes**, and adapt strategy using AI-enabled insights.

The following table describes a real-life roadmap example:

Phase	Initiative	Impact Timeline
Phase 1: 0–3 months	Virtual agent for password resets	Immediate
Phase 2: 3–6 months	Smart routing + auto-prioritization	Short-term ROI
Phase 3: 6–12 months	Predictive alerting (AIOps)	Mid-term efficiency
Phase 4: 12–24 months	AI-enabled self-healing + dynamic CMDB	Long-term innovation

Table 3.6: *Real-Life Roadmap Example*

AI success in ITSM does not demand massive upfront investments or overnight overhauls. It begins with smart, strategic steps that solve pressing challenges and build internal trust. By combining quick wins with a long-term roadmap, organizations can evolve from reactive service providers to proactive, intelligent service partners, turning ITSM into a powerhouse of continuous value creation.

Conclusion

AI is no longer a futuristic add-on to ITSM–it is a present-day necessity that enables service management to evolve from reactive support to intelligent, value-driven engagement. Throughout this chapter, we have explored the persistent operational challenges that limit ITSM effectiveness and how AI addresses them through automation, insight, and prediction. Whether it is eliminating repetitive tasks, improving resolution accuracy, or proactively preventing incidents, AI delivers tangible outcomes across the ITSM lifecycle.

By starting with quick, low-risk wins and progressively scaling toward long-term transformation, organizations can build a resilient, scalable, and future-ready ITSM ecosystem. The road to smarter service management does not require a revolution–it requires a commitment to evolve, one intelligent step at a time!

In the next chapter, we will discuss the key AI concepts in service management context. We will try to explain how these technologies work in simple terms and how they power every day ITSM functions.

Multiple Choice Questions

1. What is one of the biggest contributors to inefficiency in traditional ITSM operations?
    a. Complex budgeting processes
    b. High employee turnover
    c. Manual handling of repetitive tasks
    d. Lack of mobile apps
2. How does AI help in reducing SLA breaches in ITSM?
    a. By outsourcing tasks to third-party vendors
    b. By predicting and preventing incidents before they escalate
    c. By increasing the number of IT support staff
    d. By limiting user access during peak hours
3. Which of the following is considered a quick win in AI adoption for ITSM?
    a. Implementing a full AIOps architecture
    b. Deploying AI-driven dynamic CMDB updates
    c. Using chatbots for password resets
    d. Replacing legacy ticketing systems
4. What role does AI play in improving ticket accuracy and resolution?
    a. It replaces human agents completely.
    b. It creates more escalations for better visibility.
    c. It offers contextual recommendations and pattern-based analysis.
    d. It reduces the number of ticket categories.
5. What is a key benefit of AI in managing data overload in ITSM environments?
    a. It archives all incoming alerts for future use.
    b. It reduces the number of monitoring tools.
    c. It applies contextual filtering to highlight actionable insights.
    d. It deletes duplicate logs automatically.

Answers

1. c
2. b
3. c
4. c
5. c

Questions

1. Explain why repetitive tasks in ITSM are ideal candidates for AI-driven automation. Provide examples from real-world scenarios discussed in the chapter.
2. How does AI improve the accuracy of incident categorization and ticket routing compared to manual methods?
3. Describe the role of anomaly detection and predictive analytics in transforming ITSM from reactive to proactive.
4. What are the primary differences between quick wins and long-term AI transformations in ITSM? Provide examples of each.
5. How can AI help in resolving the issue of data overload in ITSM environments?
6. What are the business benefits of using AI-powered tools like NLP and machine learning in prioritizing IT tickets?
7. Discuss the concept of skill mismatch in ITSM and how AI helps to reduce reassignment loops.
8. How do AI dashboards and analytics tools enhance real-time visibility for IT managers and business leaders?
9. Outline a phased roadmap for implementing AI in ITSM, starting from low complexity use cases to more strategic initiatives.
10. Why is it important for organizations to combine quick wins with a long-term vision for AI adoption in ITSM?

Key Terms

- **Repetitive Tasks:** Routine and low-complexity service requests–such as password resets or software installations–that are frequently encountered in ITSM and ideal for AI-driven automation.
- **Anomaly Detection:** A machine learning technique used to identify unusual patterns or behaviors in IT systems that may indicate potential incidents or service disruptions before they occur.
- **AIOps (Artificial Intelligence for IT Operations):** The application of AI technologies (for example, machine learning, big data analytics) to enhance and automate IT operations tasks, such as performance monitoring and event correlation.
- **Virtual Agent (Chatbot):** An AI-powered tool that interacts with users in natural language to resolve common service requests or answer IT support questions without human intervention.
- **Predictive Analytics:** The use of historical and real-time data combined with AI models to forecast potential IT incidents, user behavior, or infrastructure performance issues.
- **Intelligent Routing:** AI-enabled ticket assignment based on factors such as ticket content, team skill sets, and past resolution trends, ensuring faster and more accurate service delivery.
- **Knowledge Article Recommendation:** An AI capability that suggests relevant knowledge base articles in real time based on the context of a service ticket or user query.
- **Quick Wins:** Low-complexity, high-impact AI implementations in ITSM that deliver immediate value–such as chatbot deployment or ticket categorization–without major system overhauls.
- **Skill Mismatch:** A common issue where tickets are assigned to agents or teams lacking the appropriate expertise, leading to resolution delays; AI can reduce this through intelligent assignment.
- **Proactive ITSM:** A modern approach where IT services anticipate and prevent issues using AI and data-driven insights, rather than waiting to react after incidents occur.

CHAPTER 4
Understanding AI for Service Teams

Introduction

Artificial Intelligence is no longer the domain of researchers and tech giants—it is becoming an everyday reality for IT service teams. Whether you are aware of it or not, AI is already influencing how tickets are categorized, how incidents are prioritized, and even how user sentiment is interpreted in your service desk. Yet for many professionals, the terms surrounding AI—like *machine learning*, *deep learning*, and *natural language processing*—remain shrouded in technical ambiguity.

This chapter aims to break that barrier. We will take a simple, practical approach to understanding these AI technologies, showing how they work, what they mean in plain English, and most importantly, how they apply directly to ITSM tasks. You do not need a background in data science to grasp the power of supervised or unsupervised learning. All you need is curiosity and a willingness to explore how these systems are quietly transforming service operations from behind the scenes.

Imagine a service desk tool that can learn from every past incident and suggest the next best action, or a chatbot that not only responds with the correct answer but also detects user frustration based on their language. These are not futuristic ideas—they are real applications of AI that stem from foundational concepts we will explain here.

Throughout this chapter, we will explore the logic behind these tools, beginning with how AI "learns" from data and makes decisions. We will then move into the distinctions between different learning models, and finally, map these technologies to familiarize ITSM functions such as ticket triage, automation, knowledge recommendations, and experience management.

By the end of this chapter, you will have a solid understanding of what powers intelligent service management. You will be able to look beyond the AI hype and identify how these systems truly work—and how your team can start leveraging them more effectively.

Structure

In this chapter, we will discuss the following topics:

- Machine Learning, Deep Learning, Natural Language Processing
- Supervised versus Unsupervised Learning
- Application of These Concepts in a Service Environment

Machine Learning, Deep Learning, Natural Language Processing

Artificial Intelligence is not a single technology–it is a collection of capabilities, and three of the most essential among them are **Machine Learning (ML)**, **Deep Learning (DL)**, and **Natural Language Processing (NLP)**. While these terms are often used interchangeably in casual conversation, each plays a distinct role in making IT systems smarter, more responsive, and increasingly autonomous.

Why AI Concepts Matter for Service Management

The buzz around artificial intelligence in IT service management is no longer a hype–it is a reality unfolding across service desks, operations centers, and self-service portals. However, behind the curtain of every "intelligent" recommendation or automation lies a specific type of AI technique doing the heavy lifting. Among the most influential are **Machine Learning (ML)**, **Deep Learning (DL)**, and **Natural Language Processing (NLP)**.

Understanding these concepts is critical not just for developers or data scientists, but for **service managers, analysts, and consultants** seeking to improve service performance, reduce ticket volumes, and deliver better user experiences. This chapter breaks each down into understandable terms, real-life scenarios, and practical relevance to ITSM environments

Understanding Machine Learning: Learning from Experience

Let us begin with **machine learning**, often referred to as the backbone of modern AI. At its core, machine learning is about teaching systems to learn from data. Instead of being explicitly programmed for every possible scenario, a machine learning model is trained on historical examples–like past incident tickets or user requests–and then uses that experience to make predictions or decisions when new data appears.

For example, if an ITSM tool has seen hundreds of passwords reset requests, it can eventually learn to recognize and automatically classify similar tickets without human input.

Machine learning is a subset of artificial intelligence that allows systems to **learn from data** and **make decisions or predictions** without being explicitly programmed for every rule. It relies on patterns and past experiences rather than hard-coded logic.

At its core, machine learning is like training an intern with examples. The more examples you provide–tickets, incidents, logs–the better the system becomes at recognizing patterns and making informed decisions when faced with new inputs.

Real-Life Examples in ITSM:

- **Ticket Classification:** A machine learning model trained on thousands of past tickets can automatically categorize new incidents such as *network*, *hardware*, *application issue*, and more, saving analysts valuable time.
- **Incident Prediction:** By analyzing historical patterns, ML can identify incidents that are likely to recur under specific conditions–helping prevent service disruptions.
- **SLA Breach Forecasting:** ML models can learn to spot tickets at risk of missing SLAs based on attributes such as priority, time to first response, assignee workload, and historical breach trends.

Analogy:

Imagine you are managing a service desk and have trained a new analyst by walking them through 500 example tickets. Eventually, they start to "just know" where a new issue fits. That's machine learning in action–except the system does not forget and can process thousands of cases in seconds.

We must also be aware of the **misconceptions** about **Machine Learning (ML)**.

Few prominent ones are as follows:

- **Machine learning does not need human oversight:** Many assume that once a model is trained, it can function indefinitely without intervention. In reality, models must be monitored and retrained periodically to remain effective and aligned with evolving service patterns.
- **The more the data, the better the model:** Quantity doesn't guarantee quality. Poorly labeled, outdated, or irrelevant data can negatively impact the accuracy of predictions.
- **Machine learning always gives the correct answer:** ML provides probabilities based on patterns–it is fallible. *It should assist human judgment, not replace it.*

Building on this foundation is **deep learning**, which is essentially a more advanced form of machine learning.

Understanding Deep Learning: Going Deeper with DATA

Deep learning uses artificial neural networks inspired by the human brain, with multiple layers of decision-making. This allows systems to process more complex and less structured information–such as analyzing user comments, interpreting logs, or detecting anomalies in system behavior. In ITSM, deep learning might power a predictive engine that forecasts outages based on patterns buried deep within monitoring data, something traditional scripts would likely miss.

Deep learning is a specialized branch of machine learning that uses **neural networks with many layers** (hence "deep") to model and process complex patterns. These models are inspired by the structure of the human brain and excel at working with unstructured or high-volume data–such as logs, audio, or images.

While traditional ML works well with the structured data, deep learning thrives when the patterns are nonlinear, hidden, or difficult to express with simple rules.

Real-Life Examples in ITSM:

- **Anomaly Detection in Logs**: Deep learning can sift through massive volumes of infrastructure logs to detect subtle deviations that may signal early-stage outages or cybersecurity threats.
- **Voice-to-Text and Emotion Analysis**: DL models power voice assistants and can transcribe user calls while also identifying emotional tone–useful for call center quality monitoring.
- **Intelligent Chatbots**: Deep learning enables chatbots to understand multi-turn conversations and provide contextual responses, even when users stray from predefined paths.

Analogy:

Traditional machine learning is like reading a recipe and following instructions. Deep learning, on the other hand, is like a chef who has developed instincts after years in the kitchen–it knows how to adjust on the fly even when something unexpected happens.

We must also be aware of the **misconceptions** about **Deep learning (DL)**.

Few prominent ones are as follows:

- **Deep learning is just a better version of machine learning:** Deep learning is suited for complex, unstructured data. It does not replace traditional ML; it complements it where needed.

- **Deep learning models understand logic like humans do:** Despite being inspired by the human brain, DL models do not think–they identify statistical patterns, which can sometimes lead to strange or incorrect results.
- **Deep learning models are explainable:** Most deep learning models operate as 'black boxes,' making it difficult to understand how decisions are made–a challenge in sensitive or regulated ITSM environments.

Then there is **Natural Language Processing** or **NLP**–the AI capability that enables computers to understand and interact using human language.

Understanding Natural Language Processing: Making Sense of Human Language

Natural language processing is the AI capability that enables machines to **understand, interpret, and generate human language**–whether it is written or spoken. NLP bridges the gap between structured systems and the messy, ambiguous, as well as richly contextual nature of human communication.

It combines linguistics, computational methods, and machine learning to extract the meaning from unstructured data such as emails, chats, surveys, and spoken language.

Real-Life Examples in ITSM:

- **Sentiment Analysis:** NLP models can analyze the incoming messages or feedback to detect whether a user is satisfied, frustrated, or angry – helping prioritize emotionally charged tickets.
- **Intent Detection in Self-Service Portals:** When a user types "I cannot print," NLP interprets the intent and routes the request to the right category, even if the wording is informal.
- **Knowledge Article Recommendation:** NLP helps match user-entered queries to relevant knowledge base articles, even if the words do not match exactly, improving self-resolution rates.

Analogy:

Think of NLP as a bilingual translator that understands both human and machine language. It takes the natural, unstructured way we speak or write, and transforms it into data that computers can act on.

NLP is what allows a chatbot to understand a user's query like "My laptop will not connect to Wi-Fi" and respond meaningfully, or what enables sentiment analysis to determine whether a user is angry, confused, or satisfied based on their language. In ITSM, NLP is the bridge between structured systems and unstructured, human inputs–emails, chats, voice messages, or survey feedback.

We must also be aware of the **misconceptions** about Natural Language Processing (NLP). Few prominent ones are as follows:

- **NLP understands language exactly like a human**: NLP can process syntax and extract meaning from patterns, but it doesn't comprehend context, tone, or sarcasm the way people do.
- **NLP chatbots can fully replace human support**: NLP bots can handle routine queries, but for complex or emotionally charged situations, human support remains critical.
- **NLP does not require continuous training**: Language evolves–slang, acronyms, and phrasing change. NLP models need regular updates to remain effective and relevant in communication-heavy environments.

The following table summarizes these three concepts:

Concept	Focus Area	Key Use in ITSM	Strengths
Machine Learning	Structured data, prediction	Ticket classification, SLA forecasting	Fast learning from past patterns
Deep Learning	Unstructured or complex data	Log analysis, chatbot interactions, emotion detection	Handles high-volume and subtle complexities
Natural Language Processing	Human language interpretation	Sentiment detection, chatbots, knowledge search	Bridges human input and machine response

Table 4.1: *Summarization of ML, DL, and NLP*

Together, these three technologies form the cognitive core of intelligent service management. ML helps systems learn from experience, DL helps uncover deep patterns, and NLP helps make sense of language–turning messy, human data into structured, actionable insights. Understanding them is not just about knowing the theory–it is about seeing how they power the tools your service desk uses every day, often invisibly, but with enormous impact.

Machine learning, deep learning, and natural language processing are not abstract academic ideas–they are **practical tools already embedded** in many ITSM solutions. By understanding what they are and how they work, service management teams can better assess vendor solutions, ask sharper questions during implementation, and even identify new use cases for intelligent automation.

The more familiar you are with these technologies, the more equipped you are to lead in an AI-enabled service environment–where speed, accuracy, and user experience are no longer trade-offs, but simultaneous goals.

Supervised versus Unsupervised Learning

To truly understand how machine learning operates within ITSM, it helps to explore two fundamental learning approaches: **supervised learning** and **unsupervised learning**. These terms describe how an AI model is trained–and what kind of data it needs to become effective.

Let us start with **supervised learning**, the most commonly used approach in service management applications. In this method, the AI is trained on a labeled dataset–where each input has a known, correct output. Think of it as teaching by example. For instance, if you feed the model thousands of historical incidents labeled with categories like *hardware*, *software*, *network*, or *access issue*, it will learn to recognize patterns in new tickets and automatically assign the appropriate category. This is supervision in action–the model is guided by what the correct answers should be.

Supervised learning excels in environments where structured historical data is abundant. That is why it is effective in ITSM scenarios, such as ticket classification, incident prediction, SLA breach detection, and routing to the right technician or team. As more data becomes available, the model improves its accuracy–learning from past mistakes, just like a human analyst would.

On the other hand, **unsupervised learning** works differently. Here, the data has no labels or predefined outcomes. Instead, the AI looks for hidden patterns, groupings, or relationships within the data. Imagine feeding the system all customer feedback and letting it discover clusters of similar complaints–without being told what those clusters mean. It might uncover that certain issues tend to spike after a system patch or that users in a particular department are reporting performance issues more frequently.

In ITSM, unsupervised learning is especially useful for **anomaly detection**, **trend analysis**, and **problem identification**. It can help surface unknown issues that have not been reported yet but are lurking within system logs, user behavior, or ticket metadata.

In essence, supervised learning helps AI become good at specific, repeatable tasks based on clear historical knowledge. Unsupervised learning allows it to explore the unknown, make sense of the messy data, and reveal insights that even humans may miss. Thus, both play a critical role in shaping smarter, more proactive service management systems.

Understanding the different types of learning methods in AI is crucial for applying the right approach to various ITSM problems. Two of the most widely used techniques in machine learning are supervised and unsupervised learning. This chapter explains what these learning methods are, how they work, where they fit in ITSM, and the pros and cons associated with each.

Understanding Supervised Learning

Supervised learning is a type of machine learning where the model is trained on a labeled dataset. Each training example is paired with an output label, enabling the algorithm to learn a mapping from inputs to the desired output. This method is called 'supervised' because the process of an algorithm learning from the training dataset can be thought of as a teacher supervising the learning process.

The following steps explain how Supervised Learning works:

1. Collect a dataset with input-output pairs (for example, ticket descriptions and their categories).
2. Split the dataset into training and testing sets.
3. Train the model using the training data.
4. Validate the model on the testing data to assess accuracy.
5. Deploy the model for real-time predictions.

Use Cases in ITSM

- Ticket classification based on historical labels
- Predicting SLA breaches
- Forecasting incident trends

Understanding Unsupervised Learning

Unsupervised learning deals with data that has no labels. The goal is to infer the natural structure present within a set of data points. This type of learning is useful when you want to explore the data and find hidden patterns without knowing what you are looking for in advance.

The following steps explain how Unsupervised Learning works:

1. Collect a dataset without output labels.
2. Choose an unsupervised algorithm (for example, clustering or dimensionality reduction).
3. Run the algorithm to identify patterns or groupings.
4. Analyze the results for insights or anomaly detection.

Use Cases in ITSM

- Identifying new ticket categories

- Anomaly detection in system logs
- Grouping user feedback for trends

Comparison: Supervised versus Unsupervised Learning

Supervised Learning:

- Requires labeled data
- Produces highly accurate models for known tasks
- Better for prediction and classification
- Needs continuous labeled data updates

Unsupervised Learning:

- Works with unlabeled data
- Useful for exploring unknown patterns
- Better for clustering and anomaly detection
- Interpretability can be challenging

Pros and Cons

Supervised Learning

Pros:

- Accurate and reliable predictions
- Easy to evaluate using standard metrics
- Clear objective from labeled data

Cons:

- Requires large amounts of labeled data
- Can be expensive and time-consuming to label
- Less flexible for discovering unknown patterns

Unsupervised Learning

Pros:

- No need for labeled data
- Ideal for exploring unknown structures
- Great for anomaly detection

Cons:

- Results can be harder to interpret
- No standard accuracy metrics
- May find patterns that are not meaningful

Real-Life Examples of Supervised Learning in ITSM

- A service desk at a global telecom provider uses a supervised ML model trained on 50,000 historical tickets to automatically classify new incoming tickets into categories such as 'Connectivity Issue', 'Billing Query', or 'Account Access'.
- A Managed Service Provider (MSP) uses supervised models to predict which tickets are likely to breach SLAs based on previous resolution times, ticket priorities, and agent workload.
- An enterprise IT team predicts which IT assets are most likely to fail within the next 30 days using labeled maintenance logs and incident history.

Real-Life Examples of Unsupervised Learning in ITSM

- An IT operations team uses clustering to analyze thousands of logs from different systems and identify abnormal patterns that could indicate early signs of ransomware or system misuse.
- A financial services ITSM team analyzes feedback from end-user surveys using topic modeling (an unsupervised technique) to identify recurring complaints, such as 'slow system login' or 'delayed approvals', without pre-defined tags.
- A hospital IT department applies anomaly detection on network monitoring data to identify unusual spikes in traffic that may signal configuration errors or a cyberattack.

Application of These Concepts in a Service Environment

Understanding how supervised and unsupervised learning operate is only part of the equation. To unlock their full value, we must examine how these AI methods are applied within actual service environments, particularly in IT service management (ITSM).

Supervised Learning in Service Environments

In a structured service environment, such as an IT helpdesk or service desk, supervised learning is especially useful for repetitive, rule-based tasks. It enables the automation of decisions that follow historical trends.

For example, a company that logs thousands of incidents each month can train a model using past ticket categories and resolutions. When new tickets arrive, the model automatically assigns them to the right category and team, dramatically reducing manual triage. This not only saves time but also improves consistency and speeds up response times.

In another case, an AI model is trained to predict which tickets are likely to miss their SLA deadlines. Service managers use this insight to prioritize workloads and allocate resources proactively, ensuring critical issues are resolved on time.

Supervised learning is also frequently embedded in ITSM platforms (such as, ServiceNow, BMC, or ManageEngine) as part of smart ticketing or AI-powered incident routing features.

Unsupervised Learning in Service Environments

Unsupervised learning shines in scenarios where the organization doesn't yet know what patterns exist in the data. It is particularly valuable for identifying previously unseen trends or grouping data into meaningful clusters without prior labels.

For instance, an ITSM team might apply clustering algorithms to incident logs and discover a pattern of recurring problems after a specific patch release–something that was not detected through traditional reporting. This insight can drive problem management initiatives and prevent future disruptions.

In another example, unsupervised learning is used for anomaly detection in infrastructure monitoring. The model learns 'normal' behavior from system performance data and flags deviations that could suggest early-stage failures or security threats.

Such proactive detection allows IT teams to act before issues impact end users, strengthening availability and trust in services.

In essence, supervised learning applies historical knowledge to automate known tasks, while unsupervised learning helps discover the unknown. Together, these methods support smarter, more resilient IT service environments–enabling teams to be not just reactive, but predictive and preventive.

Application in Real-World Environment

Understanding the technical foundations of AI–machine learning, deep learning, natural language processing, and their learning models–is just the beginning. The true value of these technologies comes to life when they are applied within a **real-world service environment**.

Consider the daily flood of tickets an IT support team handles. Each request needs to be understood, categorized, prioritized, and routed correctly. Without AI, this relies heavily on human intervention–slowing down response times and increasing the risk of inconsistency. With **machine learning**, however, ticket data from past incidents can train the system to automatically classify and assign new tickets based on historical patterns. The result? Faster triage and reduced load on first-line support agents.

Now take **natural language processing**. Users often describe problems in free-form text–full of jargon, typos, or emotional tones. NLP enables service tools to make sense of this unstructured input. It can extract intent ("I can't log in"), identify urgency ("ASAP! It's blocking my work"), and even detect sentiment ("I'm frustrated, this keeps happening"). This means service desk can prioritize tickets not just by category, but by the emotional state or business impact implied in the language.

Deep learning becomes powerful when layered onto more complex ITSM scenarios, such as analyzing massive logs for anomaly detection or powering intelligent chatbots that mimic human-like interactions. For example, a deep learning model can identify patterns in infrastructure alerts that suggest a brewing outage, even before users report issues.

AI also improves **self-service portals**. A well-trained ML model can suggest the most relevant knowledge articles as a user type of their issue. If a user searches "reset password," the system not only shows relevant guides but might also trigger an automated workflow to initiate the reset–saving time for both user and support staff.

Even **problem and change management** benefit from AI. By scanning historical incidents, AI can spot recurring issues that point to a deeper root cause–supporting the proactive side of ITSM. In change enablement, AI can assess the risk of proposed changes by comparing them to past outcomes, helping change managers make better-informed decisions.

These examples illustrate that AI is no longer theoretical. It is already embedded in many service management tools, quietly optimizing everything from response times to user satisfaction. The challenge for service teams is no longer whether AI should be used–but **how well they understand its capabilities and limitations** to get the most out of it.

Artificial Intelligence is transforming how IT service environments operate. Concepts such as Machine Learning (ML), Deep Learning (DL), Natural Language Processing (NLP), and learning methods such as Supervised and Unsupervised Learning are not just theoretical–they are being used to solve real problems, reduce workload, and enhance user satisfaction. This chapter explores how each of these AI techniques is utilized in service environments, with examples and situational insights.

Let us understand utilization of ML, DL, and NLP in Service Environments individually.

Machine Learning (ML)

ML models are primarily used for tasks that require pattern recognition, classification, and prediction. In service management, this translates to classifying tickets, forecasting SLA violations, or predicting ticket volumes.

Example: A global IT support center uses ML models trained on historic tickets to categorize incoming issues automatically, reducing the manual triage burden and improving assignment accuracy.

Deep Learning (DL)

DL is especially useful for analyzing large volumes of unstructured data such as system logs, user behavior, and voice inputs. It powers advanced use cases such as anomaly detection and voice-based service interfaces.

Example: A financial institution applies deep learning to infrastructure logs to identify subtle patterns that signal potential failures, enabling proactive remediation before service outages occur.

Natural Language Processing (NLP)

NLP enables machines to understand and act upon human language, making it ideal for enhancing user interactions. It powers chatbots, sentiment analysis, and intent detection in service portals.

Example: A telecom company deploys an NLP-powered chatbot that understands user queries like 'my internet is down' and routes them to the correct service queue while providing real-time status updates to users.

Let us also discuss the Supervised and Unsupervised Learning in Service Environments.

Supervised Learning

Supervised learning is used when there is historical data with labeled outcomes. It is well-suited for repeatable, high-volume tasks such as ticket classification or SLA prediction.

Example: An ITSM tool uses supervised learning to predict if a new incident will breach SLA based on inputs such as ticket category, priority, time of day, and historical agent performance.

Unsupervised Learning

Unsupervised learning is used when there are no labels and the goal is to discover hidden patterns or groupings. It is excellent for trend detection, anomaly detection, and clustering.

Example: A healthcare IT team applies unsupervised learning to end-user feedback forms and discovers an unexpected cluster of complaints related to the EMR login process, prompting a UI redesign.

Selecting the Right AI Technique Based on Problem, Type, and Context

- Use ML when you have labeled historical data and need predictions or classifications.
- Use DL when working with large and complex unstructured data, such as logs, audio, or video.
- Use NLP when interacting with users through chat, email, or voice and need to interpret intent or emotion.
- Use supervised learning for well-defined problems with historical outcomes.
- Use unsupervised learning to explore new patterns, group data, or identify unknown issues.

AI learning concepts are more than technological jargon—they are real enablers of efficiency, accuracy, and user satisfaction in service environments. Understanding which technique to apply and when empower ITSM teams to design smarter systems, deliver faster responses, and proactively manage IT operations.

Conclusion

As we have explored in this chapter, artificial intelligence is not a monolithic concept—it is an ecosystem of interrelated technologies, such as machine learning, deep learning, and natural language processing, each with unique strengths and use cases within service management. Understanding how these components work is not about turning service teams into data scientists about building awareness, confidence, and clarity around the tools shaping the future of ITSM.

We have demystified the difference between supervised and unsupervised learning, and shown how these models help AI make sense of both structured and unstructured data. From smart ticket classification to user sentiment analysis and predictive insights, these technologies are no longer theoretical–they are embedded in the systems many service teams already use, often without realizing it.

The real shift lies in perspective: moving from passive usage to intentional adoption. When service professionals understand the "why" and "how" of AI, they can actively participate in shaping smarter workflows, ask the right questions during tool evaluations, and play a more strategic role in IT transformation efforts.

In the chapters ahead, we will dive deeper into real-world implementations, examine the ethical and operational considerations of AI in ITSM, and help you build a roadmap for introducing intelligent automation into your own environment.

For now, it is enough to know this: AI is not a future ambition for service management–it is a present reality. And the more you understand its building blocks, the more empowered you are to unlock its full potential.

In the next chapter, we will discuss the prominent AI-powered tools we already use.

Multiple Choice Questions

1. What is the primary difference between supervised and unsupervised learning in AI?
    a. Supervised learning requires human intervention, unsupervised does not.
    b. Supervised learning uses labeled data, unsupervised uses unlabeled data.
    c. Unsupervised learning is faster than supervised learning.
    d. Supervised learning uses structured data, while unsupervised only uses text.
2. In the context of ITSM, what is a common use case for machine learning?
    a. Designing new chat interfaces
    b. Rewriting knowledge base articles
    c. Classifying tickets based on historical data
    d. Encrypting email communications

3. Which AI technique is best suited for interpreting unstructured text, such as emails or chat messages?
    a. Deep Learning
    b. Supervised Learning
    c. Natural Language Processing
    d. Predictive Analytics
4. What is a common misconception about deep learning in ITSM?
    a. It requires labeled datasets.
    b. It works best with structured data.
    c. It can fully explain its decision-making process.
    d. It can interpret emotional tone from text.
5. Which scenario best demonstrates the application of unsupervised learning in a service environment?
    a. Predicting if a ticket will breach SLA
    b. Auto-assigning tickets based on past resolution data
    c. Detecting unknown clusters of complaints from user feedback
    d. Recommending specific resolutions to known issues

Answers

1. b
2. c
3. c
4. c
5. c

Questions

1. Explain the differences between machine learning, deep learning, and natural language processing in the context of IT service management.
2. Describe how supervised learning works, including the steps involved in training a supervised model and its typical use cases in ITSM.

3. Discuss the types of problems best suited for unsupervised learning in a service environment and provide relevant examples.
4. How can machine learning models be used to forecast SLA breaches, and what data inputs are commonly involved in this process?
5. Provide real-world examples where deep learning has improved incident analysis or chatbot performance in ITSM.
6. What role does natural language processing play in enhancing user experience within self-service portals or service desks?
7. Outline the key misconceptions about each of the three core AI technologies (ML, DL, NLP) and explain why they are inaccurate.
8. How can AI technologies such as ML and NLP help prioritize tickets based on sentiment and urgency?
9. Compare the strengths and limitations of supervised and unsupervised learning methods in terms of data requirements, interpretability, and use cases.
10. Reflect on how a better understanding of AI concepts can empower ITSM professionals to make informed decisions about adopting intelligent automation tools.

Key Terms

- **Machine Learning (ML):** A subset of AI that enables systems to learn from historical data and make predictions or decisions without being explicitly programmed. In ITSM, it is commonly used for ticket classification and SLA forecasting.
- **Deep Learning (DL):** An advanced form of machine learning using neural networks with multiple layers to analyze complex, unstructured data. It is effective in tasks such as log analysis, voice recognition, and emotion detection.
- **Natural Language Processing (NLP):** A branch of AI that helps computers understand, interpret, and respond to human language. In service desks, it is used for sentiment analysis, chatbot conversations, and interpreting user queries.
- **Supervised Learning:** An ML approach where models are trained on labeled datasets with known outputs. It is ideal for repeatable tasks including incident categorization and SLA prediction in ITSM.
- **Unsupervised Learning:** An ML method that analyzes unlabeled data to discover hidden patterns, trends, or anomalies. It is useful in ITSM for identifying unknown issue clusters or behavior anomalies.

- **Ticket Classification:** The process of categorizing service desk tickets into predefined types using AI models. This reduces manual effort and accelerates response time by routing tickets correctly.
- **Sentiment Analysis:** An NLP technique that identifies emotions such as satisfaction or frustration in user messages. It helps prioritize emotionally charged or business-critical tickets.
- **Anomaly Detection:** A method used to identify data points or behaviors that deviate from the norm. In ITSM, it is crucial for detecting early signs of failures or cyber threats in logs and monitoring data.
- **Intent Detection:** An NLP feature that determines the underlying purpose of a user's input, such as "reset password" or "report outage." It ensures accurate ticket routing and automated support.
- **Labeled Data:** Data that is tagged with the correct output or category, essential for training supervised learning models. Examples in ITSM include tickets marked as "hardware issue" or "login problem."

CHAPTER 5
AI-Powered Tools Already in Use

Introduction

AI in ITSM is no longer just an emerging trend or a promise for the future–it is already embedded in the tools many teams rely on every day. You may not always notice it, but AI is quietly working behind the scenes, classifying tickets, analyzing sentiment, suggesting responses, and even resolving common issues before a technician gets involved.

By now, you have explored the foundational concepts of AI, understood its relevance to service management, and seen where traditional ITSM models fall short without intelligent support. But theory is only half the story. What is equally important is understanding how these concepts are being brought to life in the real tools you already use.

From powerful platforms like ServiceNow and ManageEngine to collaborative environments such as Jira, AI features are being introduced in ways that feel familiar yet transformative. You have likely encountered predictive ticket fields, chatbots that understand context, or recommendations that learn from previous patterns–all of which are driven by AI capabilities.

This chapter peels back the curtain on those features. We will examine what's genuinely powered by AI, what's vendor hype, and what is becoming a standard part of modern ITSM workflows. We will also introduce you to the emerging role of **generative AI**, including tools such as ChatGPT, and how they are beginning to reshape service desk conversations, self-service portals, and knowledge creation.

Rather than viewing these tools as futuristic add-ons, it is time to recognize them as part of the current ITSM landscape. You are not preparing for an AI-driven future–you are already living in it.

By the end of this chapter, you will gain a clearer, more grounded understanding of how AI is applied in popular ITSM platforms, how it adds value to daily operations, and how to discern real innovation from marketing buzz. Let us begin by exploring how these intelligent capabilities are already woven into the service tools you use every day.

Structure

In this chapter, we will discuss the following topics:

- Introduction to Generative AI
- Exploring the Capabilities of ChatGPT and Similar TOOLs in a Service Context
- How AI Features Appear in ServiceNow, ManageEngine, Jira, and many more
- Examples: Ticket Classification, Sentiment Analysis, Auto-Remediation
- Vendor-Neutral Perspective on Capabilities

Introduction to Generative AI

Until recently, AI in ITSM was largely about **prediction and classification**—determining ticket categories, routing issues, flagging anomalies, and forecasting trends. But a new branch of AI has entered the mainstream and it is **Generative AI (GenAI)**. Unlike traditional AI models that analyze or sort data, **generative AI can create entirely new content**, whether it's a sentence, an image, a knowledge article, or a workflow template.

Generative AI (GenAI) has transformed how humans interact with machines—shifting from rule-based automation to **natural, creative, and even conversational intelligence**. It enables systems not just to respond to structured inputs, but to **understand context, synthesize information**, and **generate meaningful outputs** in real time.

Understanding Generative AI

Generative AI refers to algorithms—often powered by Large Language Models (LLMs)—that can generate text, code, images, audio, or other forms of content based on patterns in training data. At its core, GenAI leverages models such as **GPT (Generative Pre-Trained Transformer)**, **PaLM (Pathways Language Model)**, or **Claude**, which are trained on vast datasets comprising books, web pages, code repositories, IT logs, FAQs, knowledge articles, and many more.

In the ITSM context, this means AI that can:

- Draft responses to user queries
- Generate new knowledge base articles
- Translate incidents into problem records

- Offer summaries of lengthy tickets
- Create shell scripts or runbooks for automation

Understanding The Building Blocks

Generative AI is typically powered by:

- **Large Language Models (LLMs):** Trained on massive text corpora (plural of corpus) to understand and generate human-like language.
- **Prompt Engineering:** Input phrasing or instruction that influences the AI's output.
- **Transformer Architecture:** A neural network design that excels at sequence modeling (for example, predicting the next word in a sentence).
- **Fine-Tuning and Context Injection:** Customizing the model with organization-specific data such as past tickets or internal KBs (Knowledge Base).

These models don't "think" like humans. Instead, they **predict the next most likely word or action** based on training data–yet with surprising depth, fluency, and adaptability.

Real-World Applications in ITSM

The power of generative AI is already being embedded in many service management platforms and use cases. Examples include:

- **Knowledge Article Generation**: Based on a resolved incident or change record, the AI drafts an initial knowledge base entry.
- **Conversational AI for Tier 0 Support**: Tools such as ChatGPT or ITSM-integrated chatbots handle Level 1 queries conversationally, often resolving without escalation.
- **Ticket Summarization**: Long email threads or ticket comments are summarized automatically for faster handoffs.
- **Runbook and Script Generation**: Admins describe a desired action in plain language, and AI suggests a shell or PowerShell script.
- **Policy Drafting and Communication**: Service teams can generate communication templates for outages, updates, or SLAs in a professional tone.

The following table describes comparison between generative AI and traditional AI in ITSM based on features:

Feature	Traditional AI (Predictive)	Generative AI
Output Type	Labels, scores, decisions	Text, scripts, KBs, conversations

Typical Use Case	Routing, prioritization, forecasting	Response generation, KB creation
Data Requirement	Structured data, historical logs	Unstructured and semi-structured data
Customization	Model tuning	Prompt tuning and fine-tuning
Example Tool	ML-based classification in ServiceNow	ChatGPT-like interface in Jira

***Table 5.1:** Comparison between Generative AI and Traditional AI in ITSM Based on Features*

Limitations and Ethical Considerations

As organizations embrace generative AI in ITSM, it is crucial to acknowledge its limitations and ethical implications. Powerful as it is, AI must be used with caution to avoid risks related to accuracy, privacy, bias, and accountability.

While generative AI is powerful, it comes with its own set of **risks and limitations**:

- **Hallucination**: AI may generate content that is grammatically correct and plausible but factually wrong or outdated.
    - **Example:** A service desk agent asks an AI assistant to generate steps to reset a VPN connection. The AI suggests a configuration process that includes registry edits no longer supported by the latest Windows OS update. As a result, following the AI-generated instructions leads to network misconfiguration and escalates the issue.
- **Data Privacy**: Sensitive enterprise data can be exposed if user prompts or ticket content is sent to external, cloud-based AI tools without safeguards.
    - **Example:** An engineer pastes the full content of a confidential incident report–including usernames and IP addresses–into a generative AI tool to summarize it. The tool, connected to a public LLM API, stores or uses that data for future training, violating internal compliance and data residency policies.
- **Bias and Relevance**: AI may favor certain patterns based on its training data, leading to skewed or irrelevant recommendations.
    - **Example:** An AI assistant trained mostly on U.S.-based ITSM data repeatedly suggests solutions that involve tools such as Slack or Zendesk, even for a Middle Eastern organization using Arabic language interfaces and local tools. The recommendations ignore regional service tool preferences, leading to poor user adoption.
- **Auditability**: AI-generated outputs often lack clear traceability on how decisions or recommendations were made.

- **Example:** An AI bot suggests that a ticket be marked as "Resolved - Known Issue," but the support supervisor is unable to trace why or how this conclusion was reached. With no audit trail or logic tree, the team cannot validate the AI's decision, posing compliance and accountability concerns during internal audits.

Responsible usage requires **human oversight**, **access controls**, and ideally, **fine-tuning on private ITSM data**.

Getting Started: How to Explore GenAI in ITSM Safely

Adopting generative AI in ITSM requires a cautious, well-structured approach to ensure safety and value. By starting small, testing in controlled environments, and involving human oversight, organizations can explore GenAI responsibly and effectively.

Organizations interested in generative AI should:

- **Start with non-sensitive use cases** (for example, email draft generation or public KB articles).
- **Use sandboxed environments** to test AI responses before deploying them to production.
- **Educate teams** on prompt engineering and model limitations.
- **Iteratively refine** inputs and outputs through human-in-the-loop workflows.

The Road Ahead: Strategic Implications

Generative AI will not replace ITSM teams—but it will **augment and elevate their capabilities**. The future of service management will involve **collaboration between humans and AI**—where AI handles the repetitive drafting, summarizing, or searching, and humans make final decisions as well as manage exceptions.

Organizations that successfully integrate generative AI will see:

- Lower MTTR (Mean Time to Resolution)
- Higher agent productivity
- Better user experience
- Richer and faster knowledge curation

Summary

Generative AI marks a paradigm shift in how IT services are delivered, supported, and improved. From crafting smart replies to co-authoring policies and procedures, this technology is reshaping the service desk's role and the user's experience. Understanding it, testing it responsibly, and integrating it into ITSM workflows can unlock massive gains in both efficiency and satisfaction.

Exploring the Capabilities of ChatGPT and Similar TOOLs in a Service Context

This section builds naturally upon the previous one on Generative AI and focuses on **real-world, practical applications of tools such as ChatGPT** (and similar models such as Claude, Gemini, or CoPilot) in IT service management. It combines explanation, use cases, and strategic insight—aligned with your narrative tone.

From Conversational Curiosity to Service Desk Powerhouse

Once seen as a novelty or productivity aid, tools like **ChatGPT** have rapidly evolved into serious enablers of enterprise operations. In the ITSM world, where users seek quick answers and support teams juggle high volumes, these tools are not just add-ons—they are game-changers. What makes ChatGPT unique is its ability to **understand natural language, contextualize queries**, and **generate human-like responses**—in milliseconds.

In a service context, which means it can assist end users, empower agents, support knowledge workers, and even bridge gaps between technical documentation and real-world action.

Key Capabilities of ChatGPT-Like Tools for ITSM

Generative AI tools such as ChatGPT are more than just chatbots—they bring a wide range of practical capabilities to ITSM. From automating ticket handling to assisting agents with knowledge retrieval and scripting, these tools enhance both efficiency and user experience across service operations.

Let us explore how these tools translate into tangible capabilities in a service environment:

- **Natural Language Understanding (NLU)**
    - Understands human input even when it is vague or unstructured.

    - Converts "I cannot log into my laptop" into an actionable incident or suggestion.
- **Conversational Ticketing**
    - Engages users via chat to log incidents or requests without needing a formal ticket form.
    - Automates triage by asking follow-up questions, gathering essential metadata.
- **Knowledge Retrieval and Summarization**
    - Searches across internal KBs or documentation and delivers concise, conversational summaries.
    - Saves time for agents who would otherwise sift through long documents.
- **Drafting Responses**
    - Drafts initial replies to tickets or user queries in a polite, professional tone.
    - Adapts to context, urgency, and organizational style.
- **Training and Onboarding Support**
    - Acts as an interactive tutor for new agents, explaining policies, tool usage, and procedures.
    - Answers common internal queries 24/7.
- **Process and Script Guidance**
    - Generates shell scripts, PowerShell commands, or troubleshooting steps based on natural language prompts.
    - Supports backend automation scripting for advanced users.

Real-World Scenarios

To truly grasp the impact of generative AI in ITSM, it helps to see how these capabilities play out in real-life scenarios. The following examples illustrate how AI-driven tools can streamline support, enhance responsiveness, and reduce manual workload in everyday service situations.

Let us bring these capabilities to life through examples:

Scenario 1: End-User Support via Chat

A user types: "*My email is not syncing on my phone.*"

ChatGPT-enabled chatbot:

- Asks what device and email app are being used.

- Offers a step-by-step fix or logs a ticket if manual intervention is needed.

Scenario 2: Agent Sidekick

An L1 agent is unsure how to respond to a ticket about a legacy VPN issue. They type into an internal ChatGPT tool: "*How to fix Cisco AnyConnect not connecting on Windows 11?*"

The tool replies with a set of verified steps pulled from internal documentation and public KBs.

Scenario 3: Knowledge Base Drafting

After resolving a new issue involving printer drivers, an agent describes it in simple terms.

The tool converts it into a formatted knowledge article, complete with headings, solution steps, and tags.

The following table lists the benefits in a service context:

Capability	**Impact on Service Teams**
Conversational Ticket Creation	Reduces barriers for users; increases adoption
Response Drafting	Saves time; ensures consistency
Contextual Assistance	Boosts L1 agent confidence and quality
Process Acceleration	Speeds up workflows, from triage to resolution
Intelligent Escalation	Reduces unnecessary escalations

Table 5.2: *Benefits in a Service Context*

Challenges and Considerations

While the promise of generative AI in ITSM is compelling, it comes with important challenges that must be addressed. Accuracy, security, governance, and contextual relevance are critical factors organizations must manage to ensure safe and effective deployment.

Accuracy and Hallucination

- ChatGPT may confidently generate incorrect information.
- Must be integrated with **validation layers** or **human oversight** in production environments.

Security and Data Privacy

- Sensitive data shared with public models may pose risks.
- Best practice: Use **enterprise versions** with private LLM hosting or integrate via secure APIs.

Auditability and Governance

- Responses should be logged and explainable, especially in regulated industries.
- Must align with compliance and audit frameworks.

Training on Organization-Specific Context

- Out-of-the-box models lack knowledge of internal tools, terms, or acronyms.
- Solution: Fine-tune models or inject context dynamically via **Retrieval-Augmented Generation (RAG).**

Integrating These Tools Within Organizations

Leading organizations are already embedding generative AI into their ITSM ecosystems to enhance service delivery and user experience. From built-in assistants in major ITSM platforms to custom-trained GPTs, these integrations showcase the practical and scalable adoption of AI in real-world environments.

- **ServiceNow**: Embedding GenAI to summarize incidents, generate reports, and automate agent responses.
- **Atlassian (Jira)**: AI Assistants now help draft issues, auto-label them, and suggest solutions from Confluence.
- **ManageEngine**: Offers Zia, a virtual assistant for self-service and smart replies.
- **Custom GPTs**: Organizations create tailored ChatGPT interfaces trained on internal KBs, service catalogs, and standard operating procedures.

Future Potential

The future of generative AI in ITSM holds exciting possibilities that go beyond today's capabilities. As these tools evolve, they are poised to deliver more proactive, intuitive, and intelligent service experiences through voice, real-time analysis, and emotion-aware automation.

ChatGPT-like tools are likely to expand further into:

- **Voice-based ticketing** (voice-to-text interactions)
- **Real-time root cause analysis assistance**

- **Proactive service suggestions** (for example, "You are running low on storage - open a request to expand?")
- **Sentiment-driven escalation logic**

As these tools evolve, **their role will move from passive responders to active participants** in ITSM workflows.

Summary

ChatGPT and similar tools represent more than just chatbot upgrades–they are shaping a new paradigm in service management where conversations replace forms, guidance replaces guesswork, and intelligent collaboration becomes the norm. When deployed wisely, they act as **assistants, accelerators, and advisors**–bridging human skill with scalable intelligence.

Organizations that embrace these tools, while managing their risks, will find themselves operating faster, more consistently, and with greater user satisfaction.

Using AI features in ServiceNow, ManageEngine, Jira, and Other Platforms

Modern ITSM platforms are no longer just systems of record–they are transforming into intelligent ecosystems. Leading tools such as **ServiceNow**, **ManageEngine**, and **Jira Service Management** are embedding AI to streamline operations, reduce ticket volumes, boost agent productivity, and enhance user experience. But how these AI features manifest–and how mature or customizable they are–varies significantly across platforms.

In this section, we will explore **how AI is actually built into popular ITSM tools**, what those features do, and what buyers and practitioners should look out for.

ServiceNow: The Front-Runner in AI-Powered ITSM

ServiceNow has positioned itself as a pioneer in AI-driven service management, primarily through its **Now Platform** and **AI/ML-powered workflows**.

Key AI Features are as follows:

- **Predictive Intelligence**: Uses machine learning to **auto-categorize**, **prioritize**, and **assign tickets** based on historical data.

- **Virtual Agent**: A conversational chatbot that handles common user queries (for example, password resets, status checks), freeing agents from routine tasks.
- **Performance Analytics with Forecasting**: Uses historical trends to **predict SLA breaches**, capacity issues, or surge in incidents.
- **AI Search**: Intelligently surfaces relevant knowledge base articles based on user behavior and context.
- **Document Intelligence**: Extracts and categorizes information from unstructured documents (for example, emails or PDFs) into structured ticket fields.

Example: When a user types, "My printer is not working again," the Virtual agent automatically engages, checks known fixes, and logs an incident if needed–with Predictive Intelligence assigning it to the appropriate support group.

Maturity Level: High - ServiceNow offers robust AI integrations but often requires **data training and tuning** for best results.

ManageEngine ServiceDesk Plus: Practical AI for Mid-Market

ManageEngine, especially through **Zia**, its AI assistant, provides accessible AI capabilities aimed at small and medium enterprises.

Key AI Features are as follows:

- **Zia (AI Assistant)**: Conversational interface that can help users log tickets, get FAQs, or query knowledge articles.
- **Auto-Assignment Rules**: Based on past trends, tickets are **intelligently routed** to the most suitable technician.
- **Smart Suggestions**: Suggests solutions from the knowledge base or past tickets while agents are working.
- **Anomaly Detection**: Identifies unusual ticket trends or volumes that could indicate problems.
- **Sentiment Analysis** (limited deployment): Flags negative user sentiment for priority handling.

Example: When a user asks Zia, "*Why cannot I connect to Wi-Fi?*," it replies with known solutions from past incidents or offers to log a new ticket.

Maturity Level: Moderate – Ideal for organizations starting their AI journey, though deeper learning models or full customization may be limited.

Jira Service Management: Agile + AI

Jira Service Management (by Atlassian) is increasingly integrating AI into its **Atlassian Intelligence** layer, especially in collaboration-heavy environments.

Key AI Features are as follows:

- **AI Assistant (Beta)**: Drafts responses, automates repetitive replies, and summarizes long conversations.
- **Smart Search**: Uses natural language processing to improve query results across issues and knowledge base articles.
- **Auto-Triage**: Classifies and prioritizes tickets based on rules and machine learning.
- **AI-Generated Insights**: Highlights incident patterns, dependencies, and related changes.
- **Conversational Ticketing via Slack/MS Teams**: End-users can raise requests in chat, and AI routes them appropriately.

Example: A team lead asks in Slack, "*Can someone look at the* VPN *outage*?" Jira's conversational bot logs the incident, extracts key details, and links related issues.

Maturity Level: Growing – Atlassian's AI is rapidly evolving, especially around **team collaboration**, **DevOps visibility**, and **automated responses**.

The following table lists the comparison of AI across platforms based on feature/capability:

Feature/Capability	ServiceNow	ManageEngine	Jira Service Management
Virtual Agent Chatbot	Yes (Advanced)	Yes (Zia)	Yes (Conversational UI)
Predictive Ticket Routing	Yes (ML-based)	Yes (Rule/Pattern-based)	Yes (ML + Rule-based)
Knowledge Suggestions	Yes (Contextual AI)	Yes	Yes
Auto-Response Drafting	Yes	Limited	Yes (in beta)
Sentiment Analysis	Yes (with scoring)	Emerging	Not yet widely deployed
Anomaly Detection	Yes	Yes	Yes
Natural Language Search	Yes	Moderate	Yes (Advanced)

Custom AI Models	Supported	Limited	Developing
Enterprise Readiness	Very High	Moderate	Moderate to High

***Table 5.3**: Comparison of AI across Platforms Based on Feature/Capability*

Other Emerging Platforms with AI Capabilities

Beyond the well-known players, several other ITSM platforms are rapidly integrating AI to enhance their capabilities. These emerging solutions bring unique strengths—ranging from self-healing automation to intuitive AI assistants—catering to diverse organizational needs and scales.

Freshservice (Freshworks)

- Offers Freddy AI for ticket summarization, auto-categorization, and agent suggestions.
- Emphasis on intuitive use and quick deployment.

BMC Helix

- Provides cognitive service management using NLP, ML, and intelligent automation.
- Targets large enterprises needing deep ITOM and ITSM integration.

Ivanti Neurons

- AI-powered self-healing, anomaly detection, and automation workflows across ITAM and ITSM.
- Leverages sensor data for proactive actions.

Challenges in Evaluating AI Features

Evaluating AI features in ITSM tools requires more than accepting vendor claims at face value. Organizations must critically assess the depth, transparency, and adaptability of AI capabilities to ensure they align with operational needs and compliance requirements.

While many tools offer AI, it is important to cut through **marketing hype** and ask:

- Is the model **trained on your data**, or is it generic?
- Are results **auditable and explainable**?
- Can you **fine-tune or override** the AI decisions?
- Is there a **feedback loop** to improve performance over time?

Organizations should also weigh **costs**, **integration complexity**, and **data residency** concerns when choosing platforms.

Strategic Takeaways for Service Leaders

To truly benefit from generative AI, service leaders must approach adoption with strategic intent. Success lies in targeting real value, embedding AI into workflows, and building trust through transparency and user involvement.

- **Don't chase AI for the sake of AI:** Focus on use cases that reduce effort, improve speed, or enhance accuracy.
- **Look beyond features–assess workflows:** AI is only useful if embedded into daily operations.
- **Choose platforms that allow flexibility:** To scale, retrain, or integrate with other systems as your needs evolve.
- **Involve users and agents early:** Adoption improves when teams trust AI suggestions and see their value.

Summary

AI in ITSM is no longer a premium feature–it is becoming an expectation. Whether you are using **ServiceNow's deep learning modules**, **ManageEngine's Zia assistant**, or **Jira's conversational interface**, these tools are **paving the way for a more responsive, intelligent service desk**.

As platforms race to integrate AI, service teams must **look beyond the surface**–seeking capabilities that are not only intelligent but also **reliable, explainable, and useful** in the day-to-day grind of IT operations.

Examples: Ticket Classification, Sentiment Analysis, Auto-Remediation

In earlier sections, we explored how AI is reshaping service management with concepts such as machine learning, natural language processing, and generative AI. But theory alone doesn't drive value–**practical application does**. This section dives deep into three of the most impactful, real-world uses of AI in ITSM today:

- **Ticket Classification**
- **Sentiment Analysis**
- **Auto-Remediation**

Each of these capabilities directly influences how service teams operate, how fast they resolve issues, and how consistently they deliver value to users.

Ticket Classification: From Chaos to Clarity

Ticket classification is the process of automatically tagging or categorizing tickets based on their content–whether it is the subject line, description, or attached data. Traditional systems required users or agents to manually select the category and subcategory, often leading to inconsistencies, misrouted tickets, or delays in triage.

How AI Enhances Ticket Classification

Using **machine learning**, modern systems learn from historical ticket data and identify patterns in language, frequency, and resolution paths. AI models can then predict:

- **Category**
- **Priority**
- **Assignment group**
- **SLA tier**

Real-Life Example - A global retailer uses ServiceNow's predictive intelligence to auto-categorize incidents like "My badge doesn't work" into **Facilities > Access Control**, reducing manual errors by nearly 70%.

Benefits:

- Faster triage and response
- Reduced L1 workload
- Fewer escalations due to misrouted issues
- Better analytics due to consistent classification

Considerations:

- Requires **training on quality historical data**
- Misclassification can impact SLA adherence
- Needs human override mechanisms

Sentiment Analysis: Listening between the Lines

Sentiment analysis is the use of natural language processing to determine the **emotional tone** behind user messages. This could apply to:

- Incident/request descriptions

- Emails or chat logs
- Survey feedback

AI evaluates the content and assigns a **sentiment score** (for example, positive, neutral, negative) or labels including *frustrated, confused,* or *satisfied.*

Let us understand the rationale behind the **sentiment analysis is important and critical in ITSM.**

Many service desks focus on SLAs and ticket volumes–but miss **user emotions** entirely. Sentiment analysis helps surface hidden dissatisfaction or urgency, enabling proactive action even if the ticket appears routine on the surface.

Real-Life Example - An IT support team at a university integrates sentiment scoring into ManageEngine. A request like "My laptop crashed before my exam, and no one helped me last time" gets flagged as high priority despite being a simple hardware request.

Benefits:

- Identify high-risk or escalated cases early
- Improve VIP or critical user experience
- Prioritize beyond just technical severity
- Measure agent performance in user interactions

Considerations:

- Sentiment models need tuning for **industry-specific language**
- May misread sarcasm or cultural variations
- Requires alignment with escalation rules

Auto-Remediation: Closing the Loop Without Human Intervention

Let us understand auto-remediation. Auto-remediation refers to **automated resolution of IT issues** using predefined or AI-triggered actions–without needing a human technician to intervene. This can range from:

- Restarting a service
- Resetting a user password
- Running a diagnostic script
- Triggering cloud resource scaling

AI-powered auto-remediation systems go beyond simple scripts. They use pattern recognition to:

- Detect recurring issues
- Propose solutions based on similar resolved cases
- Execute actions via orchestration tools such as Ansible, SCCM, or native ITSM workflows

Following is the list of where it applies:

- Endpoint management
- Network troubleshooting
- Cloud infrastructure (auto-healing)
- Software deployment or patch issues

Real-Life Example - A financial firm uses Ivanti Neurons to detect when disk usage exceeds 90% on end-user machines. The system **automatically clears temporary files**, sends a notification, and closes the ticket—all without user involvement.

Following is the list of few prominent benefits:

- Zero-touch resolution
- Reduced Mean Time to Resolve (MTTR)
- Improved service availability and consistency
- Greater operational scalability

Considerations:

- Must include **approval gates** or **rollback options**
- Requires extensive **testing and scripting discipline**
- Complex failures still need human diagnosis

The following table presents the comparison of manual process and AI enabled outcomes:

Capability	Manual Process	AI-Enabled Outcome
Ticket Classification	Prone to errors, delays	Fast, consistent, auto-assigned tickets
Sentiment Analysis	Ignored user emotion	Empathy-driven prioritization
Auto-Remediation	Wait for technician	Automated fixes for known issues

***Table 5.4:** Comparison of Manual Process and AI Enabled Outcomes*

Bringing It Together: The Intelligent Service Desk

When combined, these capabilities build the foundation for a **proactive, data-driven, and user-aware service desk**. Imagine a workflow like this:

1. A user submits a vague request: "*My internet keeps disconnecting.*"
2. AI classifies it as a **Wi-Fi connectivity issue**, assigns it to the correct support team, and suggests a known fix.
3. The system detects past frustrations from this user and elevates the priority.
4. If auto-remediation is enabled, a script runs to reset network drivers or push an updated config.
5. The ticket is closed, the user is notified, and a survey is triggered—ready for sentiment analysis.

Each step is faster, smarter, and less error-prone—delivering measurable value to both IT and the business.

Summary and Next Steps

AI is no longer confined to dashboards or predictions. It is now **acting**, **responding**, and **resolving** within ITSM platforms. Ticket classification, sentiment analysis, and auto-remediation are tangible use cases that show how intelligence is driving operational excellence.

As organizations mature in their AI journey, these features become not just enhancements—but **expectations**. For service leaders, the task is to:

- Identify where these features are most impactful
- Integrate them thoughtfully into workflows
- Monitor outcomes, refine continuously, and expand their reach

Because the future of ITSM is not just managed, it is intelligently automated.

Vendor-Neutral Perspective on Capabilities

As AI becomes a core component of ITSM solutions, vendors are aggressively marketing their platforms as "AI-powered," "intelligent," or "autonomous." While many of these platforms do embed real AI capabilities, **buyers and service leaders must cut through the hype** to focus on what actually delivers value.

A **vendor-neutral perspective** means assessing AI features based on their functionality, maturity, and business relevance–not just on branding, UI polish, or proprietary terminologies. This section helps IT leaders **evaluate AI in ITSM tools objectively**, with a focus on outcomes, adaptability, and alignment with service goals–**regardless of vendor**.

Principles of a Vendor-Neutral Evaluation

When evaluating AI capabilities across ServiceNow, ManageEngine, Jira, Freshservice, BMC Helix, or any other platform, keep these **core principles** in mind:

Capability Over Branding: Focus on what the AI feature *does*, not what it is *called*. A "Virtual Agent" in one tool may be equal to a "Conversational AI" in another–but the real question is: can it solve issues, escalate when needed, and learn from interactions?

Functionality Over Fancy Demos: Request proof of actual use cases–not just sandboxes or marketing demos. For example:

- Does predictive routing actually reduce resolution times?
- Does sentiment analysis influence prioritization workflows?

Integration Over Isolation: A feature has limited value if it is not integrated into everyday workflows. AI must **work within incident, request, change, knowledge, and problem modules**–not just as a bolt-on feature.

Scalability and Customization: Can the vendor:

- Train the AI on your historical ticket data?
- Fine-tune it for department-specific workflows?
- Control its decision-making thresholds?

The more adaptable the AI, the more valuable it becomes over time.

Here is a vendor-neutral breakdown of **common AI features**, what they typically do, and how to evaluate them across platforms:

AI Capability	What It Should Do	Questions to Ask (Vendor-Neutral)
Ticket Categorization	Automatically suggest or assign ticket categories based on input	Can the model be trained on our historical data?
Auto-Assignment	Route tickets to the right teams or technicians using AI	Does it adapt based on resolution performance or skill mapping?
Virtual Agent/ Chatbot	Interact with users to resolve issues or log tickets	Is it rule-based or NLP-driven? Can it escalate when needed?

Sentiment Analysis	Identify user tone/emotion in ticket text or chat	Does sentiment influence priority or escalation?
Knowledge Suggestions	Recommend KB articles based on ticket content or agent activity	Does it consider ticket resolution history, not just keywords?
Ticket Summarization	Generate brief summaries of long conversations or logs	Is the summary context-aware or just extracted content?
Auto-Remediation	Automatically resolve known issues using workflows or scripts	Are remediation actions governed, audited, and reversible?
Predictive Analytics	Forecast incidents, SLA breaches, or resource needs	Are insights real-time? Can they trigger workflow actions?
Anomaly Detection	Detect unusual behavior across metrics or services	Can it detect root causes or just flag outliers?

Table 5.5: *Vendor-Neutral Breakdown of Common AI Features*

AI Maturity Checklist: Applied across Platforms

Use the **AI Maturity Assessment Checklist** as a neutral benchmarking tool across different vendors. This gives you an unbiased way to compare:

- Breadth of AI coverage
- Model adaptability
- Workflow integration
- Data privacy governance
- User trust and adoption

Avoid vendor lock-in by ensuring any platform you select is **modular and API-driven**, allowing you to replace or integrate AI engines later as needed.

Vendor-Neutral Best Practices for AI Adoption

Whether you are using ServiceNow, Jira, Freshservice, BMC, or another tool, these **best practices** apply universally:

- **Start with Use Cases, Not Tools:** Let real service management challenges–like high ticket volumes or repeated misrouting–drive your AI adoption strategy.
- **Build Human Oversight Loops:** Ensure that auto-responses, recommendations, and auto-remediations are monitored, auditable, and adjustable.

- **Demand Explainability:** Ask how the AI reached its conclusion. A black-box model that cannot justify decisions will not be trusted by agents or auditors.
- **Train the AI on Your Data:** The best results come when AI learns from your unique incidents, workflows, and customer profiles–not from generic datasets.
- **Measure Before and After:** Track performance metrics such as MTTR, FCR, escalation rate, and CSAT before and after AI integration to prove ROI.

Real-World Comparison Scenario

Imagine two platforms offering "AI-based ticket routing."

- **Tool A** uses static rules with occasional machine learning predictions based on category.
- **Tool B** learns from ticket resolution history, team performance, and seasonal workload patterns to predict the best technician.

From a **vendor-neutral standpoint**, Tool B is more mature–**even if Tool A markets it with more buzzwords.**

This approach encourages IT leaders to make decisions based on **outcomes and operational fit**, not vendor narratives.

Summary: AI Without the Logo

An AI-driven ITSM strategy should be **platform-agnostic in principle**, even if it is platform-specific in execution. By focusing on what AI can *do*, how it fits your service goals, and how it evolves with your organization, you gain the power to:

- **Ask smarter questions**
- **Avoid buying into hype**
- **Implement with confidence**
- **Scale with intent**

Vendor neutrality does not mean avoiding vendors. It means staying focused on what matters: **capabilities, outcomes, trust, and alignment with your service vision.**

Conclusion

AI in ITSM is no longer an experiment or an optional upgrade–it is embedded, active, and rapidly evolving. From intelligent ticket classification and sentiment-driven prioritization to auto-remediation and conversational support, AI capabilities are already reshaping how service desks operate and how users experience support. As we have seen across leading platforms such as ServiceNow, ManageEngine, and Jira–and even through vendor-neutral lenses–what matters most is not the branding of the tools, but their ability to deliver meaningful, explainable outcomes.

This chapter aims to demystify what is real, what is emerging, and what is possible with AI in today's service environments. The takeaway is clear: AI is not just something you prepare for– it is something you are already using, whether consciously or not. The challenge now is to move from passive usage to strategic adoption.

In the chapters ahead, we will explore how organizations can measure the impact of AI, build trust in AI-assisted decisions, and drive continual improvement in an AI-augmented ITSM landscape. Because the smartest service teams of tomorrow are already learning how to collaborate–with both people and machines–today.

In the next chapter, we shall explore AIOPS and Intelligent Operations.

Multiple Choice Questions

1. What is a key differentiator of Generative AI compared to traditional predictive AI in ITSM?
    a. It assigns priority based on historical data.
    b. It generates new content like knowledge articles or scripts.
    c. It detects hardware failures automatically.
    d. It monitors service desk SLAs.
2. In which scenario is sentiment analysis most helpful within ITSM operations?
    a. Automating patch management
    b. Reducing licensing costs
    c. Prioritizing tickets based on user emotion
    d. Scheduling system backups
3. What does auto-remediation aim to achieve in ITSM workflows?
    a. Assign tickets to human agents
    b. Automate fixes without manual intervention
    c. Delete duplicate tickets
    d. Escalate all tickets to Level 3 support

4. Which AI capability is responsible for suggesting ticket categories based on the description provided?
   a. Anomaly Detection
   b. Knowledge Management
   c. Ticket Classification
   d. Virtual Agent
5. What is a best practice when evaluating AI features in ITSM platforms from a vendor-neutral perspective?
   a. Choose the platform with the most colorful dashboards
   b. Trust the vendor's demo video
   c. Focus on capabilities and integration with workflows
   d. Select the solution with the most expensive licensing

Answers

1. b
2. c
3. b
4. c
5. c

Questions

1. Explain the difference between traditional predictive AI and generative AI in the context of IT Service Management.
2. Describe how ChatGPT or similar tools enhance conversational ticketing and agent assistance in ITSM.
3. Discuss the practical use cases of sentiment analysis in improving IT support experiences.
4. How does auto-remediation contribute to reducing Mean Time to Resolution (MTTR) and improving operational efficiency?
5. Compare the AI capabilities of ServiceNow, ManageEngine, and Jira based on their integration and maturity.

6. What challenges should organizations consider when evaluating AI features in ITSM platforms?
7. Illustrate how ticket classification using AI improves triage and reduces manual errors in a real-world service desk scenario.
8. What are the ethical considerations associated with deploying generative AI in ITSM environments?
9. Describe the role of fine-tuning and context injection in improving the performance of generative AI tools.
10. How can service leaders adopt a vendor-neutral approach when assessing AI functionality across different ITSM tools?

Key Terms

- **Generative AI:** A branch of artificial intelligence that creates new content—such as text, scripts, or images—based on patterns in training data. In ITSM, it powers tools that draft replies, generate KB articles, and assist agents conversationally.
- **Large Language Model (LLM):** A deep learning model trained on vast text datasets to understand and generate human-like language. Examples include GPT, Claude, and PaLM, which power tools like ChatGPT.
- **Ticket Classification:** The automated process of assigning categories, priorities, or teams to support tickets using AI. It improves triage accuracy, and reduces manual intervention.
- **Sentiment Analysis:** The use of Natural Language Processing (NLP) to detect emotional tone in user messages. Helps identify urgent or dissatisfied users even when severity appears low.
- **Auto-Remediation:** The automated resolution of IT issues through AI-triggered scripts or workflows without human involvement. It reduces MTTR and boosts service availability.
- **Virtual Agent:** An AI-powered chatbot that handles routine support interactions like password resets or FAQs. It enables conversational support and deflects L1 ticket volume.
- **Prompt Engineering:** Crafting specific input instructions to guide the output of generative AI tools. Effective prompts help tailor responses in ITSM scenarios such as policy drafting or scripting.
- **Predictive Intelligence:** A feature in tools such as ServiceNow that uses historical data to forecast outcomes or suggest actions. Common use cases include ticket routing and SLA breach prediction.

- **Retrieval-Augmented Generation (RAG):** A method where generative AI combines live document retrieval with language generation. In ITSM, it enables AI to respond with up-to-date, context-specific information.
- **Vendor-Neutral Evaluation:** An approach to assess AI capabilities based on real functionality, integration, and outcomes—not on branding or proprietary terms. It helps organizations make platform-agnostic decisions.

Appendices

Appendix A

Suggestive AI Capability Maturity Levels in ITSM Platforms

Maturity Level	Label	Description
Level 1	**Foundational**	Basic rule-based automation with limited AI logic. Static workflows, keyword-based bots, and no learning capability. Often requires manual oversight.
Level 2	**Emerging**	AI features are present but limited in scope—like basic chatbots or predefined suggestions. Lacks contextual understanding and deep integration.
Level 3	**Operational**	AI assists in key workflows such as ticket triage, routing, or knowledge recommendations. Models are trained on internal data but require periodic manual fine-tuning.
Level 4	**Advanced**	AI features are dynamic, context-aware, and embedded across multiple ITSM modules. Includes predictive analytics, NLP search, and response generation.
Level 5	**Transformational**	AI is deeply integrated, self-learning, and adaptive. Features include generative AI, proactive remediation, behavioral insights, and closed-loop automation.

Appendix B

AI Scope and Feature Breadth

✓	Statement	Score
☐	Only basic automation (for example, rules for auto-assignment, keyword search)	1
☐	Includes a basic chatbot and ticket suggestions based on templates	2
☐	Offers AI-driven routing, ticket classification, and knowledge suggestions	3
☐	Provides contextual assistance, sentiment analysis, and predictive analytics	4
☐	Enables generative AI (ChatGPT-like), self-remediation, and proactive insights	5

Appendix C

Data Learning and Model Adaptability

✓	Statement	Score
☐	No learning capability; logic is static and admin-defined	1
☐	Uses historical data in a limited way; minimal learning from patterns	2
☐	Models can be trained periodically on internal data with human supervision	3
☐	AI continuously learns from new data and improves suggestions over time	4
☐	Self-learning models that adjust in real time based on behaviors and outcomes	5

Appendix D

Workflow Integration

✓	Statement	Score
☐	AI features are siloed; not embedded into ITSM workflows	1
☐	Partial integration with forms, self-service portals, or knowledge base	2
☐	AI assists in core workflows like incident, request, and change	3
☐	End-to-end workflows leverage AI across multiple stages (triage, resolution, escalation)	4
☐	AI drives workflow decisions, creates automation rules, and enables no-touch service handling	5

Appendix E

Privacy, Security, and Governance

✓	**Statement**	**Score**
☐	No controls for data usage or transparency	1
☐	Basic role-based access; no audit trail for AI decisions	2
☐	Supports logging of AI decisions; access control for sensitive outputs	3
☐	Provides explainability, feedback loop, and AI decision override options	4
☐	Fully governed AI lifecycle with enterprise data residency, compliance, and audit readiness	5

Appendix F

User Experience and Adoption

✓	**Statement**	**Score**
☐	Users are unaware of AI features or rarely engage	1
☐	Users interact with static bots or receive generic suggestions	2
☐	AI provides useful, contextual interactions with growing adoption	3
☐	AI is trusted by users; feedback loop actively improves engagement	4
☐	AI is central to daily use; users rely on it for decisions, automation, and self-service	5

Appendix G

Scoring and Maturity Levels based on the Scores from the Preceding Five Appendices

Total Score	Maturity Level	Interpretation
5–8	**Level 1 - Foundational**	Limited AI presence; mostly manual or rule-based processes
9–13	**Level 2 - Emerging**	Early AI adoption; basic automation and limited intelligence
14–18	**Level 3 - Operational**	Core workflows benefit from AI; room to scale and refine
19–23	**Level 4 - Advanced**	Well-integrated, adaptive AI that enhances productivity and user experience
24–25	**Level 5 - Transformational**	AI is driving innovation, autonomy, and continuous improvement at scale

Chapter 6
AIOps and Intelligent Operations

Introduction

Modern IT environments are dynamic, complex, and continuously generating massive volumes of alerts, logs, and telemetry data. As digital transformation accelerates, IT operations teams are under increasing pressure to move beyond reactive incident management and embrace proactive, predictive service assurance. This is where AIOps–Artificial Intelligence for IT Operations–emerges as a critical enabler. Far from being just another industry buzzword, AIOps applies practical AI techniques such as machine learning, pattern recognition, and automation to detect anomalies, correlate events, and identify root causes in real-time. It empowers IT teams to reduce alert fatigue, respond to incidents faster, and maintain resilient, high-performing systems. When aligned with ITIL4 practices such as Monitoring and Event Management, Incident Management, and Problem Management, AIOps enhances service delivery with intelligent, data-driven insights. Moreover, the integration of Generative AI is pushing the boundaries further, enabling systems to synthesize operational data and deliver contextual recommendations in human-readable language. This chapter explores the true potential of AIOps, demystifies its capabilities, and provides a clear mapping of how intelligent operations are reshaping the future of ITSM–turning data noise into actionable intelligence.

Structure

In this chapter, we will discuss the following topics:

- Understanding AIOps
- How AI Supports Event Correlation, Anomaly Detection, Root Cause Analysis
- Mapping AIOps to ITIL4's Monitoring and Event Management, Incident, and Problem Management
- Role of GenAi in Synthesizing Operational Data and Recommendations

Understanding AIOps

In today's fast-paced, digital-first environment, IT systems have grown incredibly complex. From hybrid cloud environments to microservices, IoT, APIs, and mobile apps—IT operations teams are expected to manage an ever-expanding web of interdependent components. Every device, server, service, and user interaction generates a stream of logs, metrics, traces, and events. The problem? There is simply **too much data** for humans to process and react to manually.

In today's IT landscape, complexity is the new normal. Systems span hybrid cloud environments, microservices, APIs, and countless endpoints—all working together, but not always in harmony. Every second, these systems generate a flood of logs, metrics, traces, and events. The job of making sense of this data and identifying what matters—before it becomes a problem—has outgrown traditional monitoring tools and human capacity.

This is where **AIOps**, or **Artificial Intelligence for IT Operations**, comes in. At its core, AIOps uses **artificial intelligence and machine learning algorithms** to ingest, analyze, and act upon massive volumes of operational data in real-time. But it is not just about automation. AIOps brings **intelligence** to operations—correlating signals, detecting anomalies, predicting outages, and in some cases, automatically resolving issues without human intervention.

The following table attempts to simplify the same:

Traditional IT Operations	AIOps-Enabled Operations
Alerts flood the dashboard with no context	Alerts are correlated and prioritized automatically
Humans manually sift through logs to diagnose issues	AI identifies likely root causes in real-time
Issues are discovered after users report them	Anomalies are detected and flagged proactively
Fixes often require escalation and coordination	AI can trigger automated remediation steps

Table 6.1: *Comparison between Traditional Operations and AIOps-enabled Operations*

Defining AIOps: More Than Just a Buzzword

AIOps stands for **Artificial Intelligence for IT Operations**. It refers to the **application of Artificial Intelligence (AI) and Machine Learning (ML)** techniques to automate and enhance IT operations.

But AIOps is **not just about automation**. it is about **intelligent automation**—analyzing massive amounts of data to detect patterns, predict incidents, correlate events, and

recommend or even perform actions. It empowers IT teams with **speed, visibility, and predictive insight** that traditional tools simply cannot match.

Think of it as giving your IT operations team **a smart assistant** that never sleeps, constantly learns, and spots patterns humans might miss

In simple terms, we can state that AIOps is your **virtual operations analyst**–always on, always learning, always improving.

The Key Pillars of AIOps

To understand AIOps practically, let us break it into five core functions as mentioned in the following table:

Function	What It Does
Data Ingestion	Collects data from logs, metrics, events, traces, alerts, and tools
Pattern Recognition	Identifies trends, baselines, and anomalies across the data
Event Correlation	Connects related alerts across systems to reduce noise
Root Cause Identification	Pinpoints the most likely source of an issue
Remediation/Recommendation	Suggests or initiates fixes (automated or manual)

Table 6.2: *Five Core Functions*

Requirement for AIOps

Traditional monitoring tools rely on **static thresholds and siloed dashboards**. They are excellent at reporting when something breaches a limit–but they are terrible at telling **why**, or whether it's even important.

In contrast, AIOps provides:

- **Context:** Correlates across systems to tell the whole story
- **Prioritization**: Flags the most urgent or business-critical issues
- **Prediction**: Warns of emerging problems before they escalate
- **Remediation:** Automates common fixes or escalates with context

Real-Life Example 1: A Bank's Nighttime Outage

Scenario: A large retail bank's mobile app became unresponsive late at night. By the time customers started reporting it on social media, critical alerts had already been generated in the backend–but buried among 1,500 other routine alerts. The operations team did not notice the signal in the noise until 90 minutes later.

Before AIOps:

- All alerts were treated equally.
- Engineers manually scanned logs to identify the root cause.
- The issue was escalated multiple times.
- Total downtime: 4.5 hours.

After AIOps Implementation:

- AIOps automatically correlated multiple alerts from different systems and detected an anomaly.
- It triaged the incident by severity and identified a database memory leak as the root cause.
- It triggered an automated script to recycle the affected service.
- Ops team received a single high-priority alert with diagnosis and action summary.
- Total downtime: 12 minutes

This real-world example illustrates how AIOps can dramatically reduce time-to-resolution, prevent customer impact, and lower the stress on operational teams.

Real-Life Example 2: E-Commerce Platform Outage Prevention

Scenario: A large e-commerce company experienced repeated outages during sales events. Traditional monitoring tools bombarded the operations team with hundreds of alerts–database latency, CPU spikes, network jitter–but failed to highlight a single cause.

After AIOps implementation:

- The system correlated alerts across network, DB, and front-end
- Detected an anomaly in database query times just before outages
- Recommended index optimization and scaling DB nodes prior to the next sale

Result:

- Alert volume reduced by 70%
- Outage averted during the next major sale
- Resolution time dropped from 3 hours to 20 minutes

Real-Life Example 3: Financial Institution's Login Issue

Scenario: A bank's customers were unable to log into their mobile app early in the morning. The issue was not detected until after several complaints surfaced on Twitter.

Before AIOps:

- Monitoring tools missed the early indicators
- Manual log review delayed response
- RCA took nearly a full day

With AIOps:

- Anomaly detection spotted unusual login error spikes at 4:00 AM
- Created a high-priority alert and ticket automatically
- Root cause identified as a failed dependency on a third-party authentication API
- Triggered a workflow to switch to a backup authentication path

Result:

- Issue resolved before user complaints spiked
- Business impact minimized
- New automation created for similar future scenarios

Debunking AIOps Misconceptions

AIOps is powerful, but it is important to clarify **what it is not**:

- It is not a replacement for your IT team. It augments human capability, not replaces it.
- It is not a traditional rules-based tool. AIOps learns over time and adapts to dynamic environments.
- It is not a plug-and-play magic fix. It requires proper integration, data hygiene, and continual tuning.

AIOps and the Human Element

AIOps **complements human expertise** by handling data-heavy, repetitive tasks so that skilled professionals can focus on higher-value activities. Engineers can review

AI-generated insights and act faster. Junior analysts can rely on AI to make informed decisions. Leaders can use insights for capacity planning and risk mitigation.

In short:

AIOps does not make your people less important—it makes them more effective and efficient.

The following table summarizes the AIOps advantages:

Traditional IT Ops	AIOps-Enhanced IT Ops
Reactive problem detection	Proactive, predictive alerts
Manual data analysis	Automated pattern and anomaly detection
Static rules and thresholds	Adaptive learning based on historical data
Siloed tool insights	Unified, cross-domain correlation
Human bottlenecks in triage	Fast, automated insights and suggestions

Table 6.3: *AIOps Advantages*

AIOps does not **replace** your operations team—it **augments** their capabilities so they can focus on complex problems while machines handle the noise.

The Bottom Line

AIOps is not just a tool—it is a **strategic capability** for any organization aiming to modernize its service management. As businesses become more digital, service reliability becomes more critical—and AIOps becomes the engine that powers proactive, intelligent, and resilient IT operations.

In the next chapters, we will explore how AIOps capabilities such as event correlation, anomaly detection, and root cause analysis map directly to ITIL4 practices and how they work in harmony to transform reactive IT into intelligent, predictive service delivery.

AIOps is not a magic wand, nor is it limited to the elite few with AI labs and data scientists. It is a **practical approach** to managing complexity, increasing observability, and ensuring system reliability—especially in environments where data volume, velocity, and variety have outpaced human capabilities.

As we dive deeper into the capabilities of AIOps in the next sections, you will see how these smart systems align with ITIL4 practices and help transition operations from reactive to predictive, and ultimately, autonomous.

How AI Supports Event Correlation, Anomaly Detection, Root Cause Analysis

Modern IT environments produce a staggering volume of operational data–logs, metrics, events, alerts, and traces. While this data holds valuable insights, traditional operations teams are often overwhelmed trying to make sense of it. The result? Noise overload, delayed response times, and missed opportunities for prevention.

AI steps in as a game-changer by transforming this raw data into actionable intelligence. Three foundational capabilities–**event correlation**, **anomaly detection**, and **root cause analysis**–lie at the heart of AIOps. These capabilities help IT teams move from reactive firefighting to intelligent, proactive operations.

Let us break them down one by one.

Event Correlation: From Chaos to Context

What it means: Event correlation is the process of linking multiple related alerts and events to form a coherent picture of what's really happening in the environment. AI analyzes event patterns across systems, applications, and infrastructure to reduce noise and identify the **single incident** that triggered a cascade of alerts.

Without AI: Operations teams are flooded with hundreds or thousands of alerts for the same issue–often from different monitoring tools.

With AI: AI can correlate alerts across systems (for example, application crash + server CPU spike + storage latency) and flag a **single probable cause** with context.

Real-Life Example: A global e-commerce platform experienced a sudden surge of alerts–web server failures, database connection drops, and high CPU utilization across multiple nodes. Instead of treating them as separate incidents, the AIOps engine correlated all events and linked them to a failed load balancer in a specific data center. The Ops team resolved the root issue in minutes, rather than chasing unrelated symptoms.

Value Delivered:

- Reduces alert fatigue
- Shortens time to triage
- Offers better situational awareness during incidents

Anomaly Detection: Spotting the Unusual Before It Breaks

What it means: Anomaly detection uses AI/ML algorithms to establish a baseline of "normal" behavior (e.g., CPU usage, response time, login frequency) and then flags deviations that suggest something might be wrong—even before failure occurs.

Traditional challenge: Threshold-based alerts are static and often miss issues that don't cross predefined limits.

AI Advantage: AI learns dynamic patterns and can detect **subtle shifts** or unusual spikes—indicating early warning signs that humans or static rules would miss.

Real-Life Example: A financial services company noticed an unusual login pattern for one of their backend services—logins were increasing rapidly but the system was not failing. AI flagged this as an anomaly. Upon investigation, they discovered a misconfigured API polling loop introduced by a recent update, which—if left unchecked—would have caused a major outage during trading hours.

Value Delivered:

- Predicts issues before impact
- Detects hidden problems such as memory leaks and slow degradation
- Helps in proactive incident management

Root Cause Analysis (RCA): Finding the "Why" Behind the Incident

What it means: Root Cause Analysis is the process of determining the primary reason behind a failure or incident. With AI, RCA becomes faster and more accurate, as it sifts through historical data, correlates logs, matches past incident patterns, and narrows down potential causes.

Traditional RCA: Time-consuming, reliant on tribal knowledge, and prone to guesswork.

AI-Powered RCA: AI uses historical event data, topology maps, and resolution patterns to **suggest likely causes** and even recommend fixes.

Real-Life Example: At a telecommunications provider, a recurring network issue led to frequent service degradation in a specific region. Using AI-based RCA, the tool found that a firmware bug in edge routers was causing intermittent packet drops—but only under a specific traffic load. The problem had evaded manual investigation for weeks. Once identified, the team rolled out a firmware patch and resolved the issue permanently.

Value Delivered:

- Faster Mean Time to Resolution (MTTR)
- Reduces dependency on individual expertise
- Enables faster learning from historical incidents

Combined Impact in a Service Environment

When these capabilities work together, the benefits multiply:

AI Capability	What It Does	Outcome in ITSM
Event Correlation	Reduces redundant alerts	Fewer tickets, clearer picture for L1 teams
Anomaly Detection	Identifies issues early	Preventive action, improved uptime
Root Cause Analysis	Diagnoses problems accurately	Faster resolution, reduced escalation

Table 6.4: *Combined Impacts*

Final Thoughts

AI doesn't just make operations faster–it makes them smarter. By automating signal-to-noise filtering, early warning alerts, and diagnostic insights, AI enables service teams to focus on what matters: resilience, availability, and user experience. Whether you are running a small ITSM setup or managing enterprise-scale infrastructure, these capabilities form the building blocks of **intelligent operations**.

In the next section, we will map these capabilities directly to **ITIL4 practices** such as Monitoring and Event Management, Incident Management, and Problem Management–illustrating exactly how AIOps fits into your existing service model.

Mapping AIOps to ITIL4's Monitoring and Event Management, Incident, and Problem Management

ITIL4 defines a set of well-structured practices to manage IT services efficiently. Among them, **Monitoring and Event Management**, **Incident Management**, and **Problem Management** form the backbone of operational stability and responsiveness. As organizations move toward more complex, real-time environments, traditional methods often struggle to keep pace. **AIOps bridges this gap**—injecting intelligence into these practices to elevate performance, speed, and precision.

This chapter explores how AIOps aligns with and enhances each of these core ITIL4 practices, bringing them into the era of intelligent operations.

Monitoring and Event Management: Moving from Alert Overload to Intelligent Insight

ITIL4 Definition

This practice ensures that services and infrastructure are **observed** and that **significant events** are identified and acted upon in a timely manner.

How AIOps Enhances It

AIOps transforms monitoring from a static, rules-based activity into a **dynamic, learning-driven process**. By analyzing historical and real-time data, AIOps platforms can identify what's meaningful, correlate alerts across systems, and suppress redundant or false-positive events.

The AIOps capabilities are listed in the following table:

AIOps Function	Corresponding ITIL4 Outcome
Event correlation	Accurate incident detection
Anomaly detection	Early warning of abnormal conditions
Noise reduction	Focus on critical events
Real-time observability	Enhanced visibility across distributed environments

Table 6.5: *Mapping of AIOps Capabilities*

Real-Life Example

A large retail chain implemented AIOps on top of its existing monitoring tools. Previously, a single network hiccup could generate 500+ alerts across apps, network, and databases. After deploying AIOps, alerts were automatically **correlated and de-duplicated**, reducing noise by 85%. The platform also learned from past patterns to **predict hardware failures** based on temperature and disk performance trends—triggering preventive maintenance before service impact.

Incident Management: Detecting and Resolving Faster, Smarter

ITIL4 Definition

The goal is to **restore normal service operations** as quickly as possible and minimize the impact on business operations.

How AIOps Enhances It

AIOps improves incident detection, triage, and resolution by **proactively identifying** incidents, **automating categorization**, and even **suggesting resolutions**. Through AI-driven prioritization and historical pattern matching, incidents are resolved faster and more consistently.

AIOps Capabilities are Mapped in the following table:

AIOps Function	Corresponding ITIL4 Outcome
Predictive detection	Reduced mean time to detect (MTTD)
Automated incident classification	Streamlined ticket handling
Root cause recommendation	Accelerated resolution and fewer escalations
Self-healing/auto-remediation	Reduced mean time to resolve (MTTR)

***Table 6.6**: AIOps Capabilities*

Real-Life Example

A telecom provider saw frequent outages in its customer login system. Before AIOps, the support team reacted only after user complaints flooded in. After integrating AIOps with the service desk, the system began **predicting login slowdowns** based on CPU, API call volumes, and database response times. Incidents were automatically created in the ITSM tool, pre-filled with context and suggested resolutions. In many cases, **automated remediation scripts** resolved the issue before users noticed.

Problem Management: From Guesswork to Data-Driven Prevention

ITIL4 Definition

This practice seeks to **identify and manage the root causes of incidents** to prevent recurrence.

How AIOps Enhances It

Traditional problem management relies heavily on **manual analysis** and expert knowledge. AIOps brings in **data-driven root cause analysis** by learning from incident history, identifying recurring patterns, and correlating system behaviors over time. It can surface hidden systemic issues that humans might overlook.

AIOps Capabilities are Mapped in the following table:

AIOps Function	Corresponding ITIL4 Outcome
Pattern recognition	Identification of recurring issues
Root cause analysis	Faster and more accurate RCA
Trend analysis	Discovery of underlying systemic problems
Historical resolution mapping	Recommendations based on past fixes

***Table 6.7:** AIOps Capabilities*

Real-Life Example

A banking institution faced recurring issues with their payment gateway, but manual RCA failed to reveal a root cause. With AIOps in place, historical log analysis showed that **a specific middleware component** caused delays during peak load. AIOps flagged the pattern and presented visual timelines linking events across layers. Once the faulty component was updated, the issue disappeared–and **no recurrence occurred in the next audit cycle**.

The following table presents the Summary of How AIOps Elevates ITIL4 Operational Practices:

ITIL4 Practice	Traditional Challenges	AIOps-Driven Benefits
Monitoring and Event Management	Too many alerts, false positives, siloed tools	Noise reduction, proactive detection
Incident Management	Delayed detection, manual classification	Faster triage, intelligent routing, automation
Problem Management	Manual RCA, missed trends	Data-backed insights, systemic fix prevention

***Table 6.8:** Summary of How AIOps Elevates ITIL4 Operational Practices*

Final Thoughts

AIOps is not meant to replace ITIL4–it is a **natural evolution** that complements and strengthens ITIL4 practices. By embedding intelligence into monitoring, incident, and problem processes, organizations can unlock new levels of operational agility, resilience, and efficiency. The result is a service environment that not only reacts to issues faster but actively **prevents** them, aligns with business objectives, and continuously improves.

In the following chapter, we will explore how Generative AI takes these capabilities even further—by enabling **natural language summaries**, **human-like decision support**, and **collaborative AI agents** in the operations room.

Role of GenAI in Synthesizing Operational Data and Recommendations

As organizations embrace AI for smarter service management, one emerging capability is transforming how IT operations teams understand, communicate, and act on system data: **Generative AI (GenAI)**.

Unlike traditional machine learning that focuses on classification or prediction, **Generative AI excels at creating new content**—text, summaries, explanations, even scripts—based on patterns in existing data. This unique ability makes GenAI a powerful ally for operations teams drowning in complexity, alerts, and dashboards.

But what does this mean in practice? In this chapter, we explore how Generative AI helps **synthesize complex operational data into human-friendly insights** and **generate actionable recommendations**—bringing clarity, consistency, and speed to decision-making in IT service management.

Understanding the Shift: From Data to Understanding

Operational systems already collect vast amounts of telemetry—logs, metrics, traces, alerts, configurations. However, **data abundance is not the same as insight**. IT teams often spend hours sifting through data just to understand what went wrong, where, and what to do next.

Generative AI acts as a **translator between machines and humans**. It does not just show the data—it **explains what the data means**, highlights patterns, and **suggests next steps** in natural language.

The following table lists the Key Functions of GenAI in Operations:

Function	Description
Data summarization	Converts complex multi-source logs and alerts into clear incident summaries

Root cause explanation	Translates technical diagnostics into business-relevant RCA statements
Recommendation generation	Suggests actions based on prior resolutions, topology, and impact analysis
Conversational support	Powers chat interfaces for self-service or real-time decision support
Context-aware decision guidance	Adjusts recommendations based on service criticality, SLAs, and operational context

Table 6.9: *List of Key Functions of GenAI in Operations*

Real-Life Use Case 1: Incident Summary and Action Suggestion

Scenario: An international insurance company faced a major service disruption in their customer claims portal. The operations team had over 2,000 logs and events to review, including storage latency, API timeouts, and CPU spikes.

With GenAI Integration (via ServiceNow Virtual Agent):

- The GenAI model analyzed the event stream and **summarized the incident** in one paragraph:

  "Service disruption detected in Claims API. Root cause appears to be a storage IOPS bottleneck on volume X. Similar patterns were observed during last month's high-load event."

- It **recommended immediate actions**:

  "Throttle incoming batch requests; run disk cleanup; consider moving volume to SSD-tier storage."

Outcome:

Resolution time dropped from 3 hours to 25 minutes. The operations manager noted, "It felt like having a tier-3 engineer writing a diagnosis for us."

Real-Life Use Case 2: Conversational RCA and Knowledge Capture

Scenario: A healthcare organization uses GenAI-powered chatbots embedded in their service portal. When a batch job fails, a junior analyst types:

"Why did the overnight job fail today?"

The GenAI response:

"The ETL job failed due to a mismatch in data schema version 3.2 used by the source database. This occurred at 2:13 AM, consistent with last week's change to the staging schema. Consider aligning the ETL script with the new schema definitions."

Bonus Impact:

The GenAI interface offers to automatically **generate a post-incident report** and file a **Problem Record** if the issue has recurred more than once.

Real-Life Use Case 3: Enhancing Problem Management with Recommendations

Scenario: A logistics company experiences frequent delays in its order tracking API. Instead of manually searching past incident records, their AIOps platform uses GenAI to **suggest likely solutions**.

GenAI output: "This API latency issue resembles a pattern observed in May and July 2024. Previous mitigation involved increasing the message queue buffer and deploying async logging. Would you like to apply the same patch?"

Value Delivered:

- Prevents repeat analysis work
- Reduces time to root cause
- Encourages reuse of proven fixes
- Builds institutional memory

Where GenAI Fits in the ITIL4 Service Lifecycle

GenAI can enrich multiple stages of service management:

ITIL4 Practice	GenAI Contribution
Incident Management	Summarizes incidents, recommends actions, powers virtual agents
Problem Management	Drafts RCA reports, correlates incidents, suggests preventive steps
Change Enablement	Translates change risks, drafts CAB documentation
Knowledge Management	Converts logs and chats into reusable knowledge base articles
Continual Improvement	Identifies improvement trends, suggests automation opportunities

Availability Management	Predicts service downtime using log/event patterns, drafts availability reports, recommends proactive actions to improve resilience
Performance and Capacity Management	Analyzes usage trends, forecasts demand with predictive modeling, suggests optimization strategies to prevent bottlenecks

***Table 6.10**: GenAI Contributions in Multiple Stages of Service Management*

Challenges and Considerations

While GenAI adds significant value, organizations must address the following:

- **Data Quality:** Garbage in, garbage out. Poor logs or mislabeled tickets can result in misleading summaries.
- **Explainability:** Recommendations should include traceability–how and why a suggestion was made.
- **Security:** Ensure sensitive operational data is not exposed through poorly secured AI interfaces.
- **Human Oversight:** GenAI is a co-pilot, not an autopilot. Final decisions should still rest with service professionals.

The Human-AI Partnership

The true power of GenAI lies not in replacing humans, but in **amplifying human capability**. Operations teams now spend less time decoding logs and more time making high-value decisions. Junior analysts gain contextual awareness without needing years of tribal knowledge. Senior engineers can scale their impact by codifying their expertise into generative models.

GenAI brings **clarity to complexity** and **structure to chaos**–synthesizing data and transforming it into meaningful, timely, and actionable insights.

Final Thoughts

Generative AI is redefining how we think about operational intelligence. It's not just an assistant–it's a knowledge synthesizer, a teacher, and a communicator. In the ever-noisy world of IT operations, GenAI does not shout–it explains. As organizations evolve their ITSM strategies, integrating GenAI will be key to **human-centered, data-driven service resilience**.

In the next chapter, we will explore how to assess your organization's readiness for adopting AIOps and GenAI, with a focus on cultural, technical, and governance dimensions.

Conclusion

AIOps is not just an incremental upgrade–it is a transformative shift, converting vast operational data into actionable intelligence. By seamlessly integrating event correlation, anomaly detection, and root cause analysis, AIOps empowers IT teams to transition from reactive troubleshooting to proactive, predictive service management. When aligned effectively with ITIL4 practices and further amplified by Generative AI, organizations can realize unprecedented resilience, agility, and efficiency in their operations. As we proceed, the next chapter will explore practical steps to evaluate your organization's readiness to adopt and maximize the full potential of AIOps and GenAI.

In the next chapter, we shall discuss how AI is revolutionizing Incident and Problem Management.

Multiple Choice Questions

1. What is the primary role of AIOps in IT operations?
    a. Replacing all human roles in IT operations
    b. Automating network hardware upgrades
    c. Ingesting and analyzing operational data to provide intelligent insights
    d. Running financial audits for IT departments
2. Which of the following is a core function of AIOps?
    a. Physical asset inventory tracking
    b. Manual ticket triaging
    c. Pattern recognition across data streams
    d. Email spam filtering
3. How does AIOps support Incident Management as per ITIL4?
    a. By automating service desk staffing
    b. By creating detailed business continuity plans
    c. By providing predictive detection and root cause suggestions
    d. By sending incident alerts to customers directly

4. What makes Generative AI (GenAI) different from traditional AI in IT operations?
    a. It controls physical servers remotely.
    b. It creates new content like summaries and recommendations.
    c. It replaces all monitoring tools.
    d. It eliminates the need for change enablement.
5. In the context of Problem Management, how does AIOps add value?
    a. By delaying RCA until post-incident reviews
    b. By enforcing manual data collection
    c. By identifying recurring issues and recommending fixes based on historical data
    d. By preventing all software bugs

Answers

1. c
2. c
3. c
4. b
5. c

Questions

1. Explain how AIOps transforms traditional IT operations into proactive and predictive service management.
2. Describe the five core functional pillars of AIOps and illustrate how each contributes to intelligent operations.
3. How does AIOps improve the incident detection and resolution process within the framework of ITIL4 Incident Management?
4. Discuss the role of anomaly detection in AIOps and provide an example of how it helps in early problem identification.
5. What is the significance of event correlation in AIOps, and how does it help reduce alert fatigue?

6. Compare and contrast traditional Root Cause Analysis (RCA) with AI-powered RCA in terms of speed, accuracy, and effectiveness.
7. In what ways does Generative AI enhance IT operations beyond traditional machine learning capabilities?
8. How can GenAI improve communication between IT systems and human operators during an incident?
9. Identify the challenges and considerations organizations must address while implementing GenAI in IT operations.
10. Describe how AIOps aligns with the ITIL4 practices of Monitoring and Event Management, Incident Management, and Problem Management.

Key Terms

- **AIOps (Artificial Intelligence for IT Operations)**: AIOps is the use of AI and machine learning to analyze large volumes of IT operational data in real-time. It enhances decision-making through automation, anomaly detection, and root cause analysis.
- **Event Correlation:** This process links related alerts from different systems to identify the root incident. It reduces noise and helps IT teams respond to the actual cause rather than symptoms.
- **Anomaly Detection**: AI-based anomaly detection establishes normal behavior baselines and flags unusual patterns. It enables early identification of issues before they escalate into incidents.
- **Root Cause Analysis (RCA)**: RCA determines the underlying cause of a problem. With AIOps, this becomes faster and more accurate through automated analysis of historical and real-time data.
- **Noise Reduction:** AIOps filters out redundant or irrelevant alerts, allowing teams to focus on significant events. This minimizes alert fatigue and improves operational focus.
- **Generative AI (GenAI):** GenAI creates human-readable summaries, recommendations, and responses from structured or unstructured data. It adds context and clarity to complex operational scenarios.
- **Predictive Detection**: AIOps can forecast incidents by analyzing trends and detecting weak signals. This proactive approach helps prevent service disruptions.
- **Self-Healing Systems**: These are systems that automatically detect and resolve issues without human intervention. AIOps enables self-healing by triggering remediation workflows based on analysis.

- **ITIL4 Practices**: Refers to IT service management best practices such as Incident, Problem, and Event Management. AIOps aligns with these practices to modernize and enhance service delivery.
- **Context-Aware Recommendations**: GenAI provides suggestions tailored to the service environment, considering SLAs, priorities, and impact. This supports faster and more informed decision-making.

Chapter 7
Revolutionizing Incident and Problem Management with AI

Introduction

Incident and Problem Management have long stood at the heart of ITSM, safeguarding service stability and ensuring swift recovery when things go wrong. Yet, as digital environments grow more complex, the volume, velocity, and variety of incidents continue to overwhelm traditional service desks. Service teams find themselves firefighting – chasing symptoms instead of resolving root causes, often under pressure and with limited visibility.

This is where artificial intelligence introduces a transformational shift. By bringing automation, intelligence, and contextual awareness to the incident lifecycle, AI helps organizations move from reactive firefighting to proactive problem-solving. From auto-triaging and intelligent ticket routing to early root cause prediction, AI-driven capabilities can significantly reduce human workload and accelerate resolution times.

AI also excels at identifying recurring patterns and noise across massive datasets–something traditional tools struggle with–thus aiding both Incident and Problem Management in preempting disruptions. More importantly, this transformation is not hypothetical; organizations across industries are already realizing tangible gains through AI-powered enhancements.

This chapter explores how AI elevates these foundational practices of ITSM, using real-world examples and use cases to illustrate the shift toward intelligent operations. We will examine how incident resolution is being reimagined through algorithms that learn, adapt, and even suggest next actions pushing in a new era of service desk performance and user experience.

Structure

In this chapter, we will discuss the following topics:

- Auto-Routing, Ticket Triaging, Root Cause Prediction
- Noise Reduction and Pattern Detection
- Case Studies of AI Enhancing Operational Excellence

Auto-Routing, Ticket Triaging, Root Cause Prediction

In the ever-evolving landscape of IT service management, the burden on incident and problem management teams continues to grow. Manual triage, delayed routing, and siloed diagnostics create operational bottlenecks, ultimately degrading service quality. AI doesn't just accelerate resolution–it reshapes the very fabric of how incidents are handled, classified, and resolved.

This section explores how AI transforms these core areas through intelligent automation, contextual learning, and data-driven insights.

Auto-Routing: Precision Assignment at Machine Speed

Instead of relying on rigid routing rules or manual categorization, AI analyzes incident metadata, ticket history, and even free-text descriptions to automatically route incidents to the right team or technician.

Real-Life Example

A global logistics firm implemented auto-routing using machine learning (ML) within Jira Service Management. Based on historical resolution data, technician skill profiles, and user sentiment analysis, the AI system routed high-priority tickets about warehouse system failures directly to Tier 2 infrastructure support. This slashed reassignments by 65% and significantly improved SLA compliance.

Ticket Triaging: Smarter Classification and Prioritization

AI-powered triaging systems use historical resolution data and contextual inputs to predict categories, set impact/urgency levels, and flag anomalies. This reduces the risk of misclassification and supports more accurate SLA planning.

Real-Life Example

In a large public healthcare network, ServiceNow's Virtual Agent analyzed vague tickets like "PC not responding" and correlated the issue with ongoing domain controller outages. It escalated these incidents immediately to the core IT team, auto-prioritized them as "Critical," and bypassed usual first-line queues–minimizing service disruption in ICU environments.

Automated Incident Summaries: Reducing Manual Burden

Documenting an incident's lifecycle is often neglected, especially under pressure. Generative AI models now summarize ticket conversations, technician logs, and resolution steps, making documentation seamless and consistent.

Real-Life Example

A banking organization embedded ChatGPT-like AI within their ticketing platform. Upon resolution, the AI generated a structured summary including the timeline, actions taken, and resolution outcomes. Not only did this enhance knowledge base accuracy, but it also improved audit readiness and compliance with internal IT controls.

Root Cause Prediction: Pattern Learning from Historical Data

AI systems trained on incident/problem datasets can predict probable root causes based on patterns, such as event spikes, log anomalies, or CI interdependencies. This accelerates diagnosis, enabling a shift from resolution to prevention.

Real-Life Example

A telecom enterprise using Dynatrace's AIOps framework traced recurring dropped VoIP calls to a misconfigured network switch. The AI engine predicted this with 90% accuracy by analyzing prior incidents, traffic flows, and topology data. It also recommended remediation based on similar past fixes.

Root Cause Analysis (RCA): Augmented by AI, Not Replaced

While prediction is helpful, AI-augmented Root Cause Analysis ensures deeper investigation and accuracy. AI aids RCA by aggregating logs, user reports, infrastructure telemetry, and change records, surfacing high-probability causality chains and highlighting anomalies in timeline sequences.

Real-Life Example

A fintech startup experienced intermittent API failures. Traditional monitoring yielded no conclusive results. However, an AI-powered RCA tool synthesized logs, deployment history, and CI/CD pipeline data to reveal that a minor version update in a third-party library introduced a memory leak. Human teams validated the root cause within hours instead of days. The RCA output was archived in the KEDB (Known Error Database) and helped prevent similar future occurrences.

The following table represents the Comparative Summary:

Capability	Traditional Approach	AI-Powered Approach	Key Benefit
Auto-routing	Rule-based/manual	Skill/context-aware ML model	Faster and accurate assignment
Triaging	User-input dependent	Predictive classification	Improved prioritization
Incident Summaries	Manual post-resolution	Auto-generated narratives	Saved technician time
Root Cause Prediction	Reactive diagnosis	Pattern-based probability scoring	Early intervention
Root Cause Analysis	Manual investigation	Log + telemetry correlation	Faster, data-backed RCA

Table 7.1: *Comparative Summary*

As a Closing Perspective, it can be stated that AI doesn't eliminate human decision-making in incident and problem management—it enhances it with speed, context, and predictive insight. From routing to root cause, AI empowers service teams to focus on high-value analysis while routine tasks get handled at scale. The result is a more proactive, resilient, and data-driven IT service operation.

In the next section, we will explore noise reduction and pattern detection—critical capabilities that help filter signal from noise and streamline issue resolution even further.

Noise Reduction and Pattern Detection

In today's hyper-connected IT environments, the service desk is often flooded with a deluge of alerts, notifications, and incident reports. Not all of them are meaningful, but each one demands attention. This constant stream of "noise"–false positives, redundant alerts, and repetitive tickets–can overwhelm IT teams, delay responses to real issues, and consume valuable operational bandwidth.

AI's ability to filter out noise and detect meaningful patterns has become a game-changer in ITSM. By analyzing historical data, user behavior, and system telemetry, AI can distinguish signals from noise and surface actionable insights–turning reactive service desks into proactive intelligence centers.

So, the question arises "What is "Noise" in ITSM?"

- The answer to the question is that noise includes: Duplicate or recurring alerts for the same underlying issue
- Low-priority events that don't require action
- False positives from overly sensitive monitoring tools
- Redundant incidents raised across channels (email, chatbot, portal)

While each of these may appear harmless in isolation, their cumulative impact can paralyze a service desk.

AI-Powered Noise Reduction: Precision at Scale

AI reduces noise using correlation algorithms, anomaly detection, and log analysis to suppress redundant alerts and highlight critical incidents.

These objectives are achieved by:

- Grouping related alerts into event clusters
- Suppressing duplicate alerts using temporal and contextual matching
- Identifying and muting known benign anomalies (for example, expected maintenance windows)
- Mapping alerts to existing tickets to avoid duplication

Real-Life Example

A European airline integrated AIOps into its monitoring stack. Previously, a single database outage triggered over 800 redundant alerts across applications, infrastructure, and user systems. The AI layer reduced this flood to just one actionable incident, suppressing 98% of the noise. This allowed IT teams to focus on restoration instead of filtering noise manually.

Pattern Detection: Discovering the Undiscovered

Beyond filtering alerts, AI shines in pattern recognition across time, geography, users, or systems. Pattern detection enables teams to:

- Identify underlying problems hidden beneath recurring incidents
- Detect anomalies that deviate from historical behavior
- Predict service degradation before it affects users

Real-Life Example

A global retail chain using ServiceNow's predictive analytics found that incidents tagged "slow POS response" occurred every Friday evening. AI identified a pattern linked to weekly data sync jobs initiated at that time. With this insight, IT rescheduled the job, reducing weekend escalations by 70%.

The following table lists a few Use Cases in ITIL4 Practices:

ITIL4 Practice	AI-Enabled Benefit
Monitoring and Event Management	Real-time alert deduplication and correlation
Incident Management	Grouping repetitive incidents, triggering problem investigation
Problem Management	Identifying unknown error patterns and initiating RCA
Capacity and Performance Management	Detecting usage trends (Patterns of Business Activity) and forecasting thresholds
Availability Management	Predicts service downtime using log/event patterns, drafts availability reports, recommends proactive actions to improve resilience

Table 7.2: *Use Cases in ITIL4 Practices*

Combined Power: Correlation with Context

AI's strength lies in its ability to combine multiple weak signals—that might look benign in isolation—into one strong warning. This capability helps identify multi-layered issues, such as:

- Latency spikes across microservices
- Cascading failures in distributed systems
- Gradual performance degradation tied to configuration drift

Real-Life Example

An insurance company's claims platform was facing intermittent slowdowns. Individually, system metrics showed nothing unusual. But AI detected that CPU usage, API response time, and transaction retries, all spiked during policy load times. These correlated patterns revealed a memory leak introduced by a recent application update. The fix would have been delayed for weeks if not surfaced through pattern detection.

The following table describes the recap of benefits:

Feature	Traditional Challenge	AI-Driven Advantage
Alert Filtering	Human-led, time-consuming	Real-time, rules-free suppression
Event Correlation	Manual matching, error-prone	Automated, contextual grouping
Pattern Detection	Requires tribal knowledge	Learns from historical and cross-domain data
Noise Reduction	High alert fatigue	Clean, focused, actionable dashboards

Table 7.3: *Benefits Recap*

AI-driven noise reduction and pattern detection are not just technical enhancements—they are operational necessities. By filtering irrelevant data and spotlighting what truly matters, AI empowers service teams to act faster, with greater clarity and confidence. These capabilities shift ITSM from reactive chaos to intelligent control—ensuring service stability even in the face of digital complexity.

In the next section, we will explore case studies of AI enhancing operational excellence, showing how real organizations are leveraging these capabilities to achieve tangible service performance gains.

Case studies of AI Enhancing Operational Excellence

In this section, we will go through a few ITIL4 Case Studies of AI Enhancing Operational Excellence, now with more context, background, and richer descriptions to deepen their value. These stories offer concrete insights into how AI is practically applied in ITSM settings.

Telecom Giant Cuts Alert Fatigue by 90% Using AIOps

Background: A large telecom provider with nationwide coverage was grappling with over 30,000 alerts per day from thousands of infrastructure components–routers, switches, servers, and apps.

Challenge: Most alerts were low-value or duplicates triggered by the same root incident, overwhelming the Network Operations Center (NOC).

AI Solution: They deployed an AIOps platform that used historical correlation, topology mapping, and ML-based suppression models to group related alerts and discard noise.

Outcome: Alert fatigue was reduced by 90%, enabling teams to focus on high-impact events. MTTD improved from 1 hour to 10 minutes, directly benefiting SLA compliance and uptime.

Healthcare Group Automates Ticket Triage for Clinical Systems

Background: A regional healthcare provider ran a central service desk handling IT support for clinical systems, staff devices, and patient portal infrastructure.

Challenge: Service desk agents manually classifying all incoming tickets, resulting in frequent errors, especially for clinical system disruptions.

AI Solution: They integrated ServiceNow's Virtual Agent with NLP to analyze free-text inputs, auto-classify by service type (for example, EMR, radiology systems), and prioritize based on risk to patient care.

Outcome: Over 80% of tickets were auto-classified correctly. Critical system tickets were routed within 30 seconds, cutting average response times by 35%.

Insurance Firm Uses ChatGPT Integration for Automated Summaries

Background: A mid-sized insurance provider had grown rapidly and relied on a small IT team. Incident resolution notes were inconsistent and often lacked clarity.

Challenge: Manual documentation was time-consuming and often skipped during high-pressure situations.

AI Solution: A ChatGPT-based tool was embedded into Jira Service Desk. After resolution, it generated structured summaries using the ticket description, technician notes, system logs, and resolution time.

Outcome: 70% reduction in documentation time, and post-incident reviews improved due to consistent, AI-generated summaries. It also supported the creation of a searchable internal knowledge base.

Retail Chain Detects Weekly Pattern in POS Incidents

Background: A multinational retailer with 400+ stores experienced a surge of "slow system" complaints at checkout counters during weekends.

Challenge: Despite full infrastructure uptime, support tickets spiked every Friday evening, affecting customer experience.

AI Solution: Using pattern recognition in ServiceNow Predictive Intelligence, they correlated the spike to backend data sync jobs scheduled weekly.

Outcome: After rescheduling the sync jobs to off-peak hours, weekend incidents dropped by 60%, and customer satisfaction (CSAT) improved by 20 points.

Banking Institution Predicts Root Cause of API Failures

Background: A global bank with a major mobile banking app was experiencing sporadic API failures, disrupting user transactions.

Challenge: Traditional monitoring failed to pinpoint the issue as logs appeared normal and performance metrics were within thresholds.

AI Solution: They deployed Dynatrace AIOps with automatic root cause prediction, which correlated telemetry, log sequences, and deployment history.

Outcome: The AI identified a third-party library version as the culprit, which introduced memory leaks under peak load. The problem was resolved in hours versus the typical multi-day diagnosis cycle.

Manufacturing Firm Reduces Ticket Volume via Self-Healing Scripts

Background: An industrial manufacturing company faced hundreds of repetitive tickets daily—printer errors, storage thresholds, VPN disconnections.

Challenge: L1 support was overwhelmed, and employee productivity was suffering due to delays.

AI Solution: Machine learning was used to identify repeatable incident patterns. Scripts were developed and triggered by AI rules for auto-remediation (for example, clearing spoolers, restarting services).

Outcome: 38% of incidents were resolved automatically without technician intervention. Helpdesk staff were reallocated to focus on more complex, high-impact issues.

University IT Helpdesk Improves FCR with AI-Based Auto-Routing

Background: A top university's central IT helpdesk served over 25,000 students and faculty.

Challenge: Low First Contact Resolution (FCR) due to poor ticket routing–academic vs. administrative tickets were often misrouted.

AI Solution: AI models trained on past ticket history and agent success rates automatically routed tickets to the most relevant department or individual.

Outcome: FCR increased by 40% in one semester. Support satisfaction scores for both students and staff improved significantly.

Government IT Agency Detects Anomalies in Change Management

Background: A government IT agency managing critical national systems had a formal change approval process–but some unauthorized changes were slipping through.

Challenge: The manual change review process couldn't cope with the growing volume of requests.

AI Solution: AI flagged "anomalous" change requests by comparing them to past patterns and approval trails. Risk scores were calculated in real time.

Outcome: All unauthorized or high-risk changes were flagged before implementation. Audit compliance increased, and post-change incidents dropped by 22%.

Logistics Company Prevents Downtime via Predictive Maintenance

Background: A logistics firm managing real-time vehicle tracking and dispatching experienced backend system slowdowns during seasonal peaks.

Challenge: System failures happened without warning, affecting delivery SLAs.

AI Solution: Predictive analytics monitored telemetry from application servers, usage patterns, and network traffic to forecast infrastructure strain.

Outcome: Maintenance and scaling actions were taken proactively, avoiding costly downtime. The company reported zero unplanned outages during the holiday season for the first time in five years.

Energy Utility Improves User Sentiment Monitoring

Background: A national energy provider offered online portals for billing, complaints, and outage updates.

Challenge: Despite timely responses, user escalations and complaints were rising–but the root cause was unclear.

AI Solution: NLP-driven sentiment analysis scanned chat transcripts, support calls, and ticket feedback to uncover negative tone trends and misaligned responses.

Outcome: The analysis revealed gaps in how support agents communicated resolution timelines. After training agents and updating messaging templates, escalation rates dropped by 28%, and NPS scores improved across key user segments.

This following table lists the cross-case takeaways:

Capability	**AI Contribution**	**Business Value**
Auto-routing	Matches tickets to best-fit agent/team	Faster response, higher FCR (First Contact Resolution)
Ticket triaging	Predicts and sets category, priority, urgency	Reduces misclassification, aligns with SLAs
Incident summaries	Auto-generates structured summaries	Saves technician time, improves audits
Root cause prediction	Uses ML for probable root cause identification	Faster problem resolution, fewer escalations

Table 7.4: *Cross-Case Takeaways*

The following table provides a summary:

Industry	**Key AI Application**	**Measurable Outcome**
Telecom	Event correlation and suppression	90% alert reduction
Healthcare	Auto-classification and prioritization	80% accuracy, SLA improvement
Insurance	Automated summaries (GenAI)	70% less manual effort, better KB

Retail	Pattern detection in incidents	60% fewer weekend incidents
Banking	Root cause prediction	RCA in hours, not days
Manufacturing	Self-healing automation	38% of L1 incidents auto resolved
Education	AI-based auto-routing	40% improvement in FCR
Government	AI-assisted change analysis	100% detection of unauthorized changes
Logistics	Predictive maintenance	Zero outages during peak season
Utilities	Sentiment analysis	28% reduction in escalations

***Table* 7.5:** *Summary View*

These case studies reveal a clear trend: AI is not just enhancing IT operations–it is redefining them. Whether through smarter triaging, proactive issue detection, or intelligent automation, AI helps organizations achieve measurable operational excellence while improving both user satisfaction and service resilience.

Conclusion

As digital ecosystems expand in complexity, the need for intelligent, scalable, and proactive service management practices has become undeniable. This chapter has demonstrated that **AI is not just an enhancement to Incident and Problem Management, but a transformative force**. By introducing automation, contextual understanding, and predictive capabilities, AI allows organizations to shift from a reactive, ticket-centric model to a proactive, insight-driven service environment.

Through the lens of **auto-routing**, **ticket triaging**, **root cause prediction**, **noise reduction**, and **pattern detection**, we have seen how AI augments human capabilities. No longer confined to manual workflows or static rules, today's service teams can leverage dynamic models that learn and adapt–resulting in faster resolution, higher SLA adherence, and a drastically improved user experience.

Furthermore, the **case studies across telecom, healthcare, banking, education, and more** illustrate one key truth: **AI is not theoretical; it is operational and measurable**. Organizations are already reaping tangible benefits–be it reducing alert fatigue by 90%, boosting first-contact resolution by 40%, or eliminating outages during peak seasons through predictive analytics. These aren't future promises–they are current realities made possible by intelligent automation and data-driven decision-making.

What emerges is a new paradigm where:

- Routine tasks are automated
- Anomalies are identified before they become incidents

- Root causes are uncovered with data-backed precision
- Service quality becomes predictive, not reactive

However, it is important to remember that **AI complements–not replaces–human expertise**. The best outcomes arise when skilled professionals work hand-in-hand with intelligent tools, leveraging AI insights to make informed, strategic decisions.

As we transition into the next chapter on **Change Enablement, Service Request Management, and Knowledge Management**, we will continue this exploration–demonstrating how AI is revolutionizing these domains as well. The journey toward **AI-powered service excellence** has just begun, and Incident and Problem Management is only the first frontier.

Multiple Choice Questions

1. What is a key advantage of AI-based auto-routing in Incident Management?
    a. It assigns incidents randomly to reduce technician bias.
    b. It routes tickets based solely on the requester's department.
    c. It analyzes ticket data to assign incidents to the most appropriate team or technician.
    d. It delays assignment until a manual review is complete.
2. How does AI improve Root Cause Analysis (RCA) compared to traditional methods?
    a. It eliminates the need for any human validation.
    b. It uses predictive modeling to suppress all future incidents.
    c. It aggregates data sources to probable causes faster and more accurately.
    d. It focuses only on software-related issues.
3. In the context of noise reduction, what is considered "noise" in ITSM?
    a. High-priority incidents
    b. Approved change requests
    c. Redundant alerts and duplicate tickets with no new impact
    d. Tickets generated through chatbot only

4. What benefit did the European airline experience after implementing AIOps in its monitoring system?
    a. Increased volume of alerts for improved visibility
    b. Suppression of 98% of alerts, focusing on one actionable incident
    c. Manual review of all application-level errors
    d. Reassignment of incidents to first-level support
5. Which AI capability helped a retail chain discover a recurring issue with their POS system every Friday evening?
    a. Auto-remediation scripting
    b. Log Suppression
    c. Pattern detection through historical analysis
    d. Sentiment analysis of customer complaints

Answers

1. c
2. c
3. c
4. b
5. c

Questions

1. Explain how AI-driven auto-routing enhances the efficiency of Incident Management compared to traditional rule-based routing.
2. Describe how AI-powered ticket triaging can help in better classification and prioritization of incidents. Provide a real-life example from the chapter.
3. What are the key components of AI-generated incident summaries, and how do they benefit both technicians and knowledge management?
4. Discuss the differences between root cause prediction and root cause analysis in the context of AI-enabled Problem Management.

5. Define "noise" in ITSM and elaborate on how AI helps in reducing noise to improve focus on critical incidents.
6. What techniques does AI use to perform pattern detection across systems, users, or time periods? Give an example illustrating its impact.
7. Analyze the role of AI in enabling proactive ITSM practices. How does it help organizations move from reactive to predictive service models?
8. From the case studies provided, choose two industries and explain how AI transformed their Incident or Problem Management practices.
9. How do AI capabilities align with specific ITIL4 practices such as Monitoring and Event Management, Problem Management, and Capacity Management?
10. Summarize the operational and strategic benefits organizations can achieve by integrating AI into their incident and problem workflows.

Key Terms

- **Auto-Routing:** AI-driven auto-routing uses machine learning to analyze ticket context and assign incidents to the most suitable team or technician. This reduces manual errors and accelerates response time.
- **Ticket Triaging:** AI-enabled triaging classifies and prioritizes incidents based on historical data and context, ensuring faster and more accurate categorization. It supports better SLA management and reduces misrouted tickets.
- **Incident Summary Generation:** Generative AI creates structured, human-readable summaries of resolved tickets, including actions taken and outcomes. This improves documentation quality and knowledge base consistency.
- **Root Cause Prediction:** AI identifies probable root causes of incidents by analyzing event patterns, logs, and historical incidents. It enables early intervention and reduces time to resolution.
- **Root Cause Analysis (RCA):** AI-augmented RCA synthesizes telemetry, logs, change history, and user data to pinpoint underlying causes. It enhances the accuracy and speed of traditional RCA efforts.
- **Noise Reduction:** AI filters out duplicate, low-priority, or false-positive alerts that overwhelm service desks. This allows teams to focus on genuine incidents that need attention.
- **Pattern Detection:** Machine learning algorithms detect recurring trends or anomalies across time, geography, systems, or users. It reveals hidden problems and supports proactive resolutions.

- **Event Correlation:** This process links related alerts across different systems or components into a single incident. AI-based correlation reduces alert fatigue and improves incident clarity.
- **AIOps (Artificial Intelligence for IT Operations):** AIOps platforms leverage AI to monitor, analyze, and automate IT operations. They enhance service performance through anomaly detection, automation, and predictive analytics.
- **Known Error Database (KEDB):** A KEDB stores validated root causes and workarounds for recurring issues. AI contributes by enriching the KEDB with accurate summaries and RCA insights.

CHAPTER 8

AI-Enhanced Change Enablement, Request, and Knowledge Management

Introduction

As IT environments continue to evolve in scale and complexity, service management teams face growing demands to ensure faster, safer, and more consistent delivery of IT services. Three foundational practices–Change Enablement, Deployment Management, Release Management, Service Request Management, and Knowledge Management–are central to this effort, yet they often rely on outdated or manual approaches that struggle to keep up. Artificial Intelligence (AI) brings a powerful opportunity to reimagine how these functions operate by introducing intelligence, automation, and predictive capabilities into the workflow. In Change Enablement, AI can proactively assess risk, identify potential conflicts, and even recommend mitigation plans, enabling safer and faster change implementation. In the area of Service Request Management, virtual assistants, predictive analytics, and workflow automation are transforming user experiences–offering seamless fulfillment and more intuitive self-service. Meanwhile, Knowledge Management is undergoing a quiet revolution as AI powers the creation, curation, and contextualization of knowledge articles–reducing agent effort while increasing user satisfaction. This chapter explores how AI is not just a tool, but a strategic enabler in turning these traditionally reactive functions into proactive, value-generating components of modern ITSM. We will cover real-world examples, actionable insights, and emerging best practices that demonstrate how AI can improve service speed, accuracy, and scalability–without compromising control or quality.

Structure

In this chapter, we will discuss the following topics:

- Change Risk Analysis and Automation
- Virtual Assistants and Smart Knowledge Bases
- Predicting Ticket Volumes and Request Fulfillment

Change Risk Analysis and Automation

In ITSM, Change Enablement is a double-edged sword. While change is essential for innovation and improvement, poor change decisions can lead to outages, service disruptions, or even reputational damage. Traditional change risk assessment relies heavily on subjective judgment, committee reviews, and manual inputs. With the infusion of AI, organizations can shift from intuition-based decisions to **data-driven, predictive risk analysis**—improving speed, accuracy, and reliability.

Traditional change risk assessments are often manual, subjective, and time-consuming—relying heavily on CAB decisions and individual judgment. AI-driven approaches bring consistency and speed by using historical data, dependency relationships, and real-time inputs to predict risk levels. This shift allows for more accurate evaluations and reduces unnecessary delays in change approvals.

The following table demonstrates the comparison between traditional change risk analysis and AI-powered change risk analysis:

Aspect	Traditional Approach	AI-Powered Approach
Risk Evaluation	Manual, based on change advisory board (CAB)	Automated, based on historical data and change history
Impact Assessment	Human-estimated based on CMDB	Predictive modeling using dependency graphs and past data
Risk Scoring	Subjective (High/Medium/Low)	Quantitative scoring using machine learning models
Decision-Making	CAB meetings, expert opinion	AI-generated recommendations with human oversight
Time to Evaluate	Hours to days	Seconds to minutes

Table 8.1: *Traditional versus AI-powered Change Risk Analysis*

Components of AI-Driven Risk Analysis

AI-powered risk analysis is built on a foundation of rich data and intelligent modeling. Inputs such as historical change outcomes, Configuration Item (CI) dependencies, and incident trends feed machine learning models that assign risk scores. These systems not only predict the likelihood of failure but also recommend mitigation steps, such as optimal change windows or stakeholder alerts, based on prior outcomes. The list of the components are as follows:

a. Data Inputs for Change Risk Modeling
    - Historical change records and outcomes
    - Configuration Item (CI) relationships from CMDB
    - Past incidents linked to similar changes
    - Change type (standard, normal, emergency)
    - Affected services and business criticality
b. ML-Based Risk Scoring Models
    - Classification algorithms (for example, decision trees and random forest)
    - Features such as change duration, CI count, and prior failures
    - Model outputs risk level and recommends action
c. Risk Mitigation Recommendations
    - Automated suggestions for back-out plans
    - Change window optimization based on system load
    - Notification of dependent teams and impacted services

Use Case: Real-Life Example – Telecom Enterprise

A telecom giant struggling with high change failure rates turned to predictive AI to improve reliability. By analyzing two years of change and incident data, the AI model forecasted risk levels and flagged high-impact changes before implementation. As a result, failure rates dropped significantly, routine changes were auto approved, and CAB sessions were focused only on truly high-risk initiatives.

Context: A large telecom provider managing 300+ weekly changes faced with frequent outages due to incomplete risk evaluations.

Solution Implemented:

- Leveraged AI-powered change risk engine (via ServiceNow Predictive Intelligence)
- Trained on 2 years of historical change data
- Integrated with CMDB for automated impact mapping

Results:

- 50% reduction in high-risk change failures
- 80% of low-risk changes auto approved with zero incidents
- CAB meetings reduced by 60%, focused only on high/complex risks

The following table lists the metrics used to measure the improvement:

Metric	Before AI	After AI Implementation
Change Failure Rate	12%	6%
Manual Risk Assessments/Week	300	50
Average Change Approval Time	2 days	<30 minutes
Business Impacting Outages/Month	6	1–2

***Table 8.2**: Metrics Used to Measure Improvement*

Automation Opportunities in Change Enablement

AI enables automation at multiple touchpoints in the change lifecycle. From auto-scoring low-risk changes for fast-track approval, to automatically suggesting back-out plans or scheduling optimal windows, automation improves both speed and reliability. This removes human bottlenecks for standard changes and frees up expert resources to focus on complex, business-critical transformations.

The following table lists few probable automation opportunities related to different areas:

Area	Automation Opportunity
Risk Classification	Auto-score based on past patterns and real-time factors
Change Approval	Auto-approve low-risk, standard changes
Conflict Detection	Use dependency mapping to identify overlaps or collisions in real-time
Back-Out Plan Generation	Auto-suggest rollback plans based on similar historical changes
Scheduling Optimization	AI suggests optimal change windows with least operational impact
Stakeholder Notifications	Dynamic identification and notification of impacted users and teams

***Table 8.3**: List of Automation Opportunities*

Challenges and Best Practices

While the benefits are clear, success depends on the quality of data, CMDB accuracy, and continuous model refinement. Poor data can lead to misleading predictions, and over-reliance on AI can erode human oversight. Best practices include starting small (for example, with standard changes), validating AI outputs through post-implementation reviews, and ensuring hybrid governance with both automation and human judgment. Following is the list of important and critical challenges and best practices.

List of few prominent challenges are as follows:

- Poor CMDB hygiene can undermine prediction accuracy
- Over-reliance on AI without human validation
- Initial model training requires quality historical data

List of best practices related to the challenges mentioned above are as follows:

- Start with standard and low-risk changes before scaling to normal/emergency
- Regularly retrain AI models on fresh data
- Maintain a hybrid Change Authority model with human oversight on AI decisions
- Use feedback loops from post-implementation reviews to improve predictions

Strategic Takeaways

AI transforms change enablement into a proactive, risk-aware discipline. Organizations that adopt AI-based risk analysis and automation reduce change failures, accelerate approvals, and improve compliance. Ultimately, AI allows change processes to scale safely supporting agility without compromising stability or control. The list of main and important takeaways are as follows:

- AI transforms Change Enablement from a reactive compliance task into a proactive risk management process.
- Automated risk scoring and decision support accelerate change velocity without compromising safety.
- Enterprises that embrace AI in change processes report fewer outages, improved audit compliance, and greater agility in digital transformation initiatives.

Virtual Assistants and Smart Knowledge Bases

As service desks become increasingly burdened with high ticket volumes and expectations for 24/7 support, traditional human-centric models are being stretched to their limits. Users demand instant answers, while service teams struggle with repetitive queries, limited bandwidth, and knowledge silos. Virtual assistants and AI-powered knowledge bases are stepping in–not just as automation tools–but as **intelligent service enablers** that provide real-time assistance, improve self-service experiences, and reduce operational workload. This chapter explores how conversational AI and knowledge automation are reshaping support delivery and empowering both end-users and agents with context-aware intelligence.

As ticket volumes grow and user expectations rise, traditional service desks are increasingly overwhelmed by routine queries and limited staffing. Virtual assistants and AI-driven knowledge bases have emerged as essential tools in delivering fast, scalable, and intelligent support. These technologies go beyond basic automation–offering context-aware responses, reducing manual effort, and enhancing both agent productivity and user satisfaction.

Virtual Assistants in ITSM

Virtual assistants act as intelligent conversational interfaces that interact with users in real time. They understand natural language, detect intent, and either resolve requests directly or guide users toward the right solution. With features such as automated fulfillment, escalation logic, and personalization, they serve as the first point of contact–offering 24/7 support while easing the burden on human agents.

So, what is a virtual assistant? A Virtual Assistant (VA) is an AI-powered conversational interface–often integrated as a chatbot–that interacts with users to guide, resolve, or escalate service issues intelligently.

The following table lists a few key capabilities of virtual assistants:

Capability	**Description**
Conversational Query Handling	Understands natural language to answer user questions
Request Fulfillment Automation	Triggers workflows (for example, password reset, access provisioning)
Intent Recognition and Routing	Detects user intent and routes to appropriate resolver group

Context Memory and Personalization	Remembers previous interactions, adapts to user profile
Escalation Logic	Hands off to human agent when confidence or context is low

***Table 8.4**: Key Capabilities of Virtual Assistants*

The list of mainly desirable benefits are as follows:

- Reduced L1 ticket volume by 30–50%
- 24/7 support availability without staffing overhead
- Faster issue resolution and user satisfaction

Real-Life Example: Virtual Assistant (VA) in a University IT Helpdesk

A university IT helpdesk was flooded with repetitive requests such as password resets and Wi-Fi issues, especially during semester starts. By deploying a virtual assistant through Microsoft Teams, integrated with their ITSM platform, the university reduced L1 ticket volumes by over 50%. Students received immediate help, while IT agents regained bandwidth to focus on complex issues–resulting in a marked improvement in service quality and responsiveness.

Context: A mid-sized university with 18,000 students was overwhelmed with password reset and Wi-Fi connectivity requests during semester starts.

Solution Implemented:

- Deployed a virtual assistant via Microsoft Teams integrated with ServiceNow Virtual Agent
- Trained with FAQs, reset workflows, and dynamic knowledge base links

The following table lists the important outcomes:

Metric	**Before VA**	**After Virtual Assistant (VA) Deployment**
Average Tickets/Week	2,400	1,100
First Contact Resolution	58%	88%
Manual Password Resets	1,300/week	<300/week
Human Agent Availability	Often overloaded	60% more time for complex issues

***Table 8.5**: List of Outcomes*

Smart Knowledge Bases

Modern knowledge bases, powered by AI, are evolving from static repositories into dynamic ecosystems that learn and improve over time. These smart KBs use natural language processing, user behavior analytics, and feedback loops to deliver the right knowledge at the right time. They can even auto-generate articles from incident resolution patterns, ensuring that knowledge remains fresh, relevant, and accessible.

From Static to Smart

Traditional knowledge bases are static repositories that rely on manual updates, tagging, and search. AI transforms these into **dynamic, living systems** that adapt, learn, and deliver relevant knowledge at the point of need.

The following table lists the core features of smart knowledge bases:

Smart Feature	Functionality
NLP-Based Search	Interprets queries beyond keywords, improving result accuracy
Contextual Recommendations	Suggests relevant articles based on user role and issue type
Auto-Generation of Articles	Converts resolved tickets into draft knowledge content
Article Quality Scoring	AI assigns usefulness score based on usage, feedback, and clarity
Feedback-Driven Improvement	Learns from thumbs-up/down, click-throughs, and comments

***Table 8.6**: Core Features of Smart Knowledge Bases*

The following image demonstrates a Smart KB Workflow example:

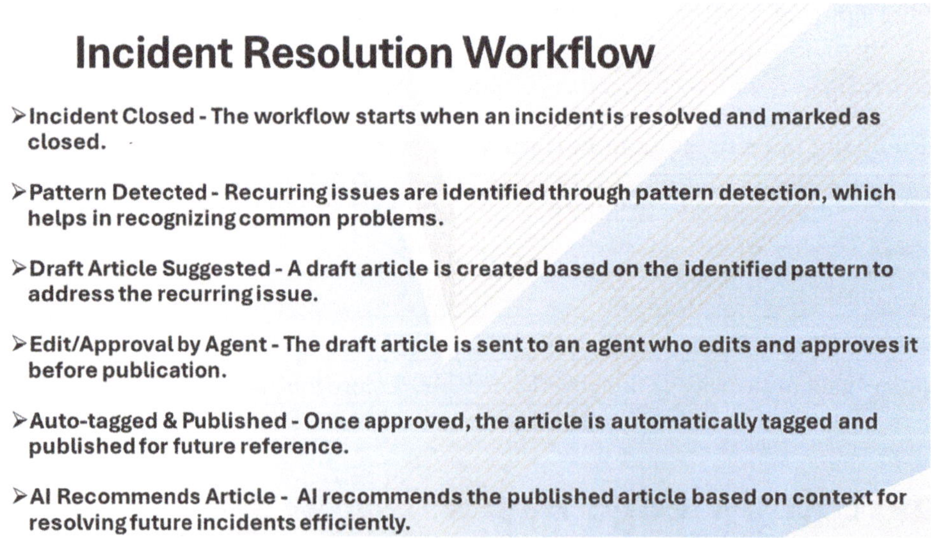

***Figure 8.1**: Smart KB Workflow Example*

Real-Life Example: Smart Knowledge Base in a Managed Services Firm

A managed service provider struggled with repeated tickets due to poor documentation. By adopting an AI-powered KB system that could suggest, tag, and update content dynamically, they reduced average resolution time by 50% and tripled their knowledge usage. Ticket deflection increased significantly, allowing their agents to operate more efficiently and effectively.

Context: A managed services firm with 500+ clients lacked structured knowledge documentation, leading to escalations and repeated resolutions.

Solution Implemented:

- Adopted ManageEngine's AI-powered knowledge module with article autosuggestions and contextual tagging
- Enabled agents to convert tickets to articles post-resolution

The following table lists the outcomes:

Metric	Before Smart KB	After Implementation
Average Resolution Time	4.2 hours	2.1 hours
Repetitive Tickets (Same issue)	28% of total volume	12%
KB Article Views per Month	600	2,300+
Ticket Deflection Rate	<5%	32%

***Table 8.7**: Metrics Used for Measuring the Improvement*

Virtual Assistants + Smart KBs = Self-service Synergy

When virtual assistants and smart knowledge bases work in tandem, they create a powerful self-service ecosystem that goes beyond automation to deliver intelligent, contextual, and scalable support. Virtual assistants act as the conversational front door—guiding users, understanding intent, and initiating workflows—while smart knowledge bases supply precise, relevant information in real time. This synergy empowers users to resolve issues independently and agents to focus on higher-value tasks. Together, they reduce ticket volumes, accelerate resolution, and enhance user satisfaction—making self-service not just efficient, but truly intelligent.

When combined, virtual assistants and smart KBs form a powerful self-service strategy. While VAs provide conversational access to support, smart KBs supply deep, relevant knowledge. The assistant acts as the guide, and the KB serves as the knowledge engine.

Together, they not only deflect tickets but also improve first contact resolution and elevate user confidence in self-service channels.

The following table lists the capabilities:

Capability	Virtual Assistant	Smart Knowledge Base
Frontend Interaction	Conversational, real-time	Search-driven or context-suggested
Intelligence Source	Natural Language + Predefined Intents	AI-surfaced, updated knowledge content
Best Use Case	Repetitive queries, password resets	Process guides, troubleshooting, how-to's
When Combined	VA offers instant answers + links to KB	KB reinforces VA with deep documentation

Table 8.8: *List of Capabilities*

Implementation Considerations

Successful deployment of VAs and smart KBs requires clean data, proper governance, and continuous learning. IT teams must ensure that knowledge content is curated and updated, that VAs are trained on relevant intents, and that feedback mechanisms are in place. Organizations should also consider multi-language support and integration with core ITSM workflows to ensure consistency and scalability across the enterprise.

- **Data quality**: Ensure well-tagged KB articles and cleaned ticket data for training VA intents
- **Continuous training**: Regularly train virtual assistants using new use cases and language variations
- **Governance**: Define ownership for VA content and KB curation to maintain relevance
- **Multi-language support**: Use NLP models that support regional languages or integrate translation engines

The key strategic takeaways are as follows:

- Virtual Assistants are becoming **first responders** in digital service desks, cutting down ticket volumes and improving SLA adherence.
- Smart Knowledge Bases drive **scalable expertise** by making useful information accessible when and where it's needed.
- Together, they form a powerful self-service strategy that balances **speed, accuracy, and cost-efficiency**.

- Organizations that invest in both AI-driven conversational agents and dynamic knowledge ecosystems position themselves to handle future IT demands with agility and intelligence.

Predicting Ticket Volumes and Request Fulfillment

Traditional service desks often function in a reactive mode–responding to user requests and incidents as they arrive, often without prior visibility into what's coming next. This creates staffing bottlenecks, SLA breaches, and user frustration. AI introduces a game-changing capability: **predictive analytics**. By analyzing historical data, patterns, seasonality, and user behavior, AI can forecast ticket volumes and request types–empowering IT teams to plan proactively, allocate resources effectively, and automate fulfillment wherever possible.

Most service desks operate reactively, responding to issues only after they occur. This results in overburdened teams and missed SLAs during unanticipated surges. Predictive analytics, powered by AI, allows IT teams to foresee upcoming ticket spikes, enabling better planning, staffing, and pre-emptive action–transforming support into a forward-looking function.

So, the question arises "What is Ticket Volume Prediction?" Ticket volume prediction involves using historical data, user behavior, and contextual signals to forecast the **number, type, and timing** of service requests or incidents over a given period.

Ticket volume prediction uses AI to analyze historical and contextual data to forecast when and what kinds of tickets are likely to be raised. This insight enables IT teams to proactively plan resources, automate responses, and mitigate risk. Unlike manual estimates, AI-driven models account for business cycles, system events, and past behavior to make accurate, actionable forecasts.

The following table describes the comparison between traditional and AI-driven approaches:

Aspect	Traditional Approach	AI-Driven Approach
Forecasting Method	Manual estimation or basic trend	ML algorithms trained on ticket and usage data
Consideration of Seasonality	Rarely included	Models incorporate cyclic trends (for example, month-end)
Granularity	Weekly or monthly	Hourly, daily, shift-based forecasts
Actionability	Post-event planning	Proactive staffing, automation, and deflection

***Table 8.9**: Comparison between Traditional and AI-Driven Approaches*

Core Components of AI-Powered Forecasting

At the heart of AI forecasting are data-rich signals–ranging from ticket history to HR calendars and device usage trends. Techniques such as time series forecasting, regression, and clustering help identify when spikes are likely and which user groups are most affected. This forms the foundation for anticipatory service planning and automated remediation workflows. The list of the core components are as follows:

Data Sources for Prediction

- Historical ticket data (volume, category, priority, requester type)
- HR and business calendars (onboarding, policy changes)
- Application deployment schedules and outages
- Device telemetry, usage patterns, sentiment trends
- External signals (for example, major OS updates, security advisories)

The following table lists the techniques used:

Technique	Application
Time Series Forecasting	Predicting daily/weekly ticket volumes using Autoregressive Integrated Moving Average (ARIMA), Long Short-Term Memory (LSTM)
Regression Analysis	Mapping ticket spikes to business or system events
Clustering	Identifying similar patterns across different user groups
Classification Models	Predicting request types based on user and system behavior
Anomaly Detection	Flagging unexpected ticket surges or volume drops

Table 8.10: *List of Techniques Used*

Predicting Request Fulfillment Patterns

AI doesn't just forecast ticket volume–it also predicts how long different requests will take to fulfill based on complexity, type, and historical performance. This enables intelligent workload balancing, SLA risk detection, and identification of automation candidates. By understanding patterns, IT can move from "first-come, first-serve" to "smartly prioritized service delivery."

AI not only forecasts volume but also:

- Estimates time-to-fulfill based on category, complexity, and past trends
- Suggests resource allocation by skill group and time window
- Recommends automation for frequently recurring requests (for example, access requests)

The following table lists the suggestions for different request types:

Request Type	Predicted Volume	Average Fulfillment Time	AI Suggestion
Password Reset	High	< 10 mins	Automate with self-service
VPN Access Request	Moderate	2–4 hours	Use pre-approved workflows
Laptop Provisioning	Low (spiky)	3–5 days	Pre-stage during onboarding
Email DL Updates	High on Mondays	30 mins	Route via VA or RPA

Table 8.11: *List of Suggestions for Different Request Types*

Real-Life Example 1: Predicting Ticket Volume in a Retail Company

A major retail chain used AI to forecast service desk workloads during sales events. By aligning IT forecasts with marketing calendars, they reduced ticket-related SLA breaches and optimized staffing levels. This predictive capability empowered the IT team to meet seasonal demand without unnecessary overtime or resource strain.

Context: A large retail chain experienced unpredictable ticket surges during promotion periods, impacting service levels.

Solution: Implemented AI-based volume forecasting using historical ticket trends and promotional calendars.

Integrated with workforce scheduler to recommend agent availability.

The following table lists the probable results:

Metric	Before AI	After AI Implementation
SLA Breach % (During Sales)	22%	4%
Ticket Spikes Missed	Frequently	None (98% prediction accuracy)
Staff Overtime Cost	High	Reduced by 35%

Table 8.12: *Metrics Used to Measure Performance*

Real-Life Example 2: Request Fulfillment Optimization in an Insurance Company

An insurance provider faced repeated fulfillment delays during new employee

onboarding. With AI-based prediction, they anticipated onboarding waves and automated common requests like email provisioning. As a result, fulfillment times dropped from days to hours, improving new hire experience and reducing IT workload during critical business periods.

Context: An insurance firm faced backlogs in user provisioning requests during quarterly hiring drives.

Solution:

- Used AI to predict spikes in IT onboarding requests.
- Pre-staged resources and automated account setups using bots.

The following table lists the results:

Metric	**Before AI**	**After AI**
Average Onboarding Fulfillment Time	3.5 days	< 24 hours
Agent Workload During Peaks	Overloaded	Balanced
Automation Rate of Fulfillment	20%	70%

Table 8.13: *Metrics Used for Performance Measurement*

Operationalizing Predictions in ITSM Tools

Many ITSM platforms now support forecasting either natively or through AI integrations. By feeding historical data into these engines and correlating it with business calendars, IT teams can visualize expected ticket trends, generate staffing alerts, and trigger automation in advance. This turns prediction into a practical, repeatable advantage in service management.

Most modern ITSM platforms (such as ServiceNow, ManageEngine, BMC) support integration with ML engines or have built-in forecasting modules.

Key Implementation Tips

- Clean and enrich historical ticket data
- Define relevant timeframes (for example, monthly spikes, day-of-week trends)
- Correlate business events (HR cycles, application releases)
- Use dashboards for visualization and alerting
- Combine with auto-routing rules and staff shift planning

The list of important and critical strategic takeaways are as follows:

- Predictive analytics moves ITSM from **reactive firefighting to proactive planning**.

- Accurate ticket forecasting ensures optimal staffing, fewer SLA breaches, and lower costs.
- Fulfillment prediction allows organizations to **automate intelligently and allocate resources** where they are needed most.
- When prediction models are connected to fulfillment workflows, IT achieves true **intelligent service orchestration**.

Conclusion

The convergence of Artificial Intelligence with ITIL practices such as Change Enablement, Service Request Management, and Knowledge Management is not merely an evolution–it represents a strategic leap in how modern service organizations operate. This chapter has explored how AI empowers these foundational ITSM functions to move beyond reactive, manual, and error-prone processes toward a new paradigm of predictive, intelligent, and scalable service delivery.

In **Change Enablement**, AI-driven risk analysis transforms decision-making from committee-led guesswork into data-informed foresight. Organizations can now anticipate the ripple effects of a change, reduce failure rates, and accelerate safe approvals through intelligent automation and historical learning models.

In **Service Request Management**, the deployment of **virtual assistants** offers always-on support, dramatically reducing L1 ticket volumes and freeing human agents for more complex tasks. These VAs, when paired with workflow automation, not only enhance user experience but also reduce operational bottlenecks–fulfilling simple requests with unprecedented speed and accuracy.

Smart knowledge bases, powered by NLP and behavior analytics, complete this transformation. No longer static repositories, they evolve continuously based on user feedback and real-world usage. This shift ensures the right knowledge reaches the right person at the right time–improving resolution quality and supporting both end-users and support agents.

AI's predictive capabilities further extend into **forecasting ticket volumes and fulfillment patterns**, allowing IT leaders to anticipate demand, optimize staffing, and pre-emptively allocate resources. This capability transforms ITSM from a reactive cost center into a proactive business enabler.

Yet, these advancements come with responsibilities. The success of AI adoption relies heavily on clean data, robust governance, and ongoing model refinement. Over-automation without oversight can introduce new risks, while poor data hygiene can reduce AI's effectiveness. Therefore, a hybrid approach–where human expertise and AI collaborate–is crucial for sustained success.

In essence, AI does not replace ITSM best practices; it **amplifies them**. When thoughtfully applied, AI becomes a powerful strategic ally, helping organizations enhance efficiency, elevate service quality, and unlock new levels of agility. By embracing AI-powered change enablement, request fulfillment, and knowledge management, organizations prepare themselves not just for the future of service management—but to lead it. In the next chapter, we will map AI's contribution across ITIL4's guiding principles and value chain activities.

Multiple Choice Questions

1. What is one key benefit of using AI for Change Risk Analysis in ITSM?
    a. It removes the need for historical data
    b. It guarantees zero change failures
    c. It enables data-driven, predictive risk scoring
    d. It eliminates the need for CAB oversight
2. Which of the following is a core feature of a Smart Knowledge Base?
    a. Static article storage
    b. CAB meeting minutes
    c. NLP-based search and contextual recommendations
    d. Manual tagging by agents only
3. What was one measurable outcome after deploying a Virtual Assistant in a university IT helpdesk?
    a. Increase in repetitive tickets
    b. Reduction in human agent availability
    c. Improvement in First Contact Resolution rate
    d. Increase in manual password resets
4. How does AI help with request fulfilment in ITSM?
    a. By reducing the number of services offered
    b. By removing the need for user input
    c. By predicting fulfilment time and identifying automation opportunities
    d. By shifting fulfilment responsibility to business users

5. What is a critical prerequisite for successful AI implementation in Change Enablement?
    a. Eliminating all human approvals
    b. Accurate CMDB and clean historical data
    c. Running only emergency changes
    d. Weekly CAB meetings

Answers

1. c
2. c
3. c
4. c
5. b

Questions

1. Explain how AI transforms traditional Change Enablement processes into proactive risk management practices.
2. Describe the components and data sources involved in AI-powered change risk analysis.
3. What are the key differences between traditional and AI-powered approaches to service request fulfillment?
4. Discuss the strategic benefits and challenges of implementing virtual assistants in IT service desks.
5. How do smart knowledge bases improve knowledge accessibility and reduce repetitive incident tickets?
6. Illustrate the synergy between virtual assistants and smart knowledge bases in creating an intelligent self-service ecosystem.
7. What role does predictive analytics play in forecasting ticket volumes, and how does it help improve SLA compliance?
8. List and explain key techniques used in AI-driven forecasting models for ITSM.
9. Describe the implementation considerations for deploying AI-based request and knowledge management tools.

10. Based on the real-life examples provided, how did AI impact operational performance in the telecom, education, and insurance sectors?

Key Terms

- **Change Risk Analysis:** A data-driven process where AI assesses the likelihood and impact of IT changes using historical data and predictive modeling. It replaces subjective risk judgments with objective scoring and mitigation suggestions.
- **Virtual Assistant (VA):** An AI-powered conversational interface that interacts with users in real-time to resolve issues or guide them to the right solution. It reduces L1 ticket volume and provides 24/7 support availability.
- **Smart Knowledge Base (Smart KB):** An AI-enabled system that evolves dynamically through NLP, user feedback, and automated article creation. It delivers contextual, relevant information at the point of need for both users and agents.
- **Predictive Analytics:** A technique that uses machine learning models and historical data to forecast future ticket volumes and service demands. It enables proactive staffing, automation, and workload balancing.
- **Change Advisory Board (CAB):** A group responsible for evaluating and approving changes in traditional ITSM. AI augments or partially replaces its functions by automating low risk change approvals.
- **Intent Recognition:** A capability of virtual assistants to interpret user requests based on natural language inputs. It helps route queries or initiate workflows accurately and efficiently.
- **Auto-Approval:** A process where AI systems approve standard or low-risk changes without human intervention. This reduces delays and improves change velocity while maintaining safety through predictive checks.
- **Knowledge Article Auto-Generation:** An AI-driven feature that converts resolved tickets into draft articles for the knowledge base. It ensures continual knowledge capture and reduces the manual burden on agents.
- **Ticket Volume Forecasting:** An AI-based method to predict the number and types of tickets likely to be raised over time. It helps IT teams plan resources, anticipate demand spikes, and avoid SLA violations.
- **Contextual Recommendations:** AI's ability to suggest knowledge articles or next actions based on user role, issue type, and interaction history. This increases first-contact resolution and enhances self-service experiences.

CHAPTER 9
AI and the ITIL4 Service Value System

Introduction

As organizations race to modernize their IT service delivery, it is no longer enough to view AI as a bolt-on technology. True transformation happens when AI becomes woven into the very fabric of service management—aligning seamlessly with ITIL4's Service Value System (SVS). This chapter explores that deeper alignment by showing how AI amplifies ITIL4's core philosophy of value co-creation, adaptability, and continual improvement. The SVS is designed to be flexible, resilient, and holistic—and AI, when applied strategically, can accelerate every element within it. From guiding principles like "optimize and automate" to governance, service design, and improvement initiatives, AI becomes a catalyst rather than a disruptor. By embedding intelligence into value chain activities, organizations can make faster, more informed decisions, reduce waste, and enhance user experiences in real time. Whether it's AI-powered risk scoring in Change Enablement, predictive insights in operations, or intelligent automation in request fulfillment, each contribution supports the unified goal of delivering consistent value. This chapter will walk readers through how AI maps to ITIL4's key components—not as a replacement, but as an enabler that strengthens and scales existing practices. Along the way, we will highlight best-fit scenarios, real-life examples, and practical considerations for integrating AI within the SVS framework. Ultimately, readers will gain a clear roadmap for embedding AI in their service ecosystem in a way that honors ITIL4's structure while driving innovation forward.

Structure

In this chapter, we will discuss the following topics:

- How AI Supports Guiding Principles: Focus on Value, Optimize, and Automate
- AI in Governance, Service Design, and Continual Improvement
- Building AI into the Service Value Chain Activities

How AI Supports Guiding Principles: Focus on Value, Optimize, and Automate

The ITIL 4 framework is grounded in seven guiding principles that provide universal recommendations for decision-making and actions in service management. When integrated thoughtfully, Artificial Intelligence (AI) serves as a powerful enabler of these principles–reinforcing strategic alignment, agility, and value delivery. In the following sections, we will examine each principle through the lens of AI in ITSM, supported by real-world applications and examples.

Focus on Value

At the heart of ITIL4 lies the principle of value creation, and AI elevates this by continuously aligning IT efforts with user needs and business priorities. AI-powered tools personalize services, predict intent, and automate low-value tasks–ensuring that service operations are always centered on outcomes that matter most to stakeholders. By using analytics to uncover pain points or preferences including waste, AI enables service providers to focus on investment where it delivers the greatest return. The result is a more relevant, efficient, and user-centric ITSM ecosystem.

How AI supports it: AI helps organizations continuously deliver value by personalizing services, optimizing experiences, and predicting needs. It enables data-driven decision-making and customer-centric automation, ensuring that efforts and investments align with what matters most to users and stakeholders.

Example: A global logistics company implemented an AI-powered virtual assistant to reduce the time field agents spent on repetitive queries, such as delivery reschedules or policy clarifications. The chatbot was trained on FAQs and real-time data feeds and integrated with their ITSM tool. This not only improved the user experience for 6,000+ employees but also reduced average ticket resolution time by 45%–delivering clear value to both users and the organization.

Start Where You Are

AI thrives on existing data–ticket history, CMDBs, resolution logs, user feedback–without requiring organizations to start from scratch. By analyzing current-state assets, AI solutions build intelligent insights that drive quick wins. For example, ML models can be trained on historical ticket categories to recommend priority rules or automation triggers. This principle reminds us that transformation doesn't require a massive overhaul; instead, AI can leverage what already exists to incrementally improve service efficiency.

How AI supports it: AI doesn't require a complete system overhaul. It thrives when organizations start with existing data, historical ticket logs, and current workflows. AI models can build on what's already available learning from past patterns to improve current operations incrementally.

Example: An insurance firm began its AI journey by feeding two years of incident and change data into a predictive engine embedded in ServiceNow. With no major platform changes, they began auto-scoring change requests and prioritizing incident triage based on historical patterns. This "start where you are" mindset enabled them to quickly gain operational benefits without disrupting ongoing services.

Progress Iteratively with Feedback

AI and iteration go hand in hand. Machine learning models and virtual assistants get smarter through continuous interaction and feedback. Organizations can deploy AI features like predictive triage or suggestions for CI/CD pipeline, or automated suggestions in a phased manner–monitoring performance, collecting feedback, and refining logic over time. This approach minimizes risk, enables user trust, and allows AI capabilities to evolve in alignment with operational maturity.

How AI supports it: AI models improve through feedback loops–be it user interactions, thumbs-up/down responses on articles, or post-resolution surveys. Organizations can deploy AI in controlled phases, learn from each iteration, and gradually expand scope and sophistication.

Example: A healthcare provider rolled out a smart knowledge base with article usefulness scoring and feedback capture. Initially launched in one department, the system collected user feedback and evolved recommendations accordingly. Over six months, it expanded enterprise-wide, improving article relevance by 60% and increasing self-service adoption through continuous, feedback-driven learning.

Collaborate and Promote Visibility

AI doesn't just work in the background; it helps make hidden service trends visible to all stakeholders. Intelligent dashboards, predictive alerts, and pattern recognition tools foster collaboration across departments by exposing shared risks, dependencies, and opportunities. For instance, predictive analytics might show how HR events impact IT requests, enabling proactive staffing decisions. AI strengthens communication by creating a shared, data-informed view of ITSM performance.

How AI supports it: AI promotes collaboration through shared insights–making patterns, dependencies, and risks more visible across departments. Dashboards powered by AI can unify metrics across silos and bring operational blind spots to the surface.

Example: A telecom provider integrated its AI-driven change risk engine with dashboards accessible to both IT and business stakeholders. This created shared visibility into upcoming high-risk changes, allowing teams to collaborate more proactively. As a result, business disruptions from failed changes were cut by 50% within one quarter.

Think and Work Holistically

Service delivery doesn't happen in silos–and neither should data analysis. AI tools are uniquely suited to connect the dots across functions–combining incident data, asset health, change history, and user behavior to uncover root causes and systemic inefficiencies. This holistic view enables service leaders to anticipate ripple effects, optimize across boundaries, and align ITSM initiatives with broader organizational goals.

How AI supports it: AI connects the dots across disparate systems–linking incidents, changes, assets, and user behaviors. It reveals cross-domain patterns that human analysis might miss, allowing for end-to-end optimization and more cohesive service delivery.

Example: A global retail chain used AI to correlate incidents with asset telemetry and application release schedules. It was discovered that POS system outages were spiking after certain deployments. By visualizing these patterns holistically, the company adjusted its release cadence and pre-emptively mitigated known issues–improving service continuity.

Keep It Simple and Practical

AI can sift through large volumes of data and recommend just the essential insights or actions. This reduces complexity for users and agents alike–enabling smarter decisions without information overload. For example, instead of generating long reports, an AI agent might highlight just three anomalous service trends with suggested actions. Simplicity and relevance are crucial for adoption, and AI–when thoughtfully deployed–delivers just enough intelligence to act confidently.

How AI supports it: AI simplifies decision-making by reducing noise, highlighting anomalies, and suggesting next-best actions. Instead of overwhelming users with dashboards and options, it can offer targeted recommendations that drive quick, effective actions.

Example: A financial institution implemented an AI agent that flagged anomalies in ticket trends and suggested automated actions for frequent issues such as password resets and VPN access. Rather than creating elaborate workflows, they focused on the top three use cases–automating 70% of L1 requests within three months and significantly improving user satisfaction.

Optimize and Automate

This principle finds its strongest ally in AI. From auto-triaging tickets and recommending fulfillment paths to intelligent workload balancing and proactive incident avoidance, AI automates high-frequency, low-complexity tasks with precision. Optimization goes further–AI continually analyzes processes to spot inefficiencies and suggest process redesigns or automation candidates. This frees up human agents to focus on complex, value-adding tasks and improves the overall agility of IT service management.

How AI supports it: This principle is almost synonymous with AI's value proposition. AI helps identify inefficiencies, recommends improvements, and automates repetitive, manual, or low-value tasks–freeing up human talent for more strategic work.

Example: A multinational bank used AI to automate access requests and provisioning. By analyzing past patterns and usage behavior, AI identified which requests were safe to automate. Combined with RPA bots, the bank achieved a 65% automation rate in service requests, cutting fulfillment times from days to minutes.

Summary Table: AI and the ITIL4 Guiding Principles

ITIL4 Guiding Principle	AI Contribution	Real-Life Outcome
Focus on Value	Personalizes and prioritizes value-generating work	Improved resolution time and user experience via virtual assistant
Start Where You Are	Leverages existing data to launch AI use cases	Predictive risk scoring with historical ticket data
Progress Iteratively with Feedback	Feedback loops improve AI models over time	Knowledge article relevance improved through user feedback
Collaborate and Promote Visibility	Dashboards unify insights across teams and services	Shared visibility into high-risk changes led to fewer business issues
Think and Work Holistically	Reveals cross-functional dependencies and service impacts	Identified root causes by correlating incidents with asset data
Keep It Simple and Practical	Offers targeted suggestions and automation for high-impact use cases	Automated resolution for top 3 common service requests
Optimize and Automate	Streamlines repetitive processes using ML, NLP, and RPA	65% of access requests automated, reducing fulfillment time drastically

Table 9.1: *AI and the ITIL4 Guiding Principles*

AI in Governance, Service Design, and Continual Improvement

As ITSM matures within enterprises, aligning AI with ITIL4's core activities–**governance**, **service design**, and **continual improvement**–becomes not just beneficial, but essential. AI is no longer confined to operational enhancements; it now plays a strategic role in enforcing policies, designing resilient services, and embedding a culture of data-driven improvement. This chapter explores how AI strengthens these three foundational pillars and provides real-life use cases that illustrate measurable impact.

AI in Governance

Governance in ITIL4 is about ensuring that policies, processes, and decisions align with the organization's goals, risks, and compliance obligations. It includes accountability, assurance, and strategic direction. AI augments governance by offering visibility, consistency, and automation in risk management, policy enforcement, and audit-readiness.

How AI Enables Governance:

- **Risk Identification and Mitigation:** AI can scan service tickets, changes, and performance metrics to flag deviations from SLAs or compliance requirements. It enables early warnings and auto-escalations for policy violations.
- **Automated Compliance Monitoring:** AI tools can monitor logs and configurations for anomalies that breach defined controls, reducing the manual burden of audit checks.
- **Data-Driven Decision Support:** Governance boards can use AI-powered dashboards to analyze trends, assess control effectiveness, and make decisions rooted in real-time data.

Real-Life Example:

Context: A multinational financial services provider needed to ensure compliance with GDPR and internal IT controls during change management processes.

Solution:

They deployed an AI-based risk engine (ServiceNow Predictive Intelligence) integrated with change records and compliance libraries.

Results:

- 90% reduction in non-compliant changes
- Real-time alerts on policy breaches
- Governance committee received weekly AI-generated dashboards on key risk indicators

AI in Service Design

Designing Service in ITIL4 is the blueprinting stage where services are planned to meet business needs effectively. AI supports this stage by introducing predictive planning, simulation, and intelligent mapping of dependencies–reducing the risks of poor design and enabling more adaptive services.

How AI Enhances Service Design:

- **Predictive Modeling for Capacity and Demand:** AI models simulate load and usage patterns to forecast future demand and optimize capacity planning.
- **Intelligent Dependency Mapping:** AI identifies underlying relationships between services, infrastructure, and users–ensuring fault-tolerant, well-integrated design.
- **Persona-Based Design Inputs:** AI analyzes behavioral data to create user personas that inform experience-focused service design.

Real-Life Example:

Context: A global retail chain was struggling with outages after launching new applications due to poorly planned capacity and demand modeling.

Solution:

They implemented an AIOps tool with predictive analytics for demand forecasting, linked to their service catalog and infrastructure telemetry.

Results:

- Reduced over-provisioning by 30%
- Application uptime increased by 22% during peak shopping seasons
- Faster time-to-market for new service launches with predictive impact analysis

AI Improving Continually

Continual Improvement is an embedded mindset and practice in ITIL4 aimed at enhancing services, processes, and outcomes over time. AI supercharges continual improvement by enabling real-time measurement, automatic anomaly detection, and intelligent recommendations based on usage patterns and service health.

How AI Drives Continual Improvement:

- **Trend and Sentiment Analysis:** NLP engines can process user feedback, surveys, and tickets to detect sentiment shifts and service dissatisfaction trends.
- **Process Mining and Optimization:** AI identifies process bottlenecks, dropped escalations, and inefficiencies across workflows–suggesting areas to improve.
- **Feedback Loop Automation:** AI integrates with CSAT tools and analytics platforms to generate automatic improvement tasks based on performance deviations.

Real-Life Example:

Context: A healthcare organization wanted to improve service desk responsiveness and satisfaction scores over a 12-month period.

Solution:

They implemented an AI-driven continual improvement engine that tracked ticket volume patterns, resolution delays, and agent feedback.

Results:

- Identified three recurring bottlenecks in incident resolution
- Average response time improved from 2.4 hours to 55 minutes
- CSAT scores rose from 76% to 91% in two quarters

Comparison Table: Traditional versus AI-Enhanced Approaches

Area	Traditional Approach	AI-Enhanced Approach
Governance	Manual audits, periodic reviews	Real-time alerts, predictive risk scoring, automated policy checks
Service Design	Static diagrams, manual capacity planning	Dynamic dependency maps, AI-based simulations, persona-informed planning
Continual Improvement	Reactive improvements based on complaints	Proactive suggestions, sentiment analysis, automated improvement initiatives

Table 9.2: *Traditional versus AI-Enhanced Approaches*

Key Implementation Tips

- **Data Hygiene is Critical:** AI decisions are only as good as the data they're built on–ensure clean, well-labeled, and contextual data.
- **Start with Strategic Use Cases:** Begin with areas such as risk monitoring or demand forecasting to show fast ROI.
- **Integrate with Governance Boards:** Feed AI dashboards into regular governance and design review meetings.
- **Build Feedback Mechanisms:** Use post-implementation reviews, CSAT surveys, and AI sentiment analysis for ongoing learning.
- **Balance AI with Human Oversight:** Ensure AI complements–not replaces–strategic human decisions in design and governance.

Now let us discuss how AI can be applied in Continual Improvement, mapped to the ITIL4 Continual Improvement Model.The ITIL4 Continual Improvement Model outlines seven logical steps that help organizations identify, plan, execute, and evaluate improvements systematically. When AI is infused into each of these steps, the improvement process becomes faster, more insightful, and increasingly autonomous. How AI enhances each of the seven steps in practice is explained as follows:

Step 1: What is the Vision?

AI's Role:

AI can align improvement opportunities with organizational vision by analyzing strategic goals, service performance metrics, and user feedback. AI-powered dashboards and NLP tools can surface recurring themes in executive communication, strategic plans, or customer satisfaction reports to identify areas that align with business direction.

Example:

A public transportation authority used AI to process city council meeting transcripts and IT usage trends to align IT improvement goals with their smart-city vision–focusing efforts on mobile ticketing and self-service.

Step 2: Where are we now?

AI's Role:

AI enables accurate current-state analysis through data mining, pattern recognition, and sentiment analysis. It can automatically assess service performance, SLA adherence, recurring incidents, and user dissatisfaction without requiring manual audits.

Example:

A healthcare network used AI-based process mining to visualize bottlenecks in patient admission and discharge ticketing systems, highlighting areas needing immediate improvement.

Step 3: Where do we want to be?

AI's Role:

AI assists in defining desired outcomes by forecasting future performance levels based on historical trends. It can also simulate the effects of specific improvements (for example, automation, training, or routing changes), helping set realistic yet ambitious targets.

Example:

A software company used AI to simulate service desk load reduction scenarios. Based on predicted deflection rates from virtual assistants, they set a goal to reduce L1 ticket volume by 40% over six months.

Step 4: How do we get there?

AI's Role:

AI suggests actionable improvement paths, such as automation candidates, changes to SLAs, or self-service opportunities. Recommendation engines can also prioritize initiatives based on impact, effort, and cost-benefit analysis.

Example:

An e-commerce firm used AI to analyze which ticket categories had the highest repeat rate. The tool recommended automating FAQs and resetting workflows, which were implemented through RPA and chatbot flows.

Step 5: Take Action

AI's Role:

AI can trigger automated workflows to implement improvements—such as launching knowledge articles, updating routing rules, or assigning ownership. It also supports change management by identifying risk areas before deploying improvements.

Example:

An insurance provider used AI bots to automatically deploy revised knowledge articles and update chatbot intents based on a new claims policy rollout—reducing training time and increasing support consistency.

Step 6: Did we get there?

AI's Role:

AI tracks key performance indicators (KPIs), analyzes trends, and validates whether improvement goals have been met. Machine learning models can identify anomalies in the post-change environment and measure user sentiment before and after interventions.

Example:

A telecom company tracked CSAT, ticket resolution time, and call volume pre/post deployment of a virtual assistant. AI-generated dashboards showed that customer satisfaction improved by 18% and agent workload reduced by 40%.

Step 7: How do we keep the Momentum going?

AI's Role:

AI facilitates continual learning by feeding insights from ongoing operations into the next cycle of improvement. It monitors evolving patterns and triggers new improvement suggestions based on real-time data and performance thresholds.

Example:

A university IT department deployed an AI-powered continual improvement assistant that auto-suggested quarterly improvement areas by analyzing system usage logs, feedback forms, and seasonal demand forecasts.

Summary Table: AI across the Continual Improvement Model

Step	AI Contribution	Example Outcome
What is the Vision?	AI analyzes strategic documents and goals to align improvement areas	Focused on mobile ticketing aligned with city vision
Where Are We Now?	AI mines performance and sentiment data to assess current state	Identified service desk bottlenecks via process mining
Where Do We Want to Be?	AI forecasts potential improvement outcomes and helps define measurable goals	Simulated chatbot impact to set a 40% L1 reduction goal
How Do We Get There?	AI recommends prioritized actions and automation paths	Identified high-impact, repetitive requests for RPA and VA implementation

Take Action	AI triggers workflows, updates knowledge, and supports safe deployment	Rolled out updated content and chatbot training during a policy change
Did We Get There?	AI validates KPIs and compares pre/post-intervention performance	Dashboards confirmed post-intervention CSAT and efficiency gains
How Do We Keep the Momentum Going?	AI continuously scans for new improvement opportunities and suggests iterations	Auto-generated quarterly improvement focus areas based on evolving usage patterns

Table 9.3: *AI across the Continual Improvement Model*

AI is no longer just a tactical tool—it is a strategic ally in ITSM governance, service design, and continual improvement. By embedding intelligence across these core areas, organizations gain agility, resilience, and the ability to course-correct in real time. Whether through smarter decisions, faster response to risk, or better user experience, AI brings the vision of intelligent service management full circle—transforming plans into action and insights into impact.

AI is a natural enabler of ITIL4's Continual Improvement Model, offering precision, automation, and real-time insight at every step. By integrating AI tools into the improvement cycle, organizations can move from reactive changes to proactive, sustainable service enhancement. With machine learning and analytics guiding each phase—from vision alignment to performance tracking—IT leaders can embed a culture of intelligent, data-driven evolution across the service lifecycle.

Building AI into the Service Value Chain Activities

The ITIL4 **Service Value Chain (SVC)** represents the core of the **Service Value System (SVS)**—a dynamic operating model that outlines key activities required to create and deliver value through IT-enabled services. AI doesn't just automate tasks within these activities; it **augments, accelerates, and improves decision-making** across the value chain. In this section, we examine how AI supports each of the six SVC activities: **Plan, Improve, Engage, Design and Transition, Obtain/Build, and Deliver and Support**—bringing intelligence and foresight into the very fabric of service delivery.

Plan

Objective: To ensure a shared understanding of the vision, current status, and improvement direction across the organization.

AI's Role:

- **Forecasting and Simulation:** AI can analyze trends, risks, and historical data to help plan capacity, demand, and budget allocations.
- **Scenario Analysis:** AI models simulate future outcomes based on different planning assumptions–enabling better strategic choices.
- **Data-Driven Strategy Formulation:** NLP engines can summarize business goals and suggest alignment with IT services.

Real-Life Example:

A multinational manufacturer used AI to simulate IT resource needs during planned factory expansions. Using historical support data and projected user growth, AI forecasted helpdesk load and infrastructure capacity needs–resulting in 35% fewer escalations post-expansion due to proactive resourcing.

Improve

Objective: To ensure continual improvement of products, services, and practices across all value chain activities.

AI's Role:

- **Trend Analysis:** AI uses ML and NLP to detect anomalies or performance degradation before they become systemic.
- **Automated Feedback Loops:** AI processes survey data, chat transcripts, and ticket notes to identify improvement opportunities.
- **Process Mining:** AI reveals hidden bottlenecks and inefficiencies across service workflows.

Real-Life Example:

A global IT services firm used AI to mine process logs from their change and incident workflows. It discovered approval delays at one department and auto-suggested process changes–cutting average change implementation time by 40%.

Engage

Objective: To foster good relationships with stakeholders, understand their needs, and ensure effective communication and collaboration.

AI's Role:

- **Sentiment Analysis:** NLP algorithms scan user interactions and feedback to identify dissatisfaction trends.

- **Virtual Assistants:** AI chatbots provide 24/7 conversational engagement and intelligent ticket creation.
- **Customer Journey Mapping:** AI visualizes user journeys and pain points to inform service design or escalation paths.

Real-Life Example:

A university implemented a Microsoft Teams-based virtual assistant integrated with their ITSM tool. It handled repetitive queries from 18,000 students, reducing L1 ticket load by over 50% and improving engagement during semester peaks.

Design and Transition

Objective: To ensure new or changed services meet expectations for quality, speed, and value while minimizing risk.

AI's Role:

- **AI-Enhanced Risk Assessment:** Predictive models evaluate change proposals based on historical data and dependency mapping.
- **Intelligent Testing:** AI supports automated testing by generating synthetic test cases and identifying failure patterns.
- **Knowledge Mapping:** AI links services to KBs and historical incidents, reducing onboarding and transition issues.

Real-Life Example:

A telecom provider used AI to score changes based on CMDB relationships and prior failure patterns. High-risk changes were flagged for CAB review, while low-risk changes were auto-approved—leading to a 50% reduction in change-related outages.

Obtain/Build

Objective: To ensure service components are available when and where needed, meeting specification and quality criteria.

AI's Role:

- **Predictive Procurement:** AI analyzes usage and inventory patterns to anticipate procurement needs.
- **Build Optimization:** AI detects coding inefficiencies or configuration issues in software builds via pattern analysis.
- **Resource Forecasting:** AI forecasts hardware/software demand aligned with release and user growth.

Real-Life Example:

An e-commerce company integrated AI with its procurement and build pipeline. Based on order history and release cycles, AI flagged a likely shortage in server licenses–allowing proactive scaling before Black Friday traffic surge.

Deliver and Support

Objective: To ensure effective delivery and support of services, meeting agreed specifications and user expectations.

AI's Role:

- **Auto-Triage and Routing:** AI classifies incidents and requests based on description, priority, and sentiment.
- **Smart Knowledge Base:** AI surfaces relevant KB articles in real time to reduce resolution time and boost self-service.
- **Predictive Ticket Volumes:** AI forecasts ticket surges to optimize staffing and SLA adherence.

Real-Life Example:

A managed services provider deployed AI-based ticket triaging and knowledge recommendation. L1 resolution increased by 60%, average ticket handling time dropped by 35%, and ticket deflection rose from 5% to 28% in three months.

Summary Table: AI Integration across Service Value Chain Activities

SVC Activity	AI Contribution	Example Outcome
Plan	Forecasting demand, simulating outcomes, aligning IT with strategy	35% fewer escalations post-expansion through AI-based resource planning
Improve	Trend detection, feedback analysis, process optimization	40% faster change cycles via process mining insights
Engage	Sentiment detection, VAs, journey analysis	50% reduction in L1 tickets through 24/7 virtual assistant
Design and Transition	Predictive risk analysis, testing insights, KB enrichment	50% drop in change-related outages with AI risk scoring

Obtain/Build	Procurement prediction, build defect detection, resource planning	Prevented license shortage before peak season
Deliver and Support	Ticket prediction, auto-triage, KB recommendations	60% increase in L1 resolution and 35% reduction in handling time

Table 9.4: *AI Integration across Service Value Chain Activities*

Now, let us discuss the same concept Contextualized for the Development of an Online Payment App.

The ITIL4 **Service Value Chain (SVC)** provides a high-level model that guides how services are created and delivered–from demand to value realization. By embedding **AI technologies** into each SVC activity, organizations can achieve higher efficiency, proactive decision-making, and intelligent automation. Using the real-life example of developing an **online payment app for a bike hire service**, we will explore how AI augments each step of the value stream: **Engage, Plan, Design and Transition, Obtain/Build, Deliver and Support, and Improve.**

Engage

(Value Stream Step 1: Understand and document the requirements of an online payment app)

AI Opportunities:

- **Conversational AI for Customer Research:** Virtual assistants can conduct scalable customer interviews or surveys, gathering qualitative and quantitative feedback in real time.
- **Sentiment Analysis:** AI can analyze customer feedback, reviews, and survey responses to understand expectations, frustrations, and emotional tone.
- **Regulatory NLP:** AI can scan and summarize financial regulations and compliance requirements for app-based transactions.

Real-Life AI Scenario:

AI-powered survey bots were deployed to engage over 1,000 users about online payment needs. Insights from natural language responses were analyzed with sentiment detection, revealing strong demand for multilingual support and digital wallet integration–critical inputs for the business case.

Plan

(Value Stream Step 2: Develop the Business Case for the App)

AI Opportunities:

- **Predictive Analytics:** AI models forecast potential ROI, adoption rates, and operating costs based on similar digital product launches.
- **Risk Modeling:** AI simulates the impact of identified risks (for example, fraud, technical debt) and suggests mitigation plans.
- **Feasibility Scoring:** Machine learning models assess the business case feasibility using data from past projects and market indicators.

Real-Life AI Scenario:

A financial analysis bot assessed cost versus benefit scenarios for introducing an online payment app. It recommended an implementation window tied to peak seasonal demand, improving adoption and shortening payback period by 30%.

Design and Transition

(Value Stream Step 3: Design and Deploy the Online Payment App)

AI Opportunities:

- **Automated Design Validation:** AI reviews designs for scalability, fault tolerance, and compliance before development.
- **Dependency Mapping:** AI identifies integration points with booking systems, payment gateways, and external APIs.
- **AI-Driven Release Planning:** Based on historic go-live data, AI suggests optimal deployment windows and user onboarding plans.

Real-Life AI Scenario:

AI simulated design blueprints and predicted latency issues in integration between the booking system and financial clearing house. The development team proactively re-architected the data flow, reducing transaction errors by 60% at launch.

Obtain/Build

(Value Stream Step 4: Build, Configure, or Buy the Online Payment App)

AI Opportunities:

- **Code Quality Inspection:** AI tools such as DeepCode or SonarQube analyze code for security vulnerabilities and logic errors in real time.

- **Smart Procurement:** AI assesses vendor proposals using historical performance and compliance benchmarks.
- **Automated Testing:** AI-driven tools perform regression, unit, and load testing faster and more comprehensively than manual efforts.

Real-Life AI Scenario:

An AI-based code scanner flagged an authentication loophole during early build stages. This prevented a security flaw before deployment, ensuring compliance with financial regulatory frameworks and avoiding a costly post-launch patch.

Deliver and Support

(Value Stream Step 5: Deploy the App and Begin Operations)

AI Opportunities:

- **Virtual Agent Support:** AI-powered service desks provide 24/7 support for early-life issues, such as password resets or failed transactions.
- **Auto-Triage and Routing:** NLP engines analyze incident descriptions and auto-route tickets to appropriate resolver groups.
- **Knowledge Recommendation:** Smart KB systems recommend resolution articles to users and agents in real time.

Real-Life AI Scenario:

Following launch, a virtual agent resolved over 65% of user queries within 30 seconds, while predictive models helped the ITSM tool detect a surge in errors after 1,000 concurrent users. The issue was mitigated in under an hour, preserving user satisfaction.

Improve

(Ongoing improvements post-launch across all activities)

AI Opportunities:

- **Feedback Loop Automation:** AI analyzes post-launch survey data, usage logs, and customer feedback to suggest iterative improvements.
- **Anomaly Detection:** AI continuously monitors user behavior and system performance, identifying issues before they are reported.
- **Process Optimization:** AI identifies delays in support processes and suggests automation or rerouting opportunities.

Real-Life AI Scenario:

Usage analytics showed a recurring spike in failed payments every Sunday evening. AI recommended auto scaling the payment gateway instance, eliminating downtime, and increasing successful transactions by 18%.

Integrated View: AI across the Payment App Value Stream

Value Chain Activity	AI Enablers	Value Realized
Engage	Sentiment analysis, virtual surveys, regulatory NLP	Deeper customer insight, improved compliance understanding
Plan	Predictive ROI, risk analysis, feasibility scoring	Better business case, reduced uncertainty in go/no-go decision
Design and Transition	Dependency mapping, AI-led validation, release optimization	Scalable design, faster and safer deployment
Obtain/Build	Code inspection, vendor scoring, AI-based testing	Secure builds, better vendor management, early error detection
Deliver and Support	Auto-triage, smart KB, virtual assistants	Faster resolution, fewer escalations, 24/7 support availability
Improve	Continuous monitoring, anomaly detection, feedback analytics	Continuous innovation, early detection of problems, adaptive operations

Table 9.5: *Integrated View: AI across the Payment App Value Stream*

The development and deployment of a service like an online payment app can benefit immensely from AI when aligned with each stage of the ITIL4 Service Value Chain. From planning to improvement, AI serves as both a compass and an engine—guiding teams with predictive insight and automating complex tasks for speed and precision. By integrating AI into the value stream, organizations can deliver smarter services, reduce risk, and meet evolving customer demands with agility and intelligence.

The Service Value Chain is the engine that powers ITIL4's promise of co-creating value. When AI is embedded thoughtfully into each activity, it adds speed, consistency, and intelligence—making every stage more responsive and resilient. From early planning to final support, AI transforms the Service Value Chain from a reactive sequence of tasks into a **real-time, adaptive value-creation engine**. Organizations that build AI into the heart of their SVC activities don't just manage services better—they redefine what modern service excellence looks like.

Conclusion

As we draw this chapter to a close, one thing is clear: Artificial Intelligence is no longer an optional enhancement—it is an essential enabler of the ITIL4 Service Value System. When embedded thoughtfully across the **guiding principles**, **governance functions**,

continual improvement practices, and each activity of the **Service Value Chain**, AI becomes the connective tissue that binds agility with control, innovation with consistency, and speed with quality.

This chapter has demonstrated how AI amplifies the impact of ITIL4's seven guiding principles—driving greater focus on value, promoting practical automation, enabling faster iterations, and fostering cross-functional visibility. From virtual assistants reducing ticket volumes to predictive engines flagging risk before failure, AI delivers tangible benefits that align directly with ITIL4's philosophy of co-creating value through services.

Governance, service design, and continual improvement—often viewed as high-level or strategic layers—are also being radically transformed by AI. Data-driven dashboards, anomaly detection, and automated compliance checks are empowering leaders to make decisions faster, safer, and with greater foresight. Through integration with continual improvement models, AI enables an always-on improvement loop that evolves alongside business demands.

Furthermore, we explored how each stage of the **Service Value Chain**—from *Engage* to *Improve*—can be supercharged with AI capabilities. Whether it's intelligent triaging in *Deliver and Support*, automated testing in *Obtain/Build*, or sentiment analytics in *Engage*, the synergy between ITIL4 and AI creates a service delivery model that is not only efficient but also predictive, adaptive, and user centric.

In the case of the **online payment app value stream**, AI was shown to add value at every milestone—from understanding customer needs to building resilient architecture and delivering continual enhancements. This example illustrates how AI can be operationalized to transform a concept into a sustainable, high-performing service.

Ultimately, AI brings ITIL4's vision to life—not by replacing best practices, but by scaling them with intelligence. Organizations that embrace this partnership between ITIL4 and AI position themselves not only to manage today's complexity but to lead in tomorrow's digital landscape. As we move forward, the question is no longer *whether* AI should be used in ITSM, but *how intelligently and strategically* it can be woven into the fabric of service management to unlock its full potential. In the next chapter, we will discuss how organizations can assess their readiness for AI, from data maturity and process standardization to cultural adoption.

Multiple Choice Questions

1. Which ITIL4 guiding principle is most closely aligned with AI's capability to automate repetitive tasks and optimize workflows?

    a. Think and work holistically

    b. Progress iteratively with feedback

c. Optimize and automate

d. Collaborate and promote visibility

2. In the context of continual improvement, what role does AI play in the "Where Are We Now?" step of the ITIL4 model?

 a. Sets long-term improvement goals

 b. Forecasts future capacity requirements

 c. Assesses current performance using data mining and sentiment analysis

 d. Suggests automation candidates for improvement

3. How does AI support the 'Engage' activity in the Service Value Chain?

 a. By simulating release windows and testing environments

 b. By performing automated procurement and vendor scoring

 c. By analyzing customer sentiment and enabling virtual assistant interactions

 d. By generating KPIs from incident logs

4. What is one way AI contributes to IT governance in the ITIL4 context?

 a. Replacing all human decision-making

 b. Automating password resets

 c. Providing real-time alerts for policy breaches and risk scoring

 d. Handling physical access requests

5. Which of the following best describes how AI supports continual improvement in the ITIL4 framework?

 a. Manually updates CMDB records

 b. Predicts potential new services through customer interviews

 c. Automatically identifies performance anomalies and improvement opportunities

 d. Creates static reports for service reviews

Answers

1. c
2. c
3. c
4. c
5. c

Questions

1. Explain how AI supports each of the seven guiding principles of ITIL4 with practical examples.
2. Describe how AI enhances the effectiveness of IT governance within the ITIL4 framework.
3. Discuss the role of AI in service design and how it helps organizations build more resilient and scalable services.
4. Outline how AI enables continual improvement using the seven steps of the ITIL4 Continual Improvement Model.
5. How does AI improve decision-making in the 'Plan' stage of the ITIL4 Service Value Chain? Provide examples.
6. Illustrate how AI-powered tools such as virtual assistants and sentiment analysis contribute to the 'Engage' activity in the value chain.
7. In what ways can AI be integrated into the 'Obtain/Build' value chain activity to improve software development and procurement processes?
8. Describe how AI transforms the 'Deliver and Support' stage of the value chain and its impact on user experience.
9. How can AI be used to track and validate performance improvements after a service change has been implemented?
10. Using the online payment app case study, explain how AI was applied across the value stream to improve planning, delivery, and support.

Key Terms

- **Service Value System (SVS):** The SVS is the foundational model in ITIL4 that integrates principles, governance, practices, and value chain activities to co-create value. AI strengthens the SVS by making it more adaptive, intelligent, and outcome focused.
- **Guiding Principles (ITIL4):** These are universal recommendations that guide organizations in decision-making and service management. AI complements principles like "optimize and automate" by offering data-driven insights and scalable automation.
- **Continual Improvement Model:** A seven-step model that provides a structured approach for service enhancement over time. AI enhances each step with forecasting, feedback loops, and anomaly detection.
- **Service Value Chain (SVC):** The SVC is a flexible operating model comprising six interconnected activities: Plan, Improve, Engage, Design and Transition, Obtain/Build, and Deliver and Support. AI can be embedded into each of these activities to increase agility and efficiency.
- **Predictive Analytics:** A branch of AI that uses historical and real-time data to forecast future trends or outcomes. It helps IT teams anticipate ticket volumes, service demands, and change risks proactively.
- **Virtual Assistant (VA):** An AI-powered chatbot that interacts with users to resolve requests, answer FAQs, and automate repetitive tasks. VAs improve engagement, reduce ticket volume, and offer 24/7 support.
- **Sentiment Analysis:** A Natural Language Processing (NLP) technique that detects the emotional tone behind user feedback or support interactions. It helps organizations understand user satisfaction and identify service pain points early.
- **Process Mining:** An AI-driven approach that analyzes logs and workflow data to visualize and improve real business processes. It helps identify bottlenecks, inefficiencies, and improvement opportunities.
- **Risk Scoring:** AI uses historical data and contextual analysis to assign quantitative risk levels to changes or incidents. This enables safer, faster, and more consistent decision-making in Change Enablement and Governance.
- **Knowledge Recommendation Engine:** An AI system that suggests relevant knowledge base articles based on ticket context or user intent. It improves first-contact resolution and empowers both users and agents with the right information instantly.

CHAPTER 10
Preparing ITSM Environments for AI Adoption

Introduction

Artificial Intelligence holds enormous promise for transforming IT service management–but realizing that promise requires more than just adopting the latest tools. Before organizations can reap the full benefits of AI, they must ask an honest question: *Are we truly ready for it?* Readiness is not just about having the right technology; it is about whether your data is clean, your processes are consistent, your teams are skilled, and your culture is open to change. Many organizations leap into AI initiatives only to discover foundational gaps–such as poor data hygiene or resistance from staff–slow down progress or derail adoption. This chapter is your guide to preparing the ground before you plant the seeds of AI. You will explore what it really means to be "AI-ready" from a service management lens, including key enablers such as data maturity, workforce competencies, and process discipline. We will also look at common barriers that hinder AI success and how to navigate around them. Through a practical checklist and phased roadmap, you will learn how to start small–focusing on quick, low-risk wins–while building toward larger, enterprise-wide AI integration. Ultimately, the goal is not just to adopt AI for ITSM, but to embed it in a way that delivers sustainable value and strengthens your digital operating model.

Structure

In this chapter, we will discuss the following topics:

- AI-Readiness Assessment
- Skills, Data, Culture, and Tooling Checklist
- How to Start Small and Scale Responsibly

AI-Readiness Assessment

Artificial Intelligence in ITSM isn't plug-and-play–it's a strategic journey. Before organizations can successfully deploy AI-driven solutions, they must assess their internal readiness across multiple dimensions: data, processes, tools, skills, governance, and organizational culture. This assessment acts as a litmus test, helping leaders identify strengths, expose weaknesses, and prioritize enablers that make-or-break AI adoption.

The Importance of Conducting an AI-Readiness Assessment

Rushing into AI initiatives without proper groundwork leads to failed pilots, wasted investment, and disillusioned teams. An AI-readiness assessment helps:

- Avoid misaligned expectations between leadership and IT teams.
- Uncover critical gaps in data quality or process standardization.
- Identify use cases suitable for AI based on current maturity.
- Ensure foundational alignment with ITIL4 practices and business strategy.

Core Dimensions of AI Readiness

AI readiness in ITSM goes beyond just having the right tools–it spans several foundational dimensions that collectively determine whether an organization can successfully adopt and scale AI. These dimensions include the quality and availability of data, the standardization of ITSM processes, the technical capability of existing tools, the skills and knowledge of the workforce, the cultural openness to change and innovation, and the governance structures that ensure responsible AI use. Each of these areas must be assessed to identify gaps, prioritize improvements, and establish a realistic roadmap for AI integration. A strong foundation across these dimensions ensures that AI initiatives are not only feasible but also sustainable and value-generating in the long term.

Process standardization refers to the consistency and clarity with which ITSM workflows–like incident handling, change enablement, and request fulfillment–are defined and executed. For AI to work effectively, it must recognize patterns within structured, repeatable processes. If incident tickets follow ad hoc paths or if change approvals vary widely, AI models struggle to learn or make accurate predictions. Standardized processes provide the scaffolding AI needs to automate decisions, identify anomalies, and suggest actions confidently. For example, an organization using a uniform five-step change process will be better equipped to leverage AI for risk prediction than one with multiple undocumented variations.

This refers to whether the ITSM environment includes tools and platforms that are technically capable of supporting AI integration. It involves more than just having a modern ITSM tool about whether that tool exposes APIs, allows for AI plugins, integrates with external analytics engines, or includes native AI features such as auto-categorization or virtual assistants. Organizations using platforms such as ServiceNow or Jira Service Management, which already embed machine learning or NLP capabilities, are often ahead in this dimension. Additionally, infrastructure such as data lakes, CMDBs, and monitoring tools that generate clean, structured logs also play a vital role in supporting AI pipelines.

Cultural readiness assesses whether the people in the organization—especially IT and service management teams—are open to adopting AI-driven ways of working. Even with the best tools and data, AI initiatives fail if employees distrust automation, resist change, or fear job displacement. Cultural readiness is about fostering trust in AI by involving teams early, educating them about the benefits, and positioning AI as an enabler, not a replacement. It also includes leadership buy-in, willingness to experiment, and a mindset of continuous improvement. For instance, a service desk that encourages agents to use AI-recommended KB articles or workflows demonstrates a higher degree of cultural readiness.

The following table lists core dimensions:

Dimension	Description	Example of Maturity
Data Quality and Availability	AI models rely on accurate, structured, and accessible data	Clean, labeled incident tickets in the ITSM tool over the last 12–18 months
Process Standardization	AI thrives on predictable workflows and clear categorization	Clearly defined incident and change workflows supported by a full spectrum of service management practices.
Tooling Infrastructure	Readiness of ITSM tools and integrations with AI engines	Existing use of ServiceNow with integrated NLP for ticket classification
Workforce Skills	Knowledge of AI, automation, and data management among IT staff	L1 agents trained in using AI-powered virtual assistants
Cultural Readiness	Openness to change, experimentation, and AI-augmented decisions	Support teams willing to rely on AI suggestions for prioritization
Governance and Ethics	Policies around data use, AI explainability, and risk management	Data privacy and audit trail policies in place for AI outputs

Table 10.1: *Core Dimensions*

Sample AI-Readiness Maturity Model

The AI-Readiness Maturity Model provides a structured framework to evaluate where an organization currently stands in its journey toward adopting AI in ITSM. It defines progressive levels of maturity–from having no foundational readiness to being fully AI-driven–based on key indicators such as data quality, process discipline, tool capabilities, and organizational mindset. Each level offers insight into what's working, what's missing, and what actions are needed to move forward. This model not only helps organizations benchmark their current state but also guides them in developing a realistic, phased roadmap for AI adoption–starting small, building trust, and scaling intelligently.

The following table lists the maturity levels:

Level	Description	Typical Traits
Level 0 - Not Ready	No AI understanding or strategy	No data strategy, poor documentation
Level 1 - Exploring	Awareness exists, but no groundwork	Sporadic data, unstructured processes
Level 2 - Foundation Set	Clean data, basic automation, some AI experimentation	Basic AI tools in use, defined processes
Level 3 - Piloting AI	AI pilots in defined areas like incident classification	Use of auto-categorization, basic ML models
Level 4 - Scaling AI	AI embedded in operations, governance in place	Predictive analytics, virtual agents, AIOps
Level 5 - AI-Driven ITSM	AI is a strategic enabler across ITSM	Autonomous remediation, AI in strategic planning

Table 10.2: *Maturity Levels*

Real-Life Examples

- **ServiceNow Customer: Telecom Sector**

  A leading telecom provider in the Middle East began their AI journey by cleaning up four years of historical ticket data. They standardized priority and category fields and implemented predictive categorization. After a successful pilot, they saw 23% reduction in triage time within three months. Their AI readiness assessment revealed high process maturity, but poor data labeling–so they addressed that first.

- **ManageEngine Use Case: Mid-sized Manufacturing Firm**

  This organization had robust automation but no data taxonomy. Their IT team often entered tickets with inconsistent categories. The AI-readiness assessment led to a six-week initiative to define service request templates, normalize field values, and retrain staff. Afterward, they implemented AI to predict resolution time, achieving 18% improvement in SLA adherence.

- **Jira Service Management: Startup Example**

  A tech startup wanted to use ChatGPT for virtual agent support. The AI-readiness check revealed they had excellent structured data but lacked clear escalation rules. By defining escalation paths and building confidence in automation, they safely introduced a GPT-based assistant that resolved 36% of L1 tickets autonomously.

Conducting the Assessment: Step-by-Step

A structured, step-by-step AI-readiness assessment ensures that organizations take a comprehensive and methodical approach before embarking on AI initiatives. This process begins by assembling a cross-functional task force and using a readiness checklist to evaluate critical dimensions including data, tools, processes, and culture. It involves stakeholder interviews, historical data reviews, and technical tool assessments to uncover strengths and gaps. The insights are then visualized using a maturity heatmap, enabling teams to prioritize areas for improvement. By following these steps, organizations can develop a clear, actionable roadmap to guide their AI journey with confidence and alignment to strategic goals.

The list of suggested steps are as follows:

1. **Form an AI Readiness Task Force:** Include ITSM leads, data engineers, automation experts, and change managers.
2. **Use a Readiness Checklist or Survey:** Assess each of the six dimensions.
3. **Interview Stakeholders**: Understand comfort levels, concerns, and use case ideas.
4. **Review Historical Data**: Evaluate volume, structure, and consistency.
5. **Rate Current Tools**: Identify which tools are AI-ready or need enhancements.
6. **Build a Heatmap**: Color-code maturity levels (Red = not ready, Yellow = partial, Green = ready).
7. **Prioritize Use Cases**: Start with low-risk, high-value areas such as ticket categorization or virtual assistants.

8. **Develop a Gap Closure Plan:** Include training, data cleansing, and process documentation.

The following table represents the Checklist for AI-Readiness:

Checklist Item	Yes/No
Do we have 12+ months of ticket data?	✅ / ❌
Is our data categorized and labeled consistently?	✅ / ❌
Are ITSM processes standardized and documented?	✅ / ❌
Have we implemented automation (for example, workflow, auto-escalation)?	✅ / ❌
Do our teams understand basic AI concepts?	✅ / ❌
Do we have tools that support AI plugins/APIs?	✅ / ❌
Is leadership supportive of AI experimentation?	✅ / ❌
Are change and risk governance frameworks in place?	✅ / ❌

Table 10.3: *AI-readiness Checklist*

AI-readiness is not a pass/fail judgment–it's a spectrum. The goal is to identify where you are today and define actionable steps to get to where AI adds measurable value. By conducting a readiness assessment early, organizations not only minimize risk but also accelerate the time-to-value of their AI investments in ITSM

Skills, Data, Culture, and Tooling Checklist

Adopting AI in ITSM isn't just about plugging in a tool–it's about aligning people, processes, technology, and mindset. Once the initial readiness assessment is complete, organizations must deep-dive into four critical enablers that determine whether AI can take root and scale: **skills**, **data**, **culture**, and **tooling**. Each of these areas serves as a foundation for responsible and effective AI integration. This chapter breaks down what to look for, what to fix, and how real organizations have addressed each dimension to move toward AI-powered service management.

Skills: Building a Future-Ready Workforce

Artificial Intelligence has the potential to revolutionize ITSM, but its success ultimately hinges on the people who use, manage, and evolve it. Building a future-ready workforce isn't optional–it's a strategic necessity. As AI becomes more deeply embedded in service operations, IT professionals must shift from routine task execution to higher-order functions such as interpreting AI insights, training machine learning models, and designing intelligent workflows. Without the right skills and mindset, AI tools remain underutilized or misapplied, leading to poor outcomes, frustration, and failed initiatives.

Moreover, a workforce that understands AI can better identify suitable use cases, spot data quality issues, and build trust in AI-driven decisions. Employees who are empowered with AI literacy are less likely to resist change and more likely to see AI as a partner in their work rather than a threat. In high-performing organizations, we see IT agents evolve into AI trainers, knowledge engineers, and automation architects–roles that didn't exist a decade ago but are now vital. Upskilling, continuous learning, and cross-functional collaboration become the pillars of sustainable innovation. In short, without a future-ready workforce, even the most advanced AI strategy will stall. With it, AI becomes a true force multiplier for service excellence.

AI thrives where human teams are prepared to understand, manage, and interact with it.

What to look for:

- Basic understanding of AI, ML, NLP concepts across IT teams
- Capability to manage and tune AI models (data analysts, automation engineers)
- Skills in data labeling, process design, and automation scripting
- Comfort with AI-driven decision support and insights

Red Flags:

- Over-reliance on external vendors for AI knowledge
- Resistance to adopting AI recommendations
- No in-house ownership for AI model tuning or performance

Real-Life Example: A government services organization using **ManageEngine ServiceDesk Plus** initiated AI use for ticket categorization. However, agents were confused by the AI's choices and often overrode suggestions without understanding the logic. The IT lead introduced a series of internal "AI literacy" workshops to train staff on how the model worked and when to trust its output. Within two months, trust in AI increased, and override rates dropped by 40%.

Data: The Fuel That Powers AI

In the world of AI-powered ITSM, data is not just an input–it's the lifeblood that fuels every intelligent decision, prediction, and action. Just as a car cannot run without fuel, AI cannot operate effectively without clean, structured, and reliable data. Whether it's auto-classifying incidents, predicting ticket volumes, or surfacing the most relevant knowledge article, AI systems rely on historical patterns and contextual signals extracted from data. But not just any data will do–the quality, consistency, and availability of that data determine whether AI delivers insights or confusion.

Many organizations rush to adopt AI tools without realizing that their data is fragmented, incomplete, or poorly labeled. Inconsistent use of categories, missing resolution codes, or reliance on free-text fields create blind spots that AI cannot interpret. On the other hand, organizations that invest in data hygiene–standardizing fields, integrating sources like CMDBs and monitoring logs, and ensuring historical completeness–find that AI becomes a powerful ally in streamlining operations and improving service delivery.

Think of data as the foundation upon which AI models learn and evolve. Without that foundation, even the best-designed algorithms will falter. But with clean, contextualized, and connected data, AI becomes capable of driving real transformation–from faster triage to proactive incident prevention. In short, data isn't just a prerequisite for AI–it's the fuel that powers its engine.

Without clean, structured, and sufficient data, AI initiatives collapse.

What to look for:

- Availability of historical ITSM records (at least 12–18 months)
- Clean categorization, resolution codes, and consistent field usage
- Integration of asset data, CMDB, monitoring logs, and user metadata
- Ongoing data hygiene and validation practices

Red Flags:

- High volume of free-text-only fields (for example, category, resolution)
- Missing or duplicate records
- Data silos across tools (monitoring, CMDB, ticketing not integrated)

Real-Life Example: A healthcare IT provider wanted to implement **predictive incident routing** in **ServiceNow**, but discovered over 60% of tickets lacked a resolution code. Their first step was a three-month project to backfill historical data and enforce mandatory resolution categories. Once the cleanup was complete, their ML model achieved a 79% routing accuracy, significantly improving resolution time for critical incidents.

Culture: The Soil Where AI Takes Root

If data is the fuel and tools are the engine, then **culture is the soil where AI truly takes root and grows**. You can invest in the smartest algorithms, the cleanest data, and the most powerful platforms–but if your organization's culture isn't ready to embrace change, AI will struggle to gain traction. Culture shapes how people perceive and interact with technology. It influences whether teams view AI as a threat to their roles or a catalyst for their growth.

In many organizations, fear of job loss, skepticism about AI decisions, and resistance to automation can quietly stall even the most promising initiatives. That's why building a culture of curiosity, trust, and openness is critical. Teams need to feel psychologically safe to experiment with AI, question its outputs, and learn from failures. Leadership plays a pivotal role here–not just by funding AI programs, but by actively championing them, celebrating quick wins, and positioning AI as a partner, not a replacement.

Organizations with a healthy culture of innovation don't treat AI as an external bolt-on–they nurture it from within. They encourage cross-functional collaboration, promote AI literacy, and create shared ownership of intelligent outcomes. Just like rich, well-tended soil allows a seed to flourish, a supportive culture allows AI to evolve from pilot projects into enterprise-wide value creation. Because in the end, it's not just about adopting AI–it's about cultivating an environment where it can grow, adapt, and thrive.

Even the best AI solution will fail if the organization isn't culturally prepared.

What to look for:

- Willingness to experiment and learn from AI outcomes
- Psychological safety for teams to trust AI-augmented decisions
- Top-down support for AI-driven service improvement
- Alignment with continuous improvement and DevOps mindsets

Red Flags:

- Fear of AI replacing human jobs
- Lack of cross-functional collaboration in AI initiatives
- IT teams perceiving AI as "just another tool" rather than a capability

Real-Life Example: A large retail chain piloting a **ChatGPT-based virtual assistant** for service requests faced backlash from the service desk team, who feared job loss. Instead of replacing roles, the organization reframed the pilot as a *tier-0 deflection strategy* and reassigned agents to handle complex L2/L3 issues. Morale improved, and the virtual assistant went on to handle 38% of user queries autonomously within six months.

Tooling: The AI-Ready ITSM Ecosystem

Even with the right skills, clean data, and an open culture, AI initiatives in ITSM won't succeed without the proper tools—because **tools form the ecosystem in which AI comes to life**. This ecosystem includes your ITSM platform, integration capabilities, data pipelines, monitoring systems, automation engines, and analytics layers. These tools must not only be modern and scalable—they must also be extensible, interoperable, and AI-capable. Simply put, **AI-readiness at the tooling level means your environment can support, sustain, and evolve intelligent workflows.**

Traditional, siloed systems that lack APIs or modularity can quickly become bottlenecks. If your service desk tool doesn't support structured data capture or can't integrate with a CMDB or AIOps platform, your AI efforts will stall before they begin. In contrast, an AI-ready toolset includes platforms including ServiceNow, Jira, or ManageEngine with native or plug-and-play AI features—such as predictive classification, NLP-driven search, or anomaly detection. These tools allow AI to analyze, act, and learn in real time.

But tooling is not just about feature checklists—it is about enablement. Can your tools ingest data from monitoring systems and turn alerts into actionable insights? Can they trigger automated remediation? Can they interact with chatbots and virtual assistants to support 24/7 service? When the tooling is aligned with the broader AI strategy, the ITSM environment becomes dynamic, adaptive, and truly intelligent. Just as ecosystems in nature must be balanced and resilient for growth, your ITSM tool ecosystem must be purposefully designed to let AI flourish and scale.

Your existing ITSM tools and supporting infrastructure must be technically capable of supporting AI.

What to look for:

- Modern ITSM tools with built-in AI capabilities or open APIs
- Integration capabilities across ITOM, APM, CMDB, and analytics
- Logging and monitoring tools feeding real-time data
- Cloud-based platforms with AI plugin support

Red Flags:

- Legacy tools with limited automation support
- Disconnected modules with no centralized data visibility
- Lack of support for ML/AI libraries, NLP engines, or RESTful APIs

Real-Life Example: A mid-sized bank running on **Jira Service Management** aimed to automate incident classification. However, they discovered their on-prem version lacked native AI modules and limited API support. After upgrading to the cloud version and integrating with an external AI engine via Atlassian Forge, they deployed a classifier that tagged tickets with 91% accuracy based on subject lines, historical patterns, and user profile metadata.

The following table presents the Checklist Summary Table:

Area	Checklist Item	Ready? (Y/N)
Skills	Are staff familiar with basic AI/ML concepts?	✅ / ❌
Skills	Do we have internal owners for AI tools/models?	✅ / ❌
Data	Do we have at least 12–18 months of clean ticket data?	✅ / ❌
Data	Are fields like category, priority, and resolution used consistently?	✅ / ❌
Culture	Do teams view AI as an enabler, not a threat?	✅ / ❌
Culture	Is leadership actively sponsoring AI adoption?	✅ / ❌
Tooling	Are our ITSM tools AI-ready or extensible via APIs?	✅ / ❌
Tooling	Are data sources (tickets, CMDB, logs) integrated?	✅ / ❌

***Table 10.4**: Checklist Summary Table*

The success of AI in ITSM is not solely dictated by the model used or the vendor chosen—it's shaped by how well your organization performs across **skills, data, culture, and tooling**. This checklist isn't a one-time exercise; it's a dynamic guide to continuously assess and improve your AI maturity. With the right preparation in these four areas, your organization can transition from isolated pilots to enterprise-grade AI adoption—confidently and sustainably.

How to Start Small and Scale Responsibly

The most successful AI journeys in IT Service Management aren't launched with massive investments or sweeping transformations—they begin with thoughtful, targeted experiments. Trying to deploy AI across your entire ITSM landscape from day one is not only risky but also unrealistic. The key to sustainable success lies in starting small—selecting the right use case, proving value quickly, learning from feedback—and then scaling responsibly with confidence. This chapter provides a practical roadmap to help organizations move from experimentation to enterprise-grade AI adoption without disruption or burnout.

Starting Small is a Strategic Approach, not a Cautious One

Starting small is not a sign of hesitation; it's a strategy rooted in agility, learning, and risk mitigation. AI introduces new dynamics—data dependencies, ethical concerns, user trust, and interpretability–that differ from traditional automation or tool upgrades. A focused pilot:

- Allows for controlled testing in a low-risk environment.
- Helps build internal understanding of AI workflows and model behavior.
- Encourages stakeholder buy-in by demonstrating tangible outcomes.
- Surfaces integration, data quality, or cultural issues early–before scaling amplifies them.

Choosing the Right "First Use Case"

Embarking on the AI journey in ITSM begins with a crucial decision: selecting the right first use case. This choice can make or break early momentum. Pick something too complex, and the project may stall under the weight of unclear scope, high risk, or unclear value. But choose wisely, and you will create a compelling proof of concept that builds confidence, delivers results, and lays the foundation for responsible scaling.

The ideal first use case is one that is simple enough to manage, yet valuable enough to matter. It should focus on a repetitive, high-volume task–such as categorizing incidents, routing tickets, or suggesting knowledge articles–where AI can demonstrate clear, measurable improvement. These areas offer predictable patterns for machine learning models to learn from, and the impact of improvement is easily quantifiable in terms of time saved or accuracy gained.

It is also important that the use case is low-risk and non-critical. Early pilots should be conducted in areas where mistakes won't cause disruption or compromise user experience. And just as important is the ability to measure success: define KPIs upfront, such as reduction in resolution time, improvement in triage accuracy, or percentage of AI recommendations accepted.

Organizations that succeed in AI adoption often start with narrow, focused pilots that yield quick wins–not just technical, but cultural. These pilots help stakeholders see AI not as a futuristic concept, but as a practical, reliable assistant in their day-to-day operations. And with that confidence, the door opens to broader transformation.

Not all ITSM processes are ideal starting points. The best pilot use cases share three characteristics:

- **Low Complexity**: Avoid areas with high regulatory or mission-critical dependencies.
- **High Volume and Repetition**: AI learns best when patterns are clear and frequent.

- **Measurable Outcomes**: Choose something where value can be quantified—like faster resolution or improved classification accuracy.

Ideal First Use Cases:

- Ticket auto-categorization
- Predictive assignment to the right team
- Knowledge base article recommendation
- Sentiment detection in user feedback
- Virtual agent for password resets

Real-Life Example: Mid-Sized Financial Institution (ServiceNow)

A regional bank with 3000 employees began its AI journey with a small but impactful goal: auto-classifying incidents based on short descriptions using ServiceNow's predictive intelligence module. Their starting point was a dataset of 18 months of tickets. Instead of involving all categories, they focused on just five high-volume service lines—email, VPN, printer, laptop, and software access.

Initial skepticism from the service desk team was addressed by making AI suggestions "advisory only" during phase one. Within six weeks, the AI model achieved 87% accuracy, and triage time dropped by 34%. This early win gave stakeholders the confidence to approve the next phase: integrating the classifier into routing logic and expanding it to other categories.

Framework for Responsible Scaling

Once the first AI use case has proven its value, the natural temptation is to scale quickly. But scaling AI in ITSM is not about adding more tools or automating everything overnight—it's about growing with intention, structure, and sustainability. That's where a framework for responsible scaling comes in. It provides a clear, phased approach to help organizations move from experimentation to enterprise-wide adoption without losing control, quality, or user trust.

The journey typically begins with a tightly scoped pilot—a single use case deployed in a controlled environment to test feasibility and gather insights. Once this proves successful, the next step is to learn and iterate—refining the model, improving data quality, addressing feedback, and ensuring the process adds real value. These insights inform the horizontal expansion, where the AI capability is extended to similar or adjacent use cases, such as applying classification AI from incidents to service requests.

As confidence and maturity grow, the focus shifts to deepening integration. AI moves from being a stand-alone feature to becoming embedded in workflows, CMDBs, chatbots, and AIOps platforms—enhancing automation and decision-making across the service value chain. The final stage is institutionalization, where AI is no longer a project but a core capability. Governance, ownership, performance metrics, and continual learning are formalized, ensuring AI evolves with the organization's needs.

Responsible scaling means not rushing the process, but expanding intelligently, guided by outcomes, feedback, and readiness. It ensures that AI remains aligned with the business, earns user trust at every stage, and delivers consistent value—without disruption or surprise.

Once a small AI initiative proves successful, scaling should be strategic and structured, not reactive. Responsible scaling follows five key stages as listed in the following table:

Stage	Focus	Action
1. Pilot	Experimentation	Select 1–2 low-risk use cases, monitor outcomes
2. Learn and Iterate	Process refinement	Gather feedback, retrain models, improve data quality
3. Expand Horizontally	More use cases	Extend AI to adjacent areas (for example, requests → incidents)
4. Deepen Integration	Embed AI into workflows	Link AI with automation, CMDB, and AIOps
5. Institutionalize	Enterprise scale	Define governance, performance metrics, and ownership

Table 10.5: *Key Stages*

Guardrails for Responsible AI Scaling

As organizations move beyond pilot projects and begin to scale AI across their ITSM landscape, maintaining control becomes just as important as driving innovation. This is where guardrails for responsible AI scaling come into play. These are not barriers—they're safeguards that ensure AI adoption is ethical, transparent, and sustainable. Without these checks in place, scaling can quickly lead to unintended consequences, such as biased decisions, broken trust, or loss of accountability.

One of the most essential guardrails is keeping a human-in-the-loop, especially in early stages. AI can assist and accelerate decisions, but final approvals or actions—particularly in change enablement, escalations, or customer-facing interactions—should remain with people. Another key safeguard is continuous monitoring of model performance. AI is not set-and-forget; models drift, data changes, and new patterns emerge. Regular audits and performance reviews ensure that AI remains accurate and aligned with business intent.

Bias is another area that demands attention. AI learns from historical data–and if that data is skewed or incomplete, the model can replicate past mistakes. Guardrails must include bias detection and correction mechanisms, especially in areas such as prioritization or resource assignment. Additionally, transparency and explainability are critical. Users need to understand why AI is recommending a particular action or classification. This builds trust and encourages adoption.

Other guardrails include audit trails, so that all AI-driven actions are traceable; feedback loops, so humans can override or validate AI decisions; and clear KPIs that tie AI performance to actual service outcomes, not just technical benchmarks.

In short, these guardrails act like the lines on a road–they do not restrict your journey, but keep it safe, ethical, and aligned with your destination. As AI scales across your ITSM ecosystem, these safeguards will ensure it does so with confidence, accountability, and lasting value.

As AI grows in scope, so does the responsibility. Scaling should be accompanied by controls that ensure fairness, transparency, and sustainability.

Key Guardrails:

- Human-in-the-loop design, especially in early phases
- Bias checks and continuous monitoring of model accuracy
- Audit trails to track decisions made by AI
- Feedback loops so users can correct or validate AI actions
- KPIs aligned to business outcomes, not just technical performance

Building Trust through Incremental Wins

Scaling responsibly is as much about building trust as it is about expanding capability. When service desk agents see AI triaging tickets correctly, or managers see trend predictions validated by reality, confidence builds naturally. These early successes become internal case studies, helping overcome resistance and generate buy-in across departments.

Example: A public transportation agency piloted an AI assistant to recommend KB articles during ticket logging. Initially, agents ignored the suggestions. But after internal reporting showed that AI-backed resolutions had a 15% higher first-time fix rate, adoption surged–and the assistant was promoted from optional to embedded.

The following table presents a sample "Start Small, Scale Smart" Checklist:

Readiness Indicator	**Status**
First use case selected based on impact and feasibility	✅ / ❌
Baseline data prepared and verified for quality	✅ / ❌
Pilot team trained and engaged	✅ / ❌
Initial KPIs defined (accuracy, speed, adoption rate)	✅ / ❌
Feedback loop in place	✅ / ❌
Scaling roadmap with phased milestones created	✅ / ❌

Table 10.6: *"Start Small, Scale Smart" Checklist*

In AI adoption, small wins pave the way for big breakthroughs. Starting small allows you to test hypotheses, fine-tune models, and align people and processes without overwhelming your system or staff. Scaling responsibly ensures that as AI becomes embedded into the fabric of ITSM, it enhances trust, transparency, and measurable value. This phased approach not only reduces risk but maximizes learning–and that's what makes AI adoption both strategic and sustainable.

Conclusion

As organizations stand on the cusp of AI-powered transformation in ITSM, it becomes clear that success isn't determined by ambition alone–it is rooted in preparedness. This chapter has illustrated that **getting ready for AI** means much more than selecting a vendor or enabling a feature. It is a holistic journey of aligning strategy, technology, people, and culture to build a strong, sustainable foundation. From assessing readiness across core dimensions such as data, tooling, skills, and culture, to identifying low-risk, high-impact starting points, we have seen how structured planning turns possibility into progress.

AI is not a magic wand; it thrives only in environments where processes are consistent, data is trustworthy, teams are skilled, and innovation is embraced. By starting small, organizations can mitigate risks, build confidence, and deliver visible results that earn stakeholder buy-in. And as these early successes compound, AI can be scaled with responsibility–guided by frameworks, feedback loops, and ethical guardrails that ensure it stays aligned with business value.

The message is clear: **AI in ITSM is not a destination–it is an evolving capability** that must be nurtured. With the right assessment, clear priorities, and a mindset of continual improvement, organizations can unlock AI's full potential to enhance service delivery, elevate customer experience, and strengthen their digital future. Let readiness be your launchpad–not your limitation.

In the next chapter, we will discuss about how to manage AI responsibility by addressing data privacy, algorithmic bias, and compliance concerns.

Multiple Choice Questions

1. What is the primary purpose of conducting an AI-readiness assessment in ITSM?
   a. To implement AI tools without delay
   b. To outsource service management processes
   c. To evaluate organizational preparedness across key enablers
   d. To select a cloud service provider for AI hosting
2. Which of the following is a red flag in assessing data readiness for AI adoption?
   a. Integration with CMDB and monitoring tools
   b. Availability of 18 months of historical ticket data
   c. Use of consistent categorization fields
   d. High volume of free-text-only fields
3. What makes a use case ideal for starting small with AI in ITSM?
   a. High regulatory complexity and financial impact
   b. Rare occurrence and unique service patterns
   c. Low complexity, high repetition, and measurable outcomes
   d. Involves executive-level decision making
4. What is one of the key guardrails to ensure responsible scaling of AI in ITSM?
   a. Avoiding human involvement at all stages
   b. Ignoring feedback to preserve model accuracy
   c. Implementing audit trails and human-in-the-loop oversight
   d. Focusing solely on technical KPIs
5. Which of the following reflects a culturally ready organization for AI adoption?
   a. Strict reliance on legacy workflows
   b. Fear among staff about automation replacing their jobs

c. Top-down support for AI experimentation and learning

d. Lack of communication between IT and business teams

Answers

1. c
2. d
3. c
4. c
5. c

Questions

1. Explain the significance of conducting an AI-readiness assessment before implementing AI in ITSM.
2. Describe the six core dimensions of AI readiness and how each one contributes to successful AI adoption.
3. How does cultural readiness influence the success or failure of AI initiatives in ITSM environments?
4. Discuss why data quality and availability are considered foundational to AI integration in ITSM.
5. What are the common red flags that indicate an organization is not yet ready for AI adoption?
6. Outline the characteristics of an ideal first use case for starting small with AI in ITSM.
7. What are the five stages of the framework for responsible AI scaling, and how does each stage support sustainable growth?
8. Explain the importance of building a future-ready workforce and how it impacts AI deployment.
9. What guardrails should organizations put in place to ensure that AI scaling remains ethical, accurate, and transparent?
10. How does starting small with AI help organizations build trust and accelerate enterprise-wide adoption?

Key Terms

- **AI-Readiness Assessment:** A structured evaluation of an organization's preparedness to adopt AI, covering aspects such as data, processes, tools, skills, and culture. It helps identify gaps, mitigate risks, and establish a realistic roadmap for responsible AI adoption.
- **Process Standardization:** The practice of defining and enforcing consistent workflows in ITSM processes such as incident, request, and change management. Standardization enables AI to detect patterns, make accurate predictions, and automate decisions effectively.
- **Data Hygiene:** The process of cleaning, structuring, and validating ITSM data to ensure accuracy and completeness. Good data hygiene is essential for training reliable AI models and generating meaningful insights.
- **Cultural Readiness:** An organization's openness to change, experimentation, and AI-augmented decision-making across teams. It influences how successfully AI is adopted and whether it is embraced as a value enabler or resisted.
- **Tooling Infrastructure:** The ecosystem of ITSM tools, APIs, integrations, and platforms that support AI functionality. An AI-ready infrastructure enables seamless data flow, intelligent automation, and scalable deployment.
- **Start Small Strategy:** A phased approach to AI adoption that begins with low-risk, high-value use cases. It helps build internal confidence, validate assumptions, and reduce resistance to broader implementation.
- **Human-in-the-Loop:** An AI design principle where human oversight is maintained, especially in critical decisions. It ensures accountability, trust, and ethical alignment in AI-driven ITSM processes.
- **AI Scaling Framework:** A structured model outlining stages involving pilot, iterate, expand, integrate, and institutionalize AI. This framework ensures AI growth is controlled, sustainable, and aligned with strategic goals.
- **Guardrails for Responsible Scaling:** Policies, practices, and controls that ensure AI adoption remains ethical, auditable, and effective. Examples include bias detection, audit trails, feedback loops, and outcome-driven KPIs.
- **Use Case Selection:** The process of identifying suitable ITSM functions for initial AI deployment. Ideal use cases are low in complexity, high in volume, and produce measurable business outcomes.

CHAPTER 11
Governance, Risk, and Ethics in AI-powered ITSM

Introduction

As organizations embrace AI to power smarter, faster, and more efficient IT service management, a new set of responsibilities emerges. AI is not just a tool—it is a powerful force that can influence decisions, automate actions, and shape user experiences in profound ways. With great potential comes equally significant risk, especially when it comes to trust, accountability, and transparency. Whether it is a chatbot handling user requests or an algorithm predicting incident patterns, every AI-driven function must be governed with care. Ethical considerations such as fairness, data privacy, algorithmic bias, and explainability can no longer be afterthoughts—they must be built into the foundation. This is particularly important in IT environments where AI systems may act on sensitive data or drive decisions that impact customers and business operations. Regulatory landscapes such as GDPR and emerging standards such as ISO/IEC 42001 (first international management system standard for Artificial Intelligence) are making it clear: compliance is not optional. ITIL4's governance and risk principles provide a strong foundation to align AI adoption with organizational values and controls. In this chapter, we explore how to strike the right balance between innovation and responsibility. By managing AI with intention, organizations can unlock its full potential—without compromising on ethics, security, or trust.

Structure

In this chapter, we will discuss the following topics:

- Ensuring Transparency, Explainability, and Fairness
- Data Privacy and Compliance (GDPR, ISO 42001, and so on)
- Aligning with Organizational Risk Frameworks

Ensuring Transparency, Explainability, and Fairness

In AI-powered ITSM, the benefits of automation, speed, and predictive intelligence can only be fully realized if users and stakeholders **trust** the system. That trust is built not just on outcomes but on **how** those outcomes are generated. This is where **transparency**, **explainability**, and **fairness** become non-negotiable pillars of ethical AI use.

How These Principles Define Responsible AI Implementation in ITSM

In the context of AI-powered ITSM, principles such as transparency, explainability, and fairness are critical to maintaining trust and control. Transparency ensures that stakeholders can see into the "black box" of AI and understand what data it uses and how decisions are made. Explainability goes a step further, enabling IT teams to trace the reasoning behind AI-driven actions–such as why an incident was prioritized as critical or a change flagged as high-risk. Fairness ensures that AI treats all users and scenarios consistently, avoiding unintended bias based on historical data or incomplete context. In service environments where timely and equitable decision-making is paramount, these principles act as safeguards, ensuring that automation supports–not undermines–user satisfaction, compliance, and operational excellence.

The following table lists the principles with the definition and relevance to ITSM:

Principle	Definition	Relevance to ITSM
Transparency	Making AI systems understandable to users and stakeholders	Helps IT teams know how decisions (example, ticket routing or risk scores) are made
Explainability	Ability to articulate why an AI model made a specific recommendation	Enables review, audit, and troubleshooting of AI-driven processes

Fairness	Ensuring decisions are unbiased, consistent, and equitable	Prevents service discrimination and ensures equitable ticket handling

Table 11.1: *List of Principles*

How These Principles Matter in ITSM

In IT service management, decisions driven by AI–such as ticket prioritization, routing, or change risk scoring–can have immediate and tangible impacts on users, teams, and business operations. Without the guiding principles of transparency, explainability, and fairness, these AI-driven decisions can feel arbitrary or even unjust, eroding user trust and causing resistance among service desk agents. Imagine a scenario where a VIP user's issue is delayed because the system misclassified it, and no one understands why–that's a governance failure, not just a technical glitch. Fairness ensures that no user segment is systematically disadvantaged, while transparency and explainability allow IT teams to validate, audit, and continuously improve AI behavior. These principles also serve as a compliance function, especially in regulated industries where decisions must be justified and documented. Most importantly, they humanize the role of AI in ITSM–ensuring it is not just accurate and efficient, but also ethical and accountable.

It is important to remember the following points:

- ITSM often involves decisions that impact users directly–such as how quickly an incident is prioritized, who handles it, or whether it escalates.
- Without clear explanations, users and service desk agents may feel AI systems are **opaque**, even when outcomes are beneficial.
- Without fairness, **bias in training data** (for example, location, language, device type) can cause systematic disadvantages for certain user groups.

The GenAI Challenge: Managing Hallucinations and Inaccuracy

As Generative AI finds its place in ITSM–powering virtual assistants, drafting knowledge base articles, or summarizing incidents–it brings remarkable efficiency, but also a new class of risks. One of the most pressing concerns is **hallucination**, where the AI confidently generates information that sounds correct but is factually inaccurate or outdated. In high-stakes environments like ITSM, even a small error–such as recommending the wrong configuration step or citing a non-existent solution–can lead to service disruption, wasted effort, or even breaches of compliance. This challenge is amplified when GenAI tools are integrated into self-service portals or decision support systems without proper controls. Ensuring **factual accuracy**, especially in technical domains, requires more than just training large language models—it demands real-time access to verified knowledge, clearly defined domain boundaries, and human oversight. Organizations must implement safeguards such as confidence scoring, source validation, and human-in-the-loop reviews to keep AI-generated content reliable. Left unchecked, hallucinations can undermine trust, confuse users, and erode the very value AI was meant to deliver. The key is not to fear GenAI, but to manage it responsibly—so that its creativity serves the service, not compromises it.

Generative AI tools such as ChatGPT, when embedded in ITSM workflows (for example, as virtual assistants or knowledge base authors), may **hallucinate**—that is, generate **plausible but factually incorrect** responses.

Real-Life Example: A virtual agent integrated with a knowledge base provides a resolution for a recurring VPN issue. Due to outdated training data, it confidently suggests a deprecated registry setting that **breaks connectivity** for remote users.

Mitigation Strategy:

- Implement **human-in-the-loop validation** for auto-generated KB articles or critical resolutions.
- Flag AI responses with confidence levels or source citations.
- Enforce **restricted domains** for GenAI to reduce speculative output (for example, only drawing from vetted internal documentation).

Use Case: Transparent Auto-Triage System

An IT organization implements an AI-based ticket triaging model that prioritizes tickets based on keywords, impact tags, and past resolution times. Initially, users and agents noticed inconsistent priority levels. A post-deployment review shows the model over-prioritizes certain software systems based on biased historical tagging.

Actions Taken:

- The model is retrained using balanced datasets that reflect current SLAs and incident patterns.
- An **explanation layer** is added—when a ticket is prioritized, the system shows which inputs influenced the decision.
- Stakeholders now **trust the model more** because they can understand *why* it acted the way it did.

Frameworks and Best Practices

To ensure ethical, reliability, and accountable use of AI in ITSM, organizations must embed robust governance frameworks and best practices into their AI adoption journey. This begins with **data governance**, ensuring that training data is diverse, up-to-date, and free from systemic bias that could skew AI behavior. Models should be accompanied by clear **documentation**–not just of how they work, but also when and why they were updated. Establishing **ethics review boards** or cross-functional oversight groups can provide valuable checkpoints before deploying AI into production environments. **User feedback loops** are equally critical, allowing agents and end-users to rate AI decisions or flag inaccuracies for review, thus fostering a culture of transparency and continuous learning. To meet regulatory and audit requirements, **decision logs and explainability tools** should be in place to trace AI actions and justify outcomes. Tools such as Explainable AI (XAI) platforms, confidence scoring engines, and version-controlled KB integration offer practical ways to operationalize these safeguards. Ultimately, frameworks and best practices serve as the guardrails that enable innovation to move fast without breaking trust. They create a structured foundation where AI can thrive–aligned with business objectives, regulatory standards, and ethical expectations.

The following table describes the possible recommendations:

Control Area	Recommendation
Data Governance	Use diverse, clean, and updated datasets to minimize historical bias
Model Documentation	Keep logs of model decisions, updates, and rationales
Ethics Review Boards	Establish an internal review mechanism for AI deployments
User Feedback Loops	Allow agents and users to rate or challenge AI decisions
Auditability	Retain logs of automated decisions for retrospective validation

***Table 11.2**: Recommendations for Control Areas*

Technology Enablers

While principles and frameworks define the *why* of responsible AI, technology enablers provide the *how*. A new generation of tools is emerging to support transparency, explainability, and fairness in AI-powered ITSM. **Explainable AI (XAI)** platforms–such as IBM Watson OpenScale, Google's What-If Tool, and Microsoft InterpretML–allow IT teams to visualize how models make decisions, offering clarity in scenarios involving ticket prioritization or change risk scoring. **Confidence scoring APIs** are another critical enabler, especially for GenAI applications, flagging low-certainty responses, and prompting human intervention before flawed advice reaches the user. **Audit trail mechanisms** embedded in platforms such as ServiceNow and Jira ensure that every automated action–whether classification, triage, or recommendation–is traceable for review and compliance. Additionally, **domain-restricted AI models** trained on curated internal knowledge reduce hallucinations by confining responses to trusted data. These tools don't just make AI smarter–they make it safer, more accountable, and easier to govern. By choosing the right enablers, organizations can harness the power of AI while preserving control, clarity, and user trust in every interaction.

The prominent enablers are as follows:

- **XAI (Explainable AI)** tools such as IBM Watson OpenScale or Google's What-If Tool can be integrated into platforms like ServiceNow to visualize decision logic.
- **Confidence Scoring APIs** help filter low-certainty outputs from GenAI models in virtual agents or KB generators.

Transparency, explainability, and fairness are not optional in AI-powered ITSM–they are the foundation for **trustworthy and responsible service automation**. As organizations scale their AI use, managing hallucinations, ensuring accuracy, and making models auditable will be key to maintaining control. Ethical ITSM is not about restricting AI but about **governing it with foresight, integrity, and clarity**.

Data Privacy and Compliance (GDPR, ISO 42001, and more)

In the era of AI-powered ITSM, data is both the engine and the risk surface. While AI thrives on large volumes of structured and unstructured service data–tickets, logs, chats, metrics–it also introduces complex challenges around **privacy, consent, and compliance**. The more intelligent our systems become, the more critical it is to understand **how they use data**, **where they get it from**, and **what safeguards are in place**. Laws like the **General Data Protection Regulation (GDPR)** in the EU, and new standards such as **ISO/IEC 42001** for AI management, are reshaping what ethical and compliant AI looks like in IT operations. In this chapter, we explore the obligations, best practices, and real-world applications of data privacy and compliance in AI-augmented ITSM environments.

Understanding GDPR: It is More Than Consent

The **General Data Protection Regulation (GDPR)** is one of the most comprehensive data privacy laws in the world. It empowers individuals with rights over their personal data and imposes strict obligations on organizations that process such data–including in AI systems.

Key GDPR Principles Relevant to ITSM AI:

- **Lawfulness, Fairness, and Transparency**: Users must know if their data is used to train or inform AI models.
- **Purpose Limitation**: Data collected for one purpose (for example, resolving a ticket) can't be reused for another (for example, training AI) without consent.
- **Data Minimization**: Only the necessary amount of data should be used.
- **Right to Explanation**: If AI makes a decision that affects a person (for example, escalation, denial of service), they have a right to understand how.

Real-Life Example: A global IT service provider implemented an AI chatbot that automatically classified user requests and offered solutions. However, it logged sensitive user input (including employee IDs and HR complaints) without redaction. Following an internal audit prompted by GDPR concerns, the firm had to anonymize logs, retrain models, and revise its data handling policy to ensure compliance.

ISO/IEC 42001: The First International AI Management Standard

ISO/IEC 42001, published in late 2023, is the **first international standard for managing AI systems**. Unlike GDPR, which is a legal framework, ISO 42001 offers a **voluntary, certifiable framework** for organizations to **govern their AI responsibly**.

Core Focus Areas are as follows:

- **AI Governance Structures**: Policies and procedures to manage risks across the AI lifecycle.
- **Accountability and Role Definition**: Clearly identifying who is responsible for what in the AI pipeline.
- **Data Quality and Integrity**: Ensuring that AI decisions are based on accurate, unbiased, and current data.
- **Monitoring and Auditing AI Behavior**: Tracking how AI performs over time, including any ethical or performance drift.

Use Case: A Middle Eastern telecom provider used ISO 42001 guidelines to build a governance layer for its AI-based fault detection engine. It established a formal committee to review training data sources, regularly audited AI decisions against KPIs, and created internal redress mechanisms for service desk personnel to challenge faulty recommendations.

Addressing Personally Identifiable Information (PII) in AI Workflows

In AI-powered ITSM, **PII can be unintentionally exposed** in chat logs, ticket notes, KB articles, or monitoring alerts. Protecting this data is not only a legal requirement but a reputational imperative.

Imagine a scenario where a GenAI tool is used to summarize ticket conversations for reporting. If not properly configured, it might include user phone numbers, internal system credentials, or personal grievances in its summaries–violating privacy laws and user trust.

Mitigation Techniques:

- **PII masking or redaction** before ingestion into AI systems
- **Role-based access controls** for viewing AI-generated insights
- **Differential privacy** and data obfuscation techniques during training
- **Audit logging** to track where PII may have been exposed or processed

Cross-Border Data Processing: Navigating Jurisdictional Complexity

Many AI models are hosted in the cloud or by third-party vendors–raising issues about **data sovereignty**. Under GDPR and similar laws, data of EU citizens cannot be freely transferred outside the EU without adequate protection.

Let us consider the following scenario:

An Indian managed service provider uses a U.S.-hosted AI service to analyze service desk trends for a European client. Without proper data processing agreements and safeguards (such as, Standard Contractual Clauses or Binding Corporate Rules), they risk non-compliance and heavy penalties.

Compliance Best Practices:

- Choose **cloud vendors with data centers in compliant jurisdictions.**
- Use **data anonymization** before transferring logs or service records.
- **Review Data Protection Impact Assessments (DPIAs)** for AI tools handling sensitive data.

Transparency, Consent, and User Communication

AI's use in ITSM is not always obvious to users. Virtual agents, predictive suggestions, and automated triage decisions must be clearly communicated.

Ethical Recommendations:

- Always disclose when AI is involved in service decisions.
- Provide opt-outs for non-critical AI-generated suggestions.
- Offer **simple language policies** explaining how user data may be used to improve systems.

Governance Integration with ITIL4

ITIL4 emphasizes **governance as a core component** of the Service Value System (SVS). AI governance should be **integrated into existing ITSM governance frameworks**, not treated as an external compliance function.

The following table lists the examples of AI privacy integration for ITIL4 Governance area:

ITIL4 Governance Area	AI Privacy Integration Example
Risk Management	AI risk registers, DPIAs, and bias audits
Governance Bodies	AI ethics councils and review boards
Policies and Controls	Data usage, logging, and consent policies for AI systems
Continual Improvement	AI performance and compliance reviews tied to CSI cycles

Table 11.3: *AI Privacy Integration Example for Different ITIL4 Governance Area*

Future Outlook: Evolving Laws and Adaptive AI Governance

The legal and ethical landscape for AI is evolving rapidly. From **India's Digital Personal Data Protection Act (DPDP)** to California's CPRA and the upcoming **EU AI Act**, the regulatory net is expanding. The expectation is shifting toward **proactive governance**, not reactive defense.

Strategic Guidance:

- Stay updated on global regulations
- Design AI systems with **privacy by design and by default**

- Encourage a culture of **AI ethics awareness** across service teams

The following table can be used as a guiding checklist for AI-powered ITSM data privacy and compliance checklist:

AI-Powered ITSM Data Privacy and Compliance Checklist

1. **Data Governance**
   - ☐ Identify and classify all personal data used in AI workflows
   - ☐ Ensure data is collected for a specific purpose and used accordingly
   - ☐ Minimize data collection–only gather what is necessary
   - ☐ Regularly clean and update training datasets to ensure accuracy and relevance
2. **AI Transparency and Consent**
   - ☐ Inform users when AI is involved in decision-making (e.g., triage, recommendations)
   - ☐ Provide simple explanations of how their data is used
   - ☐ Allow users to opt out of non-critical AI features where applicable
3. **Regulatory Compliance (GDPR, ISO 42001, and more)**
   - ☐ Conduct a Data Protection Impact Assessment (DPIA) for AI implementations
   - ☐ Mask or anonymize personally identifiable information (PII) during training and inference
   - ☐ Establish lawful data processing agreements with third-party AI or cloud vendors
   - ☐ Ensure cross-border data transfers comply with local and international regulations
4. **Auditability and Explainability**
   - ☐ Implement logging of AI decisions for audit and review
   - ☐ Use tools that support Explainable AI (XAI) for visibility into model behavior
   - ☐ Maintain documentation for training data sources, model updates, and decision logic
5. **Ethical AI Operations**
   - ☐ Create internal AI ethics or review boards for oversight
   - ☐ Establish redress mechanisms for users or agents to challenge AI-generated outputs
   - ☐ Regularly test for bias, drift, and hallucinations in AI models

- ☐ Score AI outputs for confidence and route low-certainty cases for human review

6. **Align with Governance Frameworks**
   - ☐ Integrate AI risk management into existing ITIL4 governance processes
   - ☐ Define roles and responsibilities for AI accountability
   - ☐ Tie AI performance, privacy, and compliance metrics to continual improvement (CSI) cycles

Table 11.4: *AI-Powered ITSM Data Privacy and Compliance Checklist*

Privacy and compliance are not blockers to AI adoption; they are **accelerators of trust and long-term success**. In ITSM, where personal data and automated decisions are tightly woven together, safeguarding that data and being accountable for how it's used is the only sustainable path forward. Whether you adopt GDPR-compliant workflows, implement ISO 42001 standards, or build AI policies aligned with ITIL4 governance, the message is clear: **responsible AI is good ITSM.**

Aligning with Organizational Risk Frameworks

As AI becomes deeply integrated into ITSM, it introduces a unique risk profile–ranging from data breaches and compliance violations to biased decisions and operational disruptions. These risks don't exist in isolation; they touch every part of the enterprise, from customer experience and legal exposure to brand reputation. That's why managing AI risk effectively means aligning it with the broader organizational risk management frameworks. It is not enough for service teams to manage AI risk in silos; instead, AI governance must be woven into the fabric of the Enterprise Risk Management (ERM) strategy.

Understanding Organizational Risk Frameworks

Most large enterprises follow formalized frameworks to identify, assess, monitor, and mitigate risks. These could be based on:

- **ISO 31000 – Risk Management Principles and Guidelines**

  ISO 31000 is an international standard that provides guidelines for effective risk management in any type of organization–whether public, private, or non-profit. It helps organizations identify potential risks, assess their impact, and put controls in place to manage them. The core idea is to make risk management a structured, repeatable, and integral part of decision-making–not just something you do during a crisis. ISO 31000 doesn't prescribe specific risks or solutions; instead, it gives a flexible framework that organizations can adapt based on their size, industry, and goals. In the context of AI-powered ITSM, ISO 31000 helps ensure that AI-related risks–such as data misuse, automation failures, or ethical concerns–are recognized, owned, and managed responsibly across the organization.

- **COSO ERM Framework - Enterprise Risk Management integrated with strategy and performance**

  The COSO ERM Framework (Enterprise Risk Management) is a widely accepted model that helps organizations manage risks in a strategic, structured, and integrated way. Developed by the Committee of Sponsoring Organizations of the Treadway Commission (COSO), it goes beyond just avoiding problems–it helps organizations understand how risk affects their ability to achieve goals. The framework encourages aligning risk management with business strategy, performance, and decision-making. It consists of key components including risk identification, assessment, response, monitoring, and strong governance and culture. In AI-powered ITSM, COSO ERM helps ensure that AI risks–like automation errors or bias–are viewed not just as technical issues, but as potential business risks that must be managed alongside financial, legal, and reputational risks.

- **COBIT 2019 - Specifically aligns IT risk with business goals**

  COBIT 2019 is a globally recognized framework designed to help organizations govern and manage their IT effectively. It stands for Control Objectives for Information and Related Technologies and provides principles, processes, and tools to align IT operations with business goals. Unlike frameworks that focus only on technology or service delivery, COBIT 2019 bridges the gap between business governance and IT management, ensuring that IT investments deliver value and risks are properly controlled. It includes clear roles, responsibilities, and performance metrics, making it especially useful in regulated or audit-sensitive environments. In the context of AI-powered ITSM, COBIT 2019 can help organizations govern AI use responsibly, integrate risk management, and ensure compliance with internal and external standards.

- **NIST Risk Management Framework (RMF) - Primarily used in government and regulated sectors**

  The NIST Risk Management Framework (RMF) is a structured approach developed by the National Institute of Standards and Technology (NIST) in the United States to help organizations identify, assess, and manage cybersecurity risks. It is especially used by government agencies and organizations in highly regulated industries. The RMF outlines a step-by-step process–from categorizing systems and selecting security controls to monitoring and continuously improving them. It emphasizes security, compliance, and risk awareness throughout the system's life cycle. For AI in ITSM, the NIST RMF helps ensure that AI-enabled systems are not only effective but also secure, trustworthy, and aligned with organizational risk management and regulatory requirements.

These frameworks emphasize a centralized view of risk–financial, operational, reputational, regulatory–and promote controls, accountability, and escalation paths.

Mapping AI Risks in ITSM to Enterprise Risk Domains

As organizations embed AI deeper into their ITSM workflows–from incident triage and chatbots to predictive analytics–they often focus on technical performance while overlooking the broader risk implications. Yet, each AI capability introduces potential vulnerabilities that align with core enterprise risk categories. For instance, when a generative AI tool provides incorrect remediation steps, it is not just a technical error–it is an operational risk that can disrupt service delivery. If personal data is used in training without consent, it becomes a compliance and legal risk, potentially violating regulations like GDPR. Unfair or biased ticket prioritization by an AI engine could escalate into a reputational or ethical risk, damaging stakeholder trust. When AI systems operate without clear oversight or logging, they create governance risks, making it difficult to audit or validate decisions. Even over-reliance on automation without fallback mechanisms introduces strategic risk, as service continuity becomes fragile. By recognizing and classifying these AI-specific risks within established enterprise risk domains, organizations can bring AI governance into their existing risk registers–ensuring AI is not just powerful, but also predictable and accountable.

AI introduces several new and amplified risks in the context of IT service management:

AI Risk in ITSM	Enterprise Risk Category
Model hallucinations, wrong decisions	Operational/Service Delivery Risk
Use of personal data in training sets	Legal/Compliance Risk
Bias in decision outcomes	Reputational/Ethical Risk
Lack of auditability	Governance/Internal Control Risk
Dependency on AI systems	Strategic/Continuity Risk

Table 11.5: *List of Risks in the Context of ITSM*

Let us consider the following real-life use case.

A Fortune 500 manufacturing firm deployed a GenAI-based virtual assistant to handle

L1 support tickets. While it dramatically reduced resolution times, it occasionally provided incorrect troubleshooting steps. This led to outages on production lines and raised concerns at the board level. The firm had to escalate the issue to its enterprise risk committee, which mandated stricter controls, monitoring, and AI governance alignment with its ISO 31000-based risk strategy.

Embedding AI Risk into Existing Risk Registers

To manage AI responsibly within ITSM, it is essential to move beyond ad hoc monitoring and formally embed AI-related risks into the organization's existing risk register. This means identifying where AI is used—such as in ticket classification, chatbots, or change risk scoring—and clearly documenting the specific risks it introduces. Each risk should be described in practical terms (for example, "AI misclassification may delay high-priority incidents"), evaluated for its likelihood and impact, and assigned an owner accountable for mitigation. Aligning AI risks with standard categories used across the enterprise allows them to be tracked, escalated, and reviewed alongside financial, operational, and regulatory risks. It also ensures that controls—such as redaction tools, human-in-the-loop workflows, and model monitoring—are not just implemented, but recognized as part of the formal governance landscape. By treating AI like any other strategic asset—with inherent risks and required oversight—organizations can ensure visibility, promote cross-functional collaboration, and elevate AI risk to the same level of seriousness as cybersecurity or data privacy. This integration transforms AI from a technological experiment into a governed, measurable component of enterprise resilience.

For effective alignment, AI-related risks must be:

- Identified and described clearly (for example, "Chatbot may expose sensitive customer data due to poor filtering")
- Rated based on impact and likelihood (for example, using heat maps or risk matrices)
- Linked to existing risk controls (for example, access control policies, change management reviews)
- Monitored with metrics (for example, AI error rates, model drift indicators, incident escalation trends)

This helps ensure that AI is not treated as a black box but as a visible and accountable component of enterprise operations.

Aligning Roles and Responsibilities

As AI becomes an integral part of ITSM operations, managing its risks and rewards cannot be left to technologists alone. Successful and responsible use of AI demands clear alignment of roles and responsibilities across the organization. While service owners and platform administrators may oversee implementation, risk management must be a shared effort involving data protection officers, enterprise risk managers, service desk leads, and internal auditors. Each has a vital part to play–whether it is ensuring compliance with data privacy laws, monitoring the behavior of AI models in production, or providing feedback loops from frontline service agents. Without this cross-functional clarity, gaps emerge as issues go unreported, risks are not escalated, and accountability becomes diffused. For example, if a predictive AI model starts consistently under-prioritizing certain types of incidents, who investigates–the data scientist, the ITSM lead, or the risk officer? To prevent ambiguity, organizations must assign specific ownership for AI performance, governance, compliance, and continuous improvement, aligned with existing ITIL4 and enterprise governance structures. This distributed yet coordinated model ensures that AI is not only delivering value but is also monitored, governed, and improved by the right people at the right levels.

Risk management is not just the job of the CISO or Risk Officer. In an AI-powered ITSM landscape, multiple stakeholders must own parts of the risk lifecycle:

Role	**Responsibility**
AI/ITSM Product Owner	Identify risks in AI implementation, escalate issues early
Service Desk Manager	Monitor AI performance and collect agent feedback on issues
Data Protection Officer	Ensure AI systems comply with data privacy policies and regulations
Enterprise Risk Manager	Integrate AI risks into the broader ERM strategy
Internal Audit	Review controls over AI models, decisions, and logging

Table 11.6: *Roles and Responsibilities*

Let us consider the following scenario.

An ITSM team at a healthcare organization using predictive AI for incident classification had no formal review mechanism. When the AI failed to escalate a critical EMR outage, auditors flagged this as a control gap. The organization responded by assigning clear responsibilities for monitoring, tuning, and validating AI models–aligning them under their ISO 27001 and COBIT governance structure.

Implementing Controls and Mitigations

Identifying AI risks is only the first step–implementing effective controls and mitigations is what turns awareness into action. In an AI-powered ITSM environment, these controls must span the entire lifecycle of AI deployment, from data ingestion to decision-making and user interaction. Preventive controls–such as anonymizing sensitive data, limiting access based on roles, or restricting model training to approved datasets–help reduce the chances of harm before it occurs. Detective controls, such as monitoring for model drift, analyzing false positive rates, or tracking user override frequency, help surface issues early. When things go wrong–as they inevitably will–corrective controls such as rollback mechanisms, human-in-the-loop escalation paths, and documented resolution procedures ensure that problems can be contained and learned from. For example, an AI model that begins misclassifying urgent incidents due to evolving ticket language can be flagged by an accuracy monitor and corrected through retraining. Importantly, these controls must not be ad hoc–they need to be codified into standard ITSM governance processes, subject to audit, and regularly reviewed for effectiveness. When controls are proactive, practical, and well-integrated, AI becomes not just a powerful tool, but a responsible and resilient part of the IT service ecosystem.

Once risks are identified, controls must be designed or adapted to address them:

- **Preventive Controls**: Data validation, RBAC on AI decisions, source-restricted training
- **Detective Controls:** AI drift detection, anomaly monitoring, audit logs
- **Corrective Controls:** Model rollback mechanisms, escalation paths, feedback loops

Controls should be testable, documented, and subject to periodic review as part of the organization's internal audit process.

Aligning with ITIL4 Governance Practices

As AI becomes embedded in ITSM workflows, aligning its governance with the principles of ITIL4 is not just ideal–it's essential. ITIL4 emphasizes governance as a core component of the Service Value System (SVS), ensuring that direction, oversight, and evaluation are applied consistently across all services. By integrating AI into this framework, organizations can manage it with the same rigor as other service components. This means AI-related risks, decisions, and performance should be reviewed by governance bodies, just like change approvals or service level breaches. Policies must be updated to explicitly cover AI use–defining acceptable models, data sources, escalation paths, and review cycles. For example, if an AI tool triages incidents, its logic and performance should be subject to regular evaluation, ideally as part of Continual Improvement. This alignment ensures that AI is not treated as a disconnected innovation, but rather as a governed capability–subject to strategic goals, risk appetite, and compliance requirements. By embedding AI within ITIL4's governance structure, organizations reinforce trust, transparency, and accountability in every AI-driven action taken within ITSM.

ITIL4 emphasizes a governance model within its Service Value System (SVS), which includes direction-setting, oversight, and evaluation. AI risk management can be embedded into:

- **Governance Bodies**: Ensure AI risk is a regular agenda item
- **Policies and Standards**: Include AI-specific risk clauses in ITSM policies
- **Continual Improvement**: Periodically assess AI governance effectiveness

Aligning with ITIL4 ensures traceability of decision-making and provides a platform for improvement, audit, and learning.

Reporting and Escalation

In AI-powered ITSM, effective reporting and escalation are critical to ensuring that risks, anomalies, and failures are not buried under the complexity of automation. AI decisions–especially those impacting service continuity, compliance, or user experience–must be made visible to the right stakeholders through structured reporting channels. Dashboards that track key AI metrics–such as model accuracy, false positives, escalation overrides, or hallucination rates–should be regularly reviewed by ITSM leads, risk managers, and governance bodies. When patterns emerge or thresholds are breached, there must be a clearly defined escalation path–from service desk supervisors to the enterprise risk committee, depending on severity. For instance, if a GenAI assistant begins generating inaccurate responses across multiple service areas, this must trigger an immediate escalation and investigation, not wait for user complaints to accumulate. These reporting mechanisms not only support real-time risk mitigation but also promote continuous learning and improvement, ensuring that AI systems evolve responsibly. Aligning AI insights with traditional ITSM reporting structures builds confidence across technical and non-technical stakeholders, reinforcing the message that AI is not an uncontrolled experiment–it's a monitored, governed component of strategic service delivery.

AI risks–especially those with high impact–must be visible at the right level of leadership. Risk dashboards and AI model performance metrics should be part of the monthly service reviews, steering committee meetings, and board risk reports. Use quantifiable KPIs, such as:

- % of AI-driven incidents that required human override
- % of GenAI outputs flagged for inaccuracy
- Average time to remediate AI errors

This creates organizational awareness and prevents risk from being hidden within technical silos.

Future Outlook: Toward Dynamic and Adaptive Risk Management

AI evolves rapidly as to your risk management approach. Static risk assessments are no longer sufficient. Enterprises are now moving toward continuous risk sensing, using AI to monitor AI–tracking model behavior, usage patterns, and compliance in real-time. Adaptive governance, backed by AI-native tooling and real-time alerts, will define the next generation of ITSM risk frameworks.

Aligning AI with organizational risk frameworks is not just about ticking compliance checkboxes–it's about safeguarding trust, performance, and resilience in an AI-driven service environment. By integrating AI risks into enterprise risk governance, assigning clear roles, implementing actionable controls, and reporting at the right level, organizations can ensure that AI remains an asset–not a liability. As AI continues to reshape ITSM, only a cohesive, enterprise-aligned risk posture can enable innovation with confidence

Conclusion

As artificial intelligence transforms the landscape of IT service management, it brings not only unprecedented efficiency but also significant ethical, regulatory, and operational responsibilities. This chapter has underscored a central truth: AI in ITSM is not merely a technological innovation–it is a governance imperative.

The integration of AI into incident management, change enablement, self-service portals, and analytics introduces new challenges around **transparency, explainability, fairness, and compliance**. These are not optional ideals but foundational pillars for building and maintaining **user trust and service accountability**. Whether an AI model is routing tickets, prioritizing changes, or generating knowledge articles, its actions must be traceable, justifiable, and free from bias.

Data privacy laws such as **GDPR** and emerging frameworks such as **ISO/IEC 42001** are making it clear that AI governance is now a matter of regulatory compliance, not just best practice. At the same time, traditional IT governance frameworks–**ITIL4, COBIT 2019, ISO 31000, COSO ERM, and NIST RMF**–must evolve to incorporate AI-specific risks and controls. By embedding AI risk into enterprise registers and assigning **clear roles and responsibilities**, organizations create the visibility and accountability necessary to govern AI at scale.

This chapter has also shown that ethical and effective AI is as much about culture as it is about controls. From implementing **feedback loops and redress mechanisms** to deploying **Explainable AI (XAI) tools**, organizations must foster an environment where AI decisions are monitored, challenged, and continuously improved. The future of ITSM belongs to those who can **balance innovation with integrity**, leveraging AI not only to accelerate operations but to elevate the standards of service excellence.

Thus, Responsible AI governance is not a roadblock to transformation—it is the pathway to **resilient, compliant, and human-centered service management**. Organizations that take a proactive stance in governing AI will not only minimize risk but also unlock AI's true value: **enhancing service outcomes while upholding trust, fairness, and accountability**.

In the next chapter, we will provide a strategic and tactical framework for adopting AI across ITSM.

Multiple Choice Questions

1. Which of the following principles helps ensure that AI decisions in ITSM can be audited and understood by stakeholders?
    a. Automation
    b. Explainability
    c. Speed
    d. Redundancy
2. What is one of the main risks associated with using Generative AI in ITSM workflows?
    a. Reduced ticket volume
    b. Human error
    c. Hallucinations or factually incorrect outputs
    d. Faster SLA breach detection
3. According to GDPR, which of the following is a key principle relevant to AI systems?
    a. AI models must self-learn without human input.
    b. All personal data must be publicly disclosed.
    c. Data should only be used for its original intended purpose.
    d. AI decisions should always be automated.

4. What framework provides a certifiable structure for managing AI governance within organizations?

    a. ISO/IEC 42001

    b. COBIT 5

    c. NIST 800-53

    d. ITIL V3

5. In the context of ITIL4 governance integration, which activity ensures continuous evaluation of AI performance and compliance?

    a. Service Level Management

    b. Incident Logging

    c. Continual Service Improvement (CSI)

    d. Change Authorization

Answers

1. b
2. c
3. c
4. a
5. c

Questions

1. What roles do transparency, explainability, and fairness play in building trust in AI-powered ITSM solutions?
2. How can organizations mitigate the risks of hallucinations in generative AI systems used in ITSM environments?
3. Explain how the principles of GDPR apply to AI systems integrated into ITSM workflows.
4. Describe the significance of ISO/IEC 42001 in the governance of AI systems within IT operations.
5. How can organizations align AI risks with existing enterprise risk frameworks such as ISO 31000, COSO ERM, or COBIT 2019?

6. What are some practical techniques for ensuring personally identifiable information (PII) is protected in AI-powered ITSM tools?
7. How does the concept of 'human-in-the-loop' improve the reliability and governance of AI-generated knowledge and actions?
8. What are the key elements that should be included in an AI audit trail within an ITSM platform?
9. Discuss the roles and responsibilities of different stakeholders in managing AI risk in ITSM.
10. Why is continual improvement critical in governing AI within the ITIL4 framework, and how can organizations embed it effectively?

Key Terms

- **Explainable AI (XAI):** A set of methods and tools that make an AI model's reasoning visible and understandable to humans. XAI enables auditability, helps troubleshoot errors, and strengthens stakeholder trust in automated ITSM decisions.
- **Hallucination (in GenAI):** The phenomenon where a generative AI confidently produces information that is factually incorrect or unsupported by its training data. In ITSM, hallucinations can mislead users or trigger faulty remediation steps if not governed.
- **GDPR:** Europe's General Data Protection Regulation mandates lawful, fair, and transparent processing of personal data. It gives users rights such as data minimization and the "right to explanation" for AI-driven decisions.
- **ISO/IEC 42001:** The first international standard dedicated to AI management systems. It defines governance structures, accountability, and controls for responsible AI across the entire lifecycle–ideal for certifying AI-powered ITSM environments.
- **Data Protection Impact Assessment (DPIA):** A formal risk-analysis process required under GDPR when processing personal data in ways that could impact individuals. Conducting a DPIA for AI in ITSM helps identify, mitigate, and document privacy risks.
- **AI Ethics Review Board:** A cross-functional body that vets AI use cases, training data, and deployment plans against ethical and regulatory criteria. Its oversight ensures fairness, transparency, and alignment with organizational values.
- **Model Drift:** The gradual degradation of an AI model's accuracy as real-world data diverges from the training set. Continuous monitoring and retraining are essential to prevent wrong classifications or biased outcomes in ITSM.

- **Human-in-the-Loop (HITL):** A governance approach that places human reviewers at key decision points in AI workflows. HITL validation catches low-confidence outputs, curbs hallucinations, and reinforces accountability for critical ITSM actions.
- **Risk Register (AI-Integrated):** An enterprise document that captures identified AI risks, their likelihood, impact, and mitigation owners. Integrating AI entries into the main risk register aligns service automation with broader ERM practices.
- **Continual Service Improvement (CSI):** The ITIL4 practice focused on measuring, analyzing, and enhancing services over time. Embedding AI performance, bias tests, and compliance checkpoints into CSI ensures ongoing governance and value realization.

CHAPTER 12
Building a Smarter ITSM Roadmap

Introduction

The journey toward AI-powered ITSM does not end with implementation–it evolves through strategy, maturity, and value realization. After understanding the "why" and "how" of AI in earlier chapters, this chapter pivots toward the "what next." For organizations ready to move beyond isolated use cases, a smarter ITSM roadmap becomes the compass guiding scalable, sustainable transformation. AI adoption in ITSM is not a one-size-fits-all approach–it demands alignment with organizational maturity, capability, and vision. This chapter introduces strategic and tactical models to help leaders assess where they stand and how to progress with confidence. From early-stage automation experiments to advanced predictive analytics and self-healing systems, we explore how to map AI capabilities to business outcomes. AI maturity models serve as critical tools to benchmark progress, diagnose gaps, and shape a continuous improvement mindset. Equally important are metrics that go beyond technical performance to capture value co-creation, user experience, and operational efficiency. Hence, whether you are a service desk manager, IT leader, or transformation architect, this chapter equips you with practical insights to build a future-ready ITSM strategy. Let us now explore how to move from pilots and patchwork initiatives to a unified roadmap that delivers intelligent, measurable, and meaningful service outcomes.

Structure

In this chapter, we will discuss the following topics:

- Strategic and Tactical Adoption Models
- Maturity Models and Continual Improvement Loops
- Metrics to Measure Impact and Value Realization

Strategic and Tactical Adoption Models

The adoption of AI in ITSM must be guided by deliberate strategy and grounded in tactical execution. Organizations that treat AI as a plug-and-play technology often find themselves facing fragmented results and unmet expectations. A well-structured adoption model—both strategic and tactical—ensures that AI initiatives align with business goals, ITSM maturity, and enterprise risk tolerance. This section explores layered models that bridge long-term vision with practical short-term steps, offering a structured path for sustainable AI enablement in service management.

Strategic Adoption Model: Setting the North Star

A successful AI journey in ITSM begins with a clear strategic vision—your organization's North Star. This isn't just about deploying new tools; it's about aligning AI initiatives with the broader business goals that matter most—improving customer experience, reducing operational costs, accelerating service delivery, and enabling scalable innovation. A strategic adoption model ensures that AI is not implemented in isolation but embedded into the fabric of service management transformation. It starts with defining what success looks like three to five years down the line, translating that vision into measurable outcomes such as faster resolution times or higher first-contact resolution rates. Leadership commitment plays a vital role here, as executive sponsorship creates the momentum and governance needed to sustain long-term change. Mapping organizational capabilities—such as data readiness, process maturity, and skills—helps identify realistic starting points and strategic gaps. Governance frameworks, including ITIL4's guiding principles and enterprise risk policies, provide essential guardrails to steer the AI strategy safely. A clearly defined strategy sets expectations, allocates resources wisely, and unites stakeholders around a common purpose. Without this North Star, even the most promising AI pilots risk becoming isolated experiments, failing to deliver meaningful, enterprise-wide impact.

At the strategic level, AI adoption in ITSM must be aligned with broader organizational goals, such as:

- Enhancing customer and employee experience
- Reducing operational costs
- Accelerating incident resolution
- Improving service quality and resilience
- Supporting digital transformation objectives

This approach requires executive buy-in, cross-functional collaboration, and a top-down understanding of *why* AI is being introduced into ITSM processes.

The following table lists the key components:

Component	Description
Vision	Define what "AI-powered ITSM" looks like in 3–5 years.
Outcomes	Link AI initiatives to tangible business outcomes (e.g., 30% reduction in MTTR).
Sponsorship	Appoint leadership to own and advocate the roadmap.
Governance Alignment	Ensure AI strategy aligns with ITIL4 governance and compliance policies.
Capability Mapping	Identify where the organization currently stands in terms of data, skills, and tools.

Table 12.1: *List of Key Components*

Real-Life Example: A large banking institution launched a 3-year roadmap to reduce manual ticket handling by 60%. Strategically, they aligned AI adoption with their "Digital First" transformation plan, securing board-level sponsorship. The initiative focused on customer-centric KPIs like first-contact resolution and CSAT, which guided platform investments and partner selection.

Tactical Adoption Model: Translating Vision into Action

While strategy provides direction, it is tactical execution that turns vision into reality. The tactical adoption model is all about translating high-level AI aspirations into concrete, manageable steps that deliver measurable value. It begins with assessing organizational readiness—not just in terms of data and tooling, but also in process standardization and team capability. From there, service leaders can identify the right entry points: use cases that are low-risk, high-impact, and easy to pilot, such as AI-driven ticket categorization or sentiment analysis. These pilots serve as learning labs, where teams can test hypotheses, refine workflows, and measure success against clear KPIs like MTTR or call deflection rates. Iteration is key—failures are not setbacks but insights that inform the next wave of improvements. Agile methodologies and feedback loops help course-correct quickly while building organizational confidence in AI. As maturity grows, successful pilots can be scaled across other service domains, teams, or geographies. Tactical execution thus ensures that AI initiatives are not only aligned with strategic intent but also grounded in the day-to-day realities of ITSM operations. Without this deliberate and iterative approach, even the best strategies risk stalling before meaningful change takes hold.

Tactical adoption bridges the gap between strategic intent and day-to-day execution. It focuses on incremental rollouts, agile feedback loops, and outcome tracking.

Tactical Model Phases:

Phase	Activities	Example
Assess	Conduct AI-readiness audit covering data, processes, and people.	Assess ticket data quality, chatbot usage, and process standardization in ITSM tool.
Prioritize Use Cases	Select high-impact, low-risk AI use cases to pilot.	For example, ticket auto-classification or sentiment analysis.
Implement Pilots	Launch controlled experiments with performance KPIs.	Enable NLP-powered ticket routing in a single region.
Evaluate and Iterate	Measure outcomes and refine model based on results.	Adjust classification model thresholds based on false positives.
Scale	Gradually expand to other service areas and geographies.	Extend AI routing to HR and facilities service desks.

Table 12.2: *Tactical Model Phases*

Tools and Enablers:

- AI-readiness checklists
- Kanban boards or Agile sprints
- Metrics dashboards (for example, MTTR, FCR, NPS)
- Feedback mechanisms from end-users and agents

Real-Life Scenario:

A regional government entity in Southeast Asia introduced GenAI features in its citizen-facing IT helpdesk. The pilot began with an internal HR chatbot using a curated knowledge base. After a 90-day sprint that showed 50% call deflection and 20% faster resolution, the model was expanded to citizen-facing services using the same backend framework.

Strategic versus Tactical: Complementary Forces

Strategic and tactical approaches are not opposing forces—they are two sides of the same coin, working in harmony to drive successful AI adoption in ITSM. Strategy defines the "why" and the "where to," offering a long-term vision, setting priorities, and aligning initiatives with business value and governance principles. Tactics, on the other hand, focus on the "how" and "when," translating that vision into actionable steps through pilots, iterations, and real-time learning. While the strategic layer is typically owned by senior leaders who chart the course, the tactical layer empowers operational teams to experiment, adapt, and scale solutions incrementally. Strategy ensures that efforts are purposeful and sustainable; tactics ensure they are practical and grounded in reality. The interplay between these layers creates a feedback loop–lessons from the frontlines inform strategic direction, and strategy provides guardrails for scalable, consistent action. Without strategy, tactical efforts risk becoming disconnected and short-sighted; without tactics, strategic goals remain abstract and unfulfilled. True transformation happens when both forces work together–vision guides execution, and execution refines vision. In AI-powered ITSM, this balance is the key to moving from isolated success stories to systemic, enterprise-wide evolution.

The following table lists the strategic goals:

Dimension	**Strategic**	**Tactical**
Time Horizon	Long-term (1–3 years)	Short-term (3–6 months)
Focus	Vision, governance, value realization	Implementation, iterations, feedback
Ownership	CIOs, CDOs, executive sponsors	ITSM leads, AI architects, project teams
Metrics	Value realization, strategic alignment	FCR, MTTR, pilot success rate, adoption %

Table 12.3: *List of Strategic Goals*

Both layers must work in tandem. Strategy ensures sustainability and cross-enterprise alignment, while tactics fuel momentum and learning.

Common Pitfalls and How to Avoid Them

Despite the growing enthusiasm around AI in ITSM, many organizations stumble when enthusiasm outpaces planning. One of the most common pitfalls is treating AI as just another tool rather than a transformative capability. When initiatives are driven solely by vendor features or hype, they often overlook critical foundations such as data quality, process maturity, and user readiness. Another misstep is scaling too quickly without validating success–pilots are rushed into production before key metrics or feedback are analyzed, leading to poor adoption or inconsistent performance. Equally problematic is neglecting to involve the people who matter most: service desk agents, support engineers, and end-users. When frontline input is ignored, AI solutions risk being misaligned with real-world workflows and pain points. Organizations also falter when they rely only on IT to drive adoption, missing the broader cultural and cross-functional dimensions required for success. To avoid these traps, it is essential to take a phased approach–start with well-scoped use cases, define clear KPIs, and build inclusive teams that bridge technology and service operations. AI should be co-created, not imposed. By learning from these common missteps, ITSM leaders can turn potential pitfalls into stepping stones for smarter, more sustainable transformation.

The following table lists the recommendations:

Pitfall	**Recommendation**
Treating AI as a tool, not a capability	Focus on organizational readiness and cultural shift, not just technology.
Scaling without success metrics	Define clear KPIs for each pilot before scaling.
Ignoring frontline input	Co-create with service desk agents and users to ensure relevance and usability.

Table 12.4: *Suggested Recommendations*

Integrating with Continual Improvement

To ensure that AI adoption in ITSM delivers lasting value, it must be tightly integrated with the principles of continual improvement. AI is not a one-time implementation–it evolves, learns, and matures alongside your service ecosystem. The ITIL4 Continual Improvement Model provides a structured way to guide this evolution, beginning with a clear understanding of the vision: what does success look like for AI in your context? From there, organizations must assess their current state–data quality, process readiness, and user engagement–before identifying the target outcomes they aim to achieve. Tactical actions are then mapped out in phases, allowing for experimentation, measurement, and refinement. Crucially, this cycle doesn't end with implementation; it loops back with metrics-driven reviews, stakeholder feedback, and new opportunities for optimization. AI models, just like processes, can drift or degrade over time, making regular tuning and retraining essential. Continual improvement ensures that AI remains aligned with changing business needs, emerging technologies, and evolving user expectations. By embedding AI initiatives into this improvement loop, organizations can foster a culture of agility, learning, and sustainable innovation. It's not about perfection on day one–it's about getting better every day, guided by data and driven by purpose.

Both strategic and tactical adoption must be embedded within ITIL4's Continual Improvement Model:

- What is the vision? (Strategic)
- Where are we now? (Readiness assessment)
- Where do we want to be? (Tactical goals)
- How do we get there? (Action plans)

- Did we get there? (KPI measurement)
- How do we keep the momentum? (Feedback and refinement)

We can conclude this discussion by stating that AI in ITSM is not just a technology project–it is a transformation journey. Strategic and tactical adoption models help leaders and practitioners move with purpose, clarity, and agility. By marrying long-term vision with iterative implementation, organizations can unlock the full potential of AI while minimizing risk and maximizing return. This dual approach enables ITSM teams to evolve intelligently and remain resilient in the face of rapidly changing digital expectations.

Maturity Models and Continual Improvement Loops

Adopting AI in ITSM is not an all-or-nothing endeavor. It's a journey that progresses through stages of maturity–each building on the foundations laid in the previous one. A maturity model helps organizations assess where they currently stand, identify gaps, and create a roadmap for progressive improvement. When combined with continual improvement loops from ITIL4, maturity models become powerful tools for sustaining transformation, adapting to change, and driving real value from AI-powered ITSM.

Understanding Maturity Models in AI-Driven ITSM

A maturity model provides a structured way to measure the evolution of AI integration in ITSM across dimensions such as data readiness, automation, process optimization, tooling, governance, and culture. These models help teams understand whether they are at an initial stage (experimental), transitioning (tactical), or operating at a fully optimized (strategic) level.

The following table describes an Example of 5-Level AI-Driven ITSM Maturity Model:

Level	**Description**	**Characteristics**
Level 1: Ad Hoc	AI is absent or only experimental	Manual processes, no AI strategy, unstructured data
Level 2: Opportunistic	AI pilots in isolated areas	Limited automation, scattered tooling, minimal governance
Level 3: Defined	AI aligned to business needs	Structured data, AI integrated into key processes

Level 4: Managed	AI delivers measurable outcomes	KPIs tracked, AI governance established, process optimization underway
Level 5: Optimized	AI is strategic, self-improving	Predictive insights, enterprise-wide AI, embedded continual improvement

Table 12.5: *5-Level AI-Driven ITSM Maturity Model*

Using Maturity Models to Drive Planning and Prioritization

Maturity models are more than diagnostic tools–they are essential instruments for planning and prioritization in AI-powered ITSM. By assessing the current state of AI adoption across dimensions such as data quality, automation, process consistency, and organizational culture, these models help organizations pinpoint where they truly stand. This clarity enables IT leaders to prioritize initiatives that close critical gaps while aligning with broader service management goals. Instead of chasing shiny AI features or vendor-driven hype, teams can focus on what matters most–whether it is improving ticket triage, reducing resolution time, or enhancing user satisfaction. The model provides a structured lens to identify which capabilities are ripe for development and which require foundational work before scaling. This ensures that investments are not only technically sound but strategically targeted. Real progress happens when maturity assessments guide resource allocation, pilot design, and the sequencing of improvement efforts. For example, an organization might realize it's not yet ready for AI-driven root cause analysis until it standardizes its incident categorization. By using maturity models to guide these choices, organizations avoid overreach and make smarter, more sustainable advancements in their AI journey.

Maturity models act as a diagnostic lens. They help organizations:

- Benchmark their current AI capabilities
- Identify which domains need attention (for example, data, process, skills, governance)
- Prioritize improvement areas based on business impact and feasibility
- Set realistic goals with measurable indicators of success

Real-Life Scenario: A global insurance company conducted an AI maturity assessment across ITSM. The results showed they were at Level 2–using chatbots and classification models in isolated support teams but lacking data governance and consistent KPIs. Based on this, they prioritized standardizing their data pipeline and aligning AI goals with customer experience KPIs, moving toward Level 3 within a year.

The Role of Continual Improvement Loops

AI in ITSM is not static–it requires feedback, retraining, and refinement. This makes ITIL4's Continual Improvement Model the perfect companion to the maturity model. As each AI initiative is deployed, its outcomes should feed into a loop of reassessment and optimization.

The following table lists the AI-focused actions in ITIL4 Continual Improvement Model Applied to AI:

Step	AI-Focused Actions
1. What is the vision?	Define long-term impact of AI on service quality and business value.
2. Where are we now?	Assess AI maturity, process efficiency, and adoption barriers.
3. Where do we want to be?	Set KPIs such as ticket resolution time, CSAT, or cost savings.
4. How do we get there?	Design AI enhancements (for example, new models, workflows).
5. Take action	Implement with pilot teams or environments.
6. Did we get there?	Measure improvement using dashboards and analytics.
7. How do we keep the momentum going?	Retune models, capture feedback, and feed into the next loop.

Table 12.6: *ITIL4 Continual Improvement Model Applied to AI*

Combining the Models for Maximum Impact

When maturity models and continual improvement loops are used together, they create a powerful framework for sustainable and intelligent AI adoption in ITSM. The maturity model sets the strategic direction–helping organizations understand their current capabilities, define a target state, and visualize the path ahead. Meanwhile, the continual improvement loop injects agility, ensuring that progress is made incrementally, measured consistently, and adapted over time. Alone, a maturity model can feel static or theoretical; without continuous feedback, it risks becoming outdated. Likewise, continual improvement without a maturity baseline may lead to scattered efforts without a clear end goal. But when combined, they form a dynamic system: the maturity model provides the structure and purpose, while the improvement loop drives momentum and responsiveness. With every improvement cycle, organizations can re-evaluate their maturity, adjust priorities, and recalibrate their goals–creating a virtuous cycle of learning and progress. This integration ensures that AI initiatives are not just technically implemented but are continuously evolving and aligned with changing business needs. The result is a more resilient, data-driven ITSM function that grows smarter over time–delivering on the true promise of AI-powered service management.

While the maturity model provides structure and direction, the continual improvement loop ensures agility and responsiveness. Together, they support sustainable progress.

Integrated Framework:

1. **Maturity Baseline**: Identify your current stage
2. **Target State Definition**: Define your AI goals and what maturity looks like at that stage
3. **Improvement Planning:** Use continual improvement steps to close the maturity gaps
4. **Measurement and Reflection:** Assess improvements and recalibrate efforts
5. **Loop Back**: Reassess your maturity periodically

Use Case: AI in Knowledge Management

Scenario:

A healthcare service provider introduced an AI-based knowledge assistant for its service desk, but adoption remained low after the initial rollout.

Maturity Assessment:

- Data was not standardized (Level 2)
- No process for feedback on AI-suggested articles
- No ownership defined for knowledge curation

Action Plan (Continual Improvement Loop):

1. Vision: Improve resolution quality and reduce ticket volume via self-service
2. Current State: <30% usage of AI knowledge assistant
3. Target: >60% usage, +10% CSAT increase
4. Actions:
    a. Integrate AI suggestions directly into agent workflows
    b. Create feedback loops for AI-suggested articles
    c. Assign a knowledge manager to monitor content

5. Outcome: Within 6 months, usage jumped to 65%, with a measurable improvement in FCR and agent efficiency

Common Mistakes to Avoid

As organizations embrace AI in ITSM, many well-intentioned efforts falter due to avoidable mistakes. A common misstep is treating maturity assessments as a one-time checklist rather than a living tool that evolves with the organization. When teams fail to revisit their maturity levels periodically, they risk losing sight of progress or stagnating in early stages. Another pitfall is relying solely on tool capabilities to gauge advancement, ignoring critical human and process dimensions such as user adoption, cultural readiness, and governance maturity. Some organizations also fall into the trap of celebrating early wins and assuming the work is done–overlooking the need for continuous tuning, retraining of models, and feedback loops. Others overcomplicate their models, layering in too much detail or academic rigor, making them impractical for real-world use. It is important to strike a balance: the models should be simple enough to act on, yet rich enough to guide strategic decision-making. Lastly, some teams bypass frontline involvement, leading to misaligned priorities and low trust in AI outcomes. By being aware of these common mistakes, ITSM leaders can proactively course-correct and ensure their AI initiatives remain purposeful, practical, and people-centered.

The following table lists few pro-active course-correct actions:

Pitfall	**Mitigation**
Using maturity models as a one-time exercise	Revisit maturity scores quarterly or bi-annually
Relying solely on tools to gauge maturity	Include user feedback, governance practices, and process metrics
Skipping continual improvement for "completed" AI projects	AI is not static–retraining and fine-tuning are essential
Overcomplicating models	Use a simple, understandable model tailored to your ITSM environment

Table 12.7: *Pro-Active Course-Correct Actions*

We have arrived at the conclusion that Maturity models give organizations a compass, while continual improvement loops provide the map and vehicle. Together, they create a framework that not only guides AI adoption in ITSM but sustains it through feedback, learning, and optimization. By periodically assessing progress and embedding learning cycles into AI initiatives, organizations can ensure their journey toward intelligent service management is measured, meaningful, and resilient to change.

Metrics to Measure Impact and Value Realization

In AI-powered ITSM, success is not defined merely by the deployment of algorithms or the adoption of new tools–it is defined by the tangible outcomes these technologies deliver. Without the right metrics, it becomes nearly impossible to distinguish between genuine value and superficial progress. Measuring impact and value realization is critical to demonstrating ROI, securing continued investment, and guiding iterative improvement. This chapter explores how organizations can define, track, and act on the right performance indicators to ensure that AI initiatives are delivering on their promise.

The Importance of Measurement in AI-Driven ITSM

AI in ITSM often promises improvements in efficiency, accuracy, responsiveness, and user satisfaction. However, to validate these claims, organizations must transition from anecdotal feedback to data-driven performance evaluation. Metrics provide the evidence base that guides decision-making, fosters accountability, and helps teams refine their approach. Furthermore, in the context of continual improvement and ITIL4 governance, metrics act as critical feedback loops that align operational activities with strategic objectives.

Categories of AI-Driven Metrics in ITSM

To truly understand the value of AI in ITSM, organizations must look beyond surface-level indicators and evaluate performance across multiple dimensions. AI-driven metrics fall into four key categories–each capturing a different aspect of impact. Operational efficiency metrics measure the gains in speed, productivity, and automation, helping teams quantify how AI reduces workloads and accelerates resolutions. Service quality and accuracy metrics reveal how reliably AI performs tasks such as classification, triaging, or sentiment analysis, ensuring that automation enhances–not compromises–outcomes. User experience metrics are equally critical, shedding light on satisfaction levels, adoption rates, and the real-world value users perceive in interacting with AI tools like chatbots or virtual agents. Finally, business value metrics connect AI performance to bottom-line outcomes such as cost savings, SLA adherence, and strategic KPIs. By categorizing metrics in this way, IT leaders gain a holistic view of how AI is influencing operations, enabling them to track what matters, prove impact, and identify where improvements are needed most. Each category plays a vital role in painting a complete picture of AI's contribution to a smarter, more responsive IT service environment.

To comprehensively assess AI's value, metrics should be grouped into categories that reflect both operational performance and strategic outcomes.

Operational Efficiency Metrics

These metrics reflect how AI enhances the productivity and throughput of ITSM teams:

- **Mean Time to Resolve (MTTR):** It is the average amount of time it takes to fully resolve an incident or issue after it has been reported. It includes the entire lifecycle–from the moment the ticket is logged to when the problem is completely fixed and the service is restored. A lower MTTR means faster resolution, which typically leads to happier users and less disruption to business operations. For example, if five incidents are resolved in 2, 4, 6, 8, and 10 hours respectively, the MTTR would be the average–6 hours. It is a key metric in ITSM that reflects the efficiency of support teams and the effectiveness of their tools and processes.
- **First Contact Resolution Rate (FCR):** It measures the percentage of support issues resolved during the very first interaction with the user–without the need to escalate, transfer, or follow up later. A high FCR means users are getting their problems solved quickly and efficiently, which boosts satisfaction and reduces ticket backlog. For example, if 80 out of 100 tickets are resolved during the first call or chat, the FCR is 80%.
- **Average Handle Time (AHT):** It is the average amount of time a service agent spends handling a ticket or call, from start to finish. This includes the time spent talking to the user, doing follow-up work, and updating the ticket. AHT helps measure efficiency–shorter handle times often mean faster service, but very short times could also indicate rushed or poor-quality support. It is about finding the right balance between speed and thoroughness.
- **Ticket Volume per Agent:** Ticket Volume per Agent tracks how many support tickets an individual agent handles over a given period, such as per day, week, or month. This metric gives insight into workload distribution, team productivity, and staffing needs. If one agent consistently handles far more tickets than others, it could indicate either high efficiency–or potential burnout or imbalance within the team.
- **Automation Rate (for example, % of tickets auto-triaged or auto-resolved):** Automation Rate shows how many support tickets are being handled automatically–either through AI-powered triage (assigning and categorizing tickets) or full resolution without human intervention. For instance, if 300 out of 1,000 incoming tickets are resolved by a chatbot or auto-remediation tool, the automation rate is 30%. This metric is essential for measuring how

effectively automation is reducing manual workload and speeding up service delivery.

Service Quality and Accuracy Metrics

These metrics track how AI impacts the precision and reliability of services:

- **Classification Accuracy (NLP-Based Ticket Tagging):** It refers to how correctly an AI system–especially one using Natural Language Processing (NLP)–can read and understand the content of a support ticket and assign it to the right category (such as, incident, request, or specific service area). For example, if a user submits a ticket saying "I can't access my email," the system should accurately tag it under "Email Access Issue" or "Login Problems." High classification accuracy means the system consistently gets the tagging right, helping in faster routing, quicker resolutions, and better reporting.
- **Sentiment Analysis Accuracy:** It refers to how correctly an AI system can understand the emotional tone or attitude expressed in a support ticket, email, or chat–such as whether the user is frustrated, neutral, or satisfied. For example, if a user writes "I'm really disappointed with the service," the system should accurately detect this as negative sentiment. High sentiment analysis accuracy ensures that the system can prioritize emotionally charged tickets, alert agents to unhappy users, and improve the overall customer experience
- **False Positive/Negative Rate in AI Predictions:** It refers to how often an AI system makes incorrect decisions when predicting outcomes. A false positive happens when the system wrongly flags something as an issue (e.g., marking a normal ticket as urgent), while a false negative occurs when it misses a real problem (e.g., not detecting a major incident). Lower false positive/negative rates mean the AI is making more accurate and reliable predictions, leading to better decisions and less manual correction by support teams.
- **AI Confidence Score Thresholds:** It refers to the level of certainty an AI system has in its prediction or decision–usually shown as a percentage. For example, if an AI tags a ticket as a "network issue" with 92% confidence, it means the system is highly sure of its choice. A threshold is the minimum confidence score required before the AI's decision is accepted automatically. If the confidence is below the threshold (e.g., 60%), the ticket might be flagged for human review. Setting the right threshold helps balance automation and accuracy.

User Experience Metrics

These metrics help assess how AI influences end-user satisfaction:

- **Customer Satisfaction Score (CSAT):** It measures how happy users are with a specific service interaction–like getting help from the service desk or using a chatbot. After the ticket is resolved, users are usually asked to rate their satisfaction (e.g., from 1 to 5). The higher the average score, the better the perceived service quality. For example, if most users rate their experience as 4 or 5, the CSAT score will reflect strong customer satisfaction.

- **Net Promoter Score (NPS):** NPS goes a step beyond satisfaction and asks users: "*How likely are you to recommend our service to others?*" Responses range from 0 (not at all likely) to 10 (extremely likely). Scores of 9–10 are Promoters, 7–8 are Passives, and 0–6 are Detractors. NPS is calculated by subtracting the percentage of Detractors from the percentage of Promoters. A higher NPS means users are not just satisfied–they are loyal and enthusiastic.
- **Self-Service Adoption Rate:** It measures how many users choose to use self-service options–such as knowledge base articles, FAQs, or virtual agents–instead of contacting the service desk. A high adoption rate indicates that users find the self-service tools useful and easy to navigate. For example, if 400 out of 1,000 users solve their issues using the self-service portal, the adoption rate is 40%. It is a key metric for tracking the success of automation and digital support channels.
- **Chatbot Resolution Rate:** It shows how many user queries are fully resolved by a chatbot without needing human assistance. It helps determine how effective the virtual assistant is in providing accurate and helpful answers. For example, if a chatbot handles 500 queries and fully resolves 350 of them, its resolution rate is 70%. A high rate indicates a well-trained, useful AI assistant that saves time for both users and service agents.

Business Value Metrics

These connect AI performance to financial and strategic outcomes:

- **Cost per Ticket:** Cost per Ticket refers to the average amount of money it takes to resolve a single support request. This includes staff time, tools, overhead, and other operational costs. For example, if a service desk handles 1,000 tickets in a month and spends ₹5,00,000 on resources, the cost per ticket is ₹500. Lowering this cost–without compromising service quality–is often a key goal for ITSM efficiency.
- **Cost Avoidance through Automation:** It measures how much money an organization saves by using AI or automation to handle tasks that would otherwise require human effort. For instance, if a virtual assistant handles 5,000 password reset requests that would have cost ₹500 each to manage manually, that is ₹2,50,000 in avoided cost. This metric helps demonstrate the financial return of AI investments in service operations.
- **Reduction in Escalation Volume:** Reduction in Escalation Volume tracks how many fewer tickets are being passed up to higher-level support teams–thanks

to better classification, smarter triage, or AI-driven resolution at lower levels. When AI tools help front-line agents or chatbots resolve issues faster and more accurately, fewer cases need to be escalated. This reduces pressure on Level 2 and 3 teams and keeps service delivery more agile and efficient.

- **Service Availability and SLA Adherence:** Service Availability and SLA Adherence measure whether IT services are up and running as expected, and whether performance commitments (SLAs) are being met. AI can contribute by predicting outages, automating recovery, or improving incident response times. If a service is promised to be available 99.9% of the time, SLA adherence confirms whether that standard is being achieved. These metrics are crucial for maintaining trust and accountability with users and business stakeholders.

Establishing Baselines and Benchmarks

Before measuring improvement, it is critical to establish baseline metrics–a snapshot of performance before AI implementation. Comparing post-deployment metrics to this baseline allows teams to quantify gains and identify areas needing optimization. Organizations should also leverage industry benchmarks to contextualize their performance.

Example: An IT service desk averaged an MTTR of 9 hours and a CSAT of 82% before deploying an AI-based ticket classification engine. Three months post-implementation, MTTR dropped to 5.5 hours, and CSAT rose to 89%, demonstrating measurable value and validating the AI use case.

Real-Life Scenario: Measuring Impact in a Telecom Service Desk

A leading telecom company in the Middle East introduced an AI-powered virtual assistant to deflect routine service requests (for example, password resets, data limit inquiries). The following table suggests the predicted outcome key metrics tracked before and after deployment:

Metric	Pre-AI	Post-AI (3 months)	Change
Call Volume to Service Desk	15,000/month	9,200/month	↓ 38%
Average Handle Time (AHT)	12 minutes	7 minutes	↓ 42%
First Contact Resolution Rate	64%	84%	↑ 20%
CSAT	80%	91%	↑ 11%

Table 12.8: *List of Key Metrics to be Tracked*

These metrics not only justified the investment but also informed the roadmap to scale the assistant's capabilities to handle billing and technical support.

Linking Metrics to Business Objectives

Measuring AI success in ITSM is not just about tracking performance indicators in isolation—it is about connecting those metrics to broader business objectives. When AI initiatives are aligned with strategic goals such as cost optimization, employee productivity, customer satisfaction, or operational resilience, the value becomes clearer and more compelling. For example, a reduction in Mean Time to Resolve (MTTR) is not merely a technical win; it directly contributes to improved employee uptime and overall organizational efficiency. Similarly, an increase in first-contact resolution rates and self-service adoption doesn't just reflect better AI performance—it indicates a smoother, more satisfying user experience that can drive loyalty and trust. Cost-focused metrics such as automation rate or cost per ticket support executive-level conversations about ROI and workforce optimization, while SLA adherence and classification accuracy reflect the stability and reliability of service delivery. The key is to treat each metric as a proxy for a business outcome—ensuring that technical improvements translate into meaningful, measurable impacts. By establishing this link early, AI initiatives gain greater visibility, stakeholder buy-in, and sustained investment. Ultimately, when metrics are woven into the language of business value, AI in ITSM becomes not just a technological advancement but a strategic enabler of enterprise success.

Effective measurement means tying AI performance to business-level outcomes. For example:

- A 20% reduction in MTTR may correlate with improved employee productivity.
- Higher self-service adoption may reduce dependency on support staff, freeing them for complex tasks.
- Improved classification accuracy can lead to better SLA compliance and fewer escalations.

Alignment Table:

Business Goal	AI Metric	Value Indicator
Reduce operational cost	Cost per ticket	↓ indicates higher efficiency
Improve employee experience	CSAT, FCR	↑ reflects satisfaction and faster resolution
Increase self-service usage	Chatbot success rate	↑ indicates improved digital adoption

Enhance service quality	SLA compliance, MTTR	Consistent SLA adherence shows reliability

Table 12.9: *Alignment Table*

Dashboards and Reporting Tools

In the fast-moving world of AI-powered ITSM, dashboards and reporting tools serve as the nerve center for decision-making. They translate complex, multi-dimensional performance data into clear, actionable insights that both technical teams and business leaders can understand. Dashboards offer real-time visibility into key metrics such as MTTR, automation rates, sentiment trends, and SLA compliance, allowing teams to monitor progress, detect anomalies, and act swiftly. Modern ITSM platforms such as ServiceNow, ManageEngine, and Jira, as well as BI tools including Power BI and Tableau, allow organizations to build dynamic, customizable views that segment data by service area, geography, or channel. Beyond simple charts, these tools can surface deeper insights–such as model confidence levels, false positive trends, or emerging support bottlenecks–enabling data-driven decisions for continual improvement. A well-designed dashboard does not just report numbers; it tells a story about the health, adoption, and impact of AI in service management. It also supports governance by ensuring that stakeholders–from service desk managers to CIOs–stay informed, aligned, and accountable. When dashboards are integrated into daily workflows and reviewed in regular cadence meetings, they become an indispensable tool for sustaining momentum and reinforcing the value of AI across the organization.

Organizations should leverage ITSM platforms (for example, ServiceNow, ManageEngine, Jira) and BI tools (for example, Power BI, Tableau) to visualize AI performance metrics in real time. Effective dashboards:

- Segment data by service, channel, or geography
- Allow drilling down into AI behavior (for example, model confidence, exceptions)
- Highlight trends over time to support strategic reviews

Common Pitfalls in Measuring AI Impact

As organizations strive to quantify the benefits of AI in ITSM, many fall into common measurement traps that undermine their efforts. One frequent mistake is focusing on vanity metrics–such as the number of chatbot interactions or model usage counts–without examining whether those interactions led to meaningful outcomes such as resolution, satisfaction, or cost savings. Another pitfall is measuring impact too soon before the AI solution has stabilized or users have adapted to the new workflows. This often results in skewed data that paints an incomplete or overly optimistic picture. Equally problematic is overlooking qualitative insights from service desk agents and users–valuable context that helps explain why certain metrics are rising or falling. Some teams treat measurement as a one-off exercise rather than a continuous learning process, failing to revisit KPIs regularly or adjust them as AI capabilities evolve. Others lack clear accountability for tracking and interpreting AI performance, leaving metrics underutilized or misinterpreted. To avoid these issues, it is crucial to establish a balanced mix of quantitative and qualitative indicators, track progress over time, and embed metric review into governance routines. Measuring AI impact is not just about collecting data–it is about creating clarity, credibility, and confidence in your AI journey.

The following table lists the common pitfalls:

Pitfall	How to Avoid
Tracking vanity metrics (for example, usage counts without outcomes)	Focus on KPIs linked to value
Measuring too soon	Allow time for adoption and learning curves
Ignoring qualitative feedback	Combine metrics with user feedback and frontline insights
Lack of ownership	Assign clear accountability for tracking and reporting AI KPIs

Table 12.10: *List of Common Pitfalls*

Embedding Metrics into the Continual Improvement Cycle

To unlock the full value of AI in ITSM, metrics must not be treated as static snapshots; they need to be woven into the fabric of continual improvement. Embedding metrics into the ITIL4 continual improvement cycle transforms them from passive reports into active levers for change. Each cycle begins by using metrics to assess the current state–pinpointing where AI is performing well and where it is falling short. These insights shape the vision for improvement, guide the selection of targeted initiatives, and inform the development of actionable plans. Once changes are implemented–such as retraining a classification model or refining a virtual assistant's response logic–new data is gathered to evaluate whether those actions led to better outcomes. This closes the loop and sets the stage for the next round of enhancements. By continuously monitoring performance indicators such as accuracy, adoption, and satisfaction, organizations can adapt in real time to shifting needs, evolving technologies, and unforeseen challenges. In essence, metrics fuel the feedback loop that keeps AI models relevant, services optimized, and users engaged. It is this dynamic cycle of measurement, reflection, and refinement that transforms AI from a one-time project into an engine of sustained, intelligent service excellence.

Metrics are not endpoints–they are entry points for the next cycle of improvement. AI models may drift, workflows evolve, and user expectations shift. Regular review of metrics ensures AI solutions remain effective, trusted, and aligned with service goals. The ITIL4 continual improvement model encourages periodic assessment and adjustment of KPIs as services mature or expand.

The discussion can be summarized by stating that Metrics are the bridge between AI implementation and value realization in ITSM. They ensure that progress is not only visible but measurable, defensible, and actionable. By thoughtfully selecting and continuously reviewing a mix of efficiency, accuracy, user experience, and business value metrics, organizations can guide their AI journey with confidence. In the world of AI-powered ITSM, what gets measured gets improved–and what gets improved becomes the foundation for intelligent, future-ready service delivery.

Conclusion

As organizations embrace the transformative power of AI in IT service management, the question is no longer whether to adopt AI–but how to do so intelligently, sustainably, and strategically. This chapter has laid out the foundations for moving beyond pilot experiments and tactical wins toward a unified, enterprise-wide AI roadmap that delivers measurable value.

We began by exploring the **strategic adoption model**, which provides the long-term vision, leadership commitment, and alignment with business goals necessary for meaningful transformation. This model emphasizes that AI is not just a technical upgrade–it is a capability that must be woven into the DNA of ITSM strategy. Vision-setting, outcome definition, executive sponsorship, governance alignment, and capability mapping form the blueprint for sustainable AI integration.

Complementing this is the **tactical adoption model**, which translates vision into action. Tactical execution is where strategy meets the real world–through iterative pilots, feedback loops, readiness assessments, and agile improvements. By identifying low-risk, high-impact use cases and learning from them, organizations can build confidence, gather momentum, and scale AI initiatives with clarity and control.

To guide this transformation, we examined **maturity models** that benchmark current capabilities and highlight areas for improvement. These models offer a structured way to prioritize investments and plot a realistic, staged journey toward enterprise AI maturity. When combined with **ITIL4's Continual Improvement Model**, they ensure that progress is iterative, feedback-driven, and anchored in real outcomes–not just intentions.

Equally important are the **metrics** that define success. From operational efficiency to user satisfaction and strategic value, metrics serve as the compass for AI decision-making. They illuminate what's working, what's not, and where to focus next. Embedded within continual improvement loops, these metrics drive data-driven evolution and help tie every improvement effort to business impact.

In essence, this chapter reinforces that AI in ITSM is not a one-off deployment—it is a transformation journey that requires **vision, structure, agility, and accountability**. By harmonizing strategic foresight with tactical execution, measuring what matters, and embedding continual improvement into the culture, organizations can unlock AI's full potential. The smarter ITSM roadmap is not about speed—it is about direction. And with the right map in hand, service leaders can navigate change confidently, deliver lasting value, and future-proof their IT operations for the digital era.

In the next chapter, we will explore how AI will reshape ITSM roles within ITSM- from service-desk agents to process owners.

Multiple Choice Questions

1. What is the primary purpose of a strategic adoption model in AI-powered ITSM?
    a. To implement AI tools as quickly as possible
    b. To define ticket resolution workflows
    c. To align AI initiatives with long-term business goals
    d. To monitor service desk agent performance
2. Which phase in the tactical adoption model focuses on launching controlled AI experiments with measurable KPIs?
    a. Assess
    b. Implement Pilots
    c. Evaluate and Iterate
    d. Scale
3. In the AI-driven ITSM Maturity Model, what characterizes Level 5: Optimized?
    a. Limited automation in isolated areas
    b. Manual processes with no AI integration
    c. Predictive insights and enterprise-wide AI
    d. AI used only for reporting purposes

4. Which of the following metrics best reflects operational efficiency in an AI-powered ITSM environment?
    a. Sentiment Analysis Accuracy
    b. Net Promoter Score (NPS)
    c. Mean Time to Resolve (MTTR)
    d. Chatbot Resolution Rate
5. What is a common pitfall to avoid when measuring the impact of AI in ITSM?
    a. Using continual improvement loops
    b. Tracking AI performance over time
    c. Focusing on vanity metrics without linking to outcomes
    d. Assigning ownership for KPI tracking

Answers

1. c
2. b
3. c
4. c
5. c

Questions

1. What are the key components of a strategic AI adoption model in ITSM, and why is each important for long-term success?
2. How does a tactical adoption model help organizations move from isolated AI pilots to scalable implementations?
3. Describe the differences between strategic and tactical adoption models, and explain how they complement each other.
4. What are the most common pitfalls organizations face when adopting AI in ITSM, and how can they be avoided?
5. Explain how maturity models can help organizations assess their current state and plan their AI adoption journey.

6. How does the ITIL4 Continual Improvement Model support the sustainable evolution of AI-powered ITSM?
7. Why is it important to integrate both quantitative metrics and qualitative feedback when measuring AI impact in ITSM?
8. What categories of AI-driven metrics are most relevant to tracking the value realization of AI in ITSM?
9. How can organizations use dashboards and reporting tools to improve visibility and governance of AI initiatives?
10. Describe how maturity models and continual improvement loops work together to create a dynamic framework for AI-enabled service transformation.

Key Terms

- **Strategic Adoption Model:** A long-term framework that aligns AI initiatives with organizational goals such as cost reduction, service resilience, and customer experience. It defines the vision, outcomes, leadership support, and governance alignment for AI in ITSM.
- **Tactical Adoption Model:** A practical execution model that translates AI strategy into action through pilots, use case selection, feedback loops, and iterative scaling. It focuses on readiness assessment, pilot implementation, and measurable improvements.
- **AI Readiness Assessment:** A diagnostic tool used to evaluate an organization's preparedness for AI adoption across data quality, process maturity, tooling, and team capabilities. It helps identify gaps before initiating AI projects.
- **Maturity Model:** A structured framework that measures the level of AI integration in ITSM across stages—from ad hoc experimentation to optimized, enterprise-wide AI. It helps prioritize improvement efforts and guide the transformation journey.
- **Continual Improvement Loop:** An iterative ITIL4-based approach that supports ongoing refinement of AI capabilities by regularly assessing performance, collecting feedback, and implementing changes. It ensures that AI solutions remain aligned with evolving business needs.
- **MTTR (Mean Time to Resolve):** A core operational efficiency metric that calculates the average time taken to resolve incidents. It reflects the effectiveness of AI-driven automation and process optimization in speeding up resolution.
- **FCR (First Contact Resolution):** A metric that tracks the percentage of tickets resolved during the first user interaction. High FCR indicates successful triage, accurate classification, and a positive user experience.

- **AI-Driven Metrics:** Performance indicators used to evaluate the impact of AI in ITSM, categorized into operational, service quality, user experience, and business value metrics. These metrics guide decisions and validate ROI.
- **Dashboards and Reporting Tools:** Visualization platforms such as Power BI or ServiceNow dashboards that display AI performance, usage trends, and KPIs in real time. They help drive data-informed decisions and governance alignment.
- **Vanity Metrics:** Superficial statistics like usage counts or interaction volumes that don't directly reflect value or outcomes. Avoiding vanity metrics ensures that the focus stays on impactful, meaningful performance indicators.

Chapter 13
The Evolving Role of The ITSM Professional

Introduction

The rise of AI in ITSM is not just a technological shift—it is a profound transformation of the roles, responsibilities, and realities of IT service professionals. As AI tools begin handling routine tasks, from ticket triage to knowledge article suggestions, the nature of human contribution is evolving from execution to orchestration. This chapter explores what that means for service desk agents, process owners, and ITSM leaders who now find themselves at the intersection of intelligence and empathy. Far from replacing them, AI empowers professionals to focus on high-value activities—those that require human judgment, relationship-building, and strategic thinking. But this evolution also demands new skills, new attitudes, and a willingness to collaborate with machines as intelligent partners. For many, the journey involves *unlearning old habits*, embracing a growth mindset, and acquiring fluency in AI-enabled tools and practices. It is a shift from knowing every process step to understanding how to guide, supervise, and optimize AI-supported workflows. Organizations that recognize and support this human-AI synergy will see faster adoption, better outcomes, and more resilient teams. Through real-world insights and forward-looking guidance, this chapter illuminates how ITSM professionals can not only survive—but thrive—in the age of intelligent service management.

The ITSM landscape is undergoing a quiet revolution—one did not mark by the obsolescence of human roles, but by their profound transformation. As AI steadily integrates into service management, it is not here to replace professionals, but to elevate them. Tasks that were once tedious, repetitive, and reactive are now becoming automated, allowing ITSM professionals to focus on higher-value, strategic work. This shift calls for more than just new tools; it requires a new mindset—one that embraces collaboration with intelligent systems rather than competing against them.

Service desk agents are evolving into service experience designers, process owners are becoming data-driven decision-makers, and service managers are emerging as orchestrators of human-AI synergy. In this new era, soft skills, contextual awareness, and ethical judgment become even more critical, as they complement what AI cannot replicate. Organizations that recognize and invest in this hybrid model—where humans and machines co-create value—will lead to the future of service delivery. Upskilling is no longer optional; it is a strategic imperative. But it is not just about learning to work with AI—it's about learning to think differently, act proactively, and continuously adapt. This chapter explores how roles in ITSM are evolving and what it takes for professionals to thrive in a world where intelligence is both human and artificial.

Structure

In this chapter, we will discuss the following topics:

- How AI augments - Not Replaces - Service Professionals
- Upskilling and Mindset Shifts
- The Human Side of Intelligent Service Delivery

Augmenting - Not Replacing - Service Professionals with AI

There is a common fear that AI is coming to replace human jobs. In the realm of IT Service Management (ITSM), this concern is particularly palpable among service desk agents, incident managers, and operational teams who worry that automation might render their roles obsolete. However, the truth is more nuanced—and far more hopeful. AI in ITSM is not about removing humans from the loop but about elevating human roles by reducing drudgery, augmenting intelligence, and enhancing decision-making.

AI augments service professionals by handling high-volume, repetitive, and data-intensive tasks, allowing humans to focus on empathy, judgment, and innovation. The future of ITSM is not "AI versus human," but "AI plus human."

Despite widespread concern about AI replacing human jobs, the reality in ITSM is far more collaborative. AI's true power lies in *augmentation*, not replacement. AI complements human strengths by taking over repetitive, time-consuming, and data-heavy tasks—freeing up professionals to focus on critical thinking, customer engagement, and service innovation.

So, what does "Augmentation" mean in ITSM?

Augmentation refers to the way AI complements human capabilities instead of replacing them. In ITSM, this means AI:

- Assists in repetitive workflows (for example, password resets, ticket triaging)
- Enhances decision-making by providing intelligent recommendations
- Speeds up routine tasks to free up time for strategic focus
- Learns from humans to improve its own performance through feedback loops

This human-AI partnership improves efficiency, lowers response times, and enriches the quality-of-service delivery without sacrificing human insight or control.

AI enables service professionals to move beyond routine operations. For instance, chatbots handle password resets and FAQs 24/7, but when an incident requires empathy, negotiation, or multi-system context, it is escalated to a human agent. Machine learning automates ticket classification, yet a service desk analyst still validates priority based on current business impact. Rather than eliminating roles, AI *is changing what these roles do—and how they deliver value.*

In this human-AI partnership:

- AI handles volume, speed, and pattern detection
- Humans provide context, judgment, and relationship management

So, what are the outcome? They are as follows:

- Greater productivity,
- Improved accuracy,
- More meaningful work.

The following table lists the supporting areas where AI augments humans:

AI Capability	**Human Strength it Supports**	**Resulting Impact**
Auto-triaging and classification	Decision-making and escalation handling	Faster response, fewer misrouted tickets
Sentiment analysis	Emotional intelligence, empathy	Prioritized care for frustrated users
Root cause prediction (AIOps)	Deep domain knowledge and system insight	Quicker recovery from major incidents

Smart knowledge base suggestions	Communication skills, content curation	Better self-service and resolution accuracy
Predictive analytics	Risk assessment and change planning	Safer, data-informed decisions
Chatbots and VA	Personalized, human follow-up	Hybrid, high-quality user experience

Table 13.1: *Supporting Areas where AI Augments Humans*

Real-Life Example: Service Desk at a Global Bank

Scenario: A leading multinational bank had a Tier-1 service desk inundated with tickets for account lockouts, password resets, and access issues. These made up over 40% of the total ticket volume.

AI Solution:

- A virtual assistant integrated with the bank's Identity and Access Management (IAM) tools was deployed.
- It handled password resets, email unlocks, and access-related FAQs automatically using NLP and workflow automation.

Results:

- 75% of repetitive tickets were resolved without human intervention.
- First-response time dropped from 2 hours to under 5 minutes.
- Human agents were re-trained to manage escalations, handle sentiment-sensitive queries, and analyze ticket data.

Impact:

- Not a single job was lost.
- Instead, job roles evolved: agents took on tasks such as chatbot workflow design, escalation management, and user journey analysis.
- Employee satisfaction improved due to more meaningful, less monotonous work.

The following table attempts to list a few key areas where AI augments, not replaces:

AI Capability	Human Role AI Augments	Value Delivered
Auto-classification and triaging	Service Desk Analyst	Faster routing, reduced backlog
Sentiment analysis	Customer Service Agent	Prioritization of high-emotion tickets

Virtual Assistants (Chatbots)	L1 Support Agents	24/7 support, escalation for complex cases
Predictive analytics	Change Manager/Problem Manager	Proactive risk detection, fewer disruptions
AIOps insights	Incident and Event Management Teams	Faster RCA and incident correlation
Smart knowledge suggestions	Knowledge Manager / Technical Writer	Improved self-service, content discovery

Table 13.2: *Key Areas Where AI Augments, Not Replaces*

The gist of the preceding discussion is as follows:

- AI relieves professionals from *drudgery*, not *duty*.
- It enhances decision-making, not replaces it.
- The future of ITSM is not man versus machine, but man with machine.
- Embracing AI creates opportunities for upskilling, innovation, and greater human impact.

The following image is aptly titled as "*Human-AI Synergy in ITSM*":

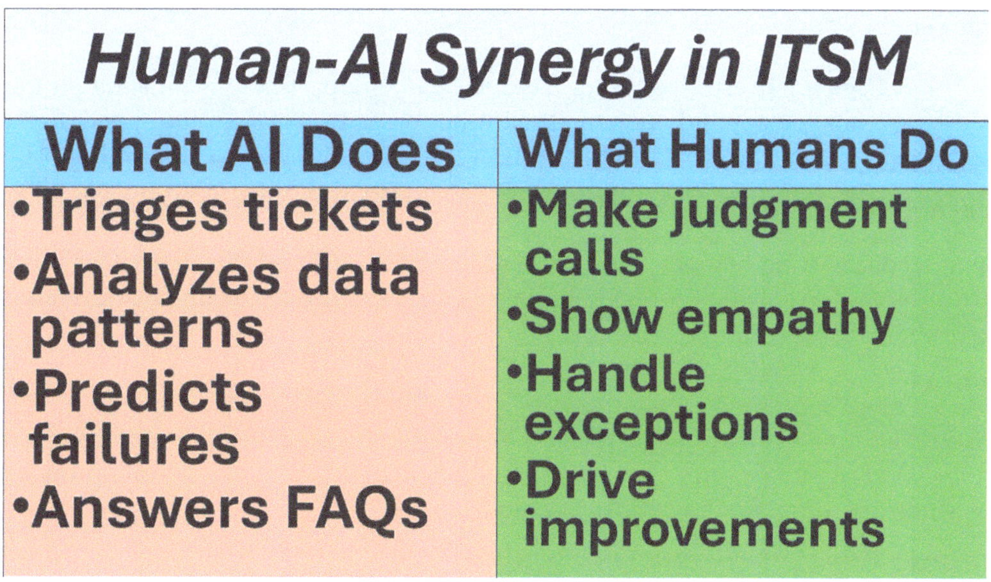

Figure 13.1: *Human-AI Synergy in ITSM*

With AI in play, traditional ITSM roles are evolving:

- Service Desk Agent → Becomes a "*Service Experience Facilitator*" using AI dashboards to monitor trends, user sentiment, and unresolved issues.

- Incident Manager → Transitions into a "*Crisis Analyst*" who interprets AI-driven root cause insights and develops response strategies.
- Change Manager → Acts as a "*Risk Orchestrator*," combining AI-driven impact assessments with business context for safe change enablement.
- Knowledge Manager → Takes on the role of a "*Content Curator*" who trains AI models on accurate KB inputs and refines AI recommendations.

These new roles blend technical skills, process knowledge, and human judgment–none of which AI can fully replicate.

Let us understand "Augmentation in Action" by living a day in the life of senior service desk analyst,

Let us follow Priya, a senior service desk analyst, working in an AI-augmented ITSM environment.

8:00 AM

Priya logs into her unified AI dashboard. The system has already classified 80% of the night's incoming tickets. Those requiring urgent human attention are flagged based on sentiment score and keyword context.

9:30 AM

An AI bot flags a pattern: five users from the same department are facing an issue accessing a finance app. Priya opens the event correlation report auto generated by the AIOps platform and escalates to the network team with precise impact details.

11:00 AM

Using feedback from her last three escalations, Priya updates the chatbot's script to better respond to complex access queries. The system suggests changes based on NLP model training data.

3:00 PM

Priya reviews AI-generated analytics on knowledge base usage. She notices one KB article is driving more support calls instead of deflecting them. She collaborates with the KB owner to rewrite it with user-centric language.

5:00 PM

Before signing off, Priya checks the AI-enabled sentiment dashboard to identify any tickets with unresolved frustration. She personally calls one VIP user whose issue is still open and assures them of timely resolution.

Takeaway: *AI didn't replace Priya. It made her work more meaningful, data-informed, and user-focused.*

The benefits of Human-AI Collaboration in ITSM are as follows:

- Increased job satisfaction: Less time spent on mundane tasks.
- Better customer experience: Faster, smarter, more empathetic support.
- Upskilling opportunities: Roles expand into AI stewardship and workflow design.
- Stronger outcomes: Improved MTTR, CSAT, FCR, and ticket resolution rates.
- Continual improvement: Humans provide feedback to train and improve AI over time.

It is very critical to understand "What AI Can't Replace."

Despite AI's rapid advancement, several uniquely human capabilities remain irreplaceable:

- Empathy and emotional intelligence
- Understanding nuanced organizational context
- Ethical reasoning and decision-making
- Cultural and language subtleties
- Leadership, mentorship, and stakeholder management

Organizations that recognize and preserve these strengths will gain the most from AI integration.

AI in ITSM is best seen not as a competitor but as a powerful ally. It empowers service professionals to shift from ticket-pushing to insight-driven, value-creating work. The augmentation of human roles by AI marks a new chapter, where ITSM becomes smarter, more responsive, and more human than ever before.

The real challenge is not whether AI will replace jobs, but whether we are ready to redefine our roles, retrain ourselves, and rise to the opportunity.

Upskilling and Mindset Shifts

As AI technologies become deeply embedded within IT Service Management (ITSM), the most crucial transformation is not technological–it is human. Success in an AI-augmented environment hinges on how well individuals and organizations can evolve their skills, mindsets, and cultural readiness.

Rather than fearing displacement, forward-thinking professionals are embracing AI as a catalyst for career evolution. From service desk agents to problem managers, roles are shifting–from execution-heavy to intelligence-led, from reactive tasks to proactive strategies.

This chapter explores the dual journey of upskilling and mindset shift–unpacking what new competencies are needed, why traditional thinking no longer suffices, and how real organizations are preparing their teams to thrive in this AI-powered landscape.

While AI is reshaping the technical landscape of ITSM, the real differentiator for professionals is how they **develop, adapt, and position their skills**. This is where SFIA—the **Skills Framework for the Information Age**—offers a powerful lens.

SFIA provides a global, structured way to define skills and levels of responsibility. It helps organizations and professionals identify **where they are today** and **what new capabilities are required** for tomorrow's AI-augmented environment. In the context of ITSM, SFIA adds clarity in three key ways:

- **Mapping Current Competence to Future Roles**
    - Service desk agents, incident managers, or problem managers can assess their existing skills (for example, *Incident Management, Service Operations*) against SFIA levels.
    - As AI automates routine tasks, these roles evolve toward higher SFIA levels emphasizing *analysis, orchestration, and leadership.*
- **Defining Upskilling Pathways**
    - **AI Literacy** links to SFIA skills in *Data Management, Analytics, and Emerging Technology Monitoring.*
    - **Workflow Automation and Integration** ties to *Systems Development and Automation.*
    - **Prompt Engineering and Human-AI Collaboration** aligns with *User Experience Analysis, Communication, and Knowledge Management.* This structured approach avoids vague training plans and builds **role-based competency roadmaps**.
- **Embedding Mindset Shifts into Competency Frameworks** SFIA does not just track technical skills; it includes dimensions such as **autonomy, influence, and complexity**. These naturally encourage mindset shifts:
    - From **Control to Collaboration** → moving up SFIA levels means operating with more autonomy and shared influence.
    - From **Fixed Roles to Fluid Capabilities** → SFIA encourages multi-skill growth across domains.
    - From **Process-First to Value-First** → SFIA levels emphasize delivering business value, not just following procedures.

Practical Example:

An organization introducing AI-based triage can map *Service Desk Analyst* roles (traditionally SFIA Level 2–3) to future roles requiring *Analytics, Problem Solving, and AI Workflow Stewardship* at Level 4–5. This gives employees a transparent growth path instead of fearing redundancy.

Takeaway:

SFIA turns "upskilling and mindset shifts" from an abstract aspiration into a **concrete, trackable competency journey**. By embedding SFIA into AI adoption programs, ITSM teams can align learning with career progression, making transformation not just necessary—but motivating and rewarding.

The Skills of the Past versus The Skills of the Future

Traditionally, ITSM roles have prioritized structured thinking, tool navigation, and procedural knowledge. While these are still important, the AI era demands a broader and deeper skillset:

From Task Execution → to Strategic Orchestration

Routine processes like ticket triage and status updates are now automated. Professionals must learn to interpret AI insights, manage AI workflows, and guide exception handling.

From Static Knowledge → to Continuous Learning

ITSM professionals must embrace lifelong learning, as AI technologies evolve rapidly. New toolkits, frameworks, and ethical challenges will require agility over rigidity.

The following table describes the key areas for upskilling in AI-Powered ITSM:

Skill Area	Description	Why It Matters in AI-Driven ITSM
AI Literacy	Basic understanding of AI/ ML/NLP, what it is and isn't	Helps professionals collaborate effectively with AI teams
Data Interpretation	Understanding AI outputs, confidence scores, trends	Enhances decision-making and action on AI-generated insights
Workflow Automation Tools	Familiarity with platforms such as Power Automate, ServiceNow Flows, or Zapier	Empowers users to design or troubleshoot automated processes
Prompt Engineering	Crafting effective prompts for tools like ChatGPT or VA interfaces	Improves the relevance and reliability of AI interactions

Ethical and Responsible AI Use	Awareness of bias, explainability, and data privacy principles	Ensures trust and accountability in AI-supported service delivery
Communication and Empathy	Explaining AI outputs to users and stakeholders clearly, with empathy	Human-centric value delivery remains a key differentiator
Collaboration with AI Systems	Operating in tandem with AI-driven tools and bots	Builds hybrid human-machine workflows for speed and efficiency

Table 13.3: *Key Areas for Upskilling in AI-Powered ITSM*

Mindset Shifts: Beyond Tools, Towards Transformation

While technical skills are teachable, mindset is what sustains transformation. Successful professionals and teams will embody these mental models:

- **From Control to Collaboration:** Instead of fearing AI as a competitor, professionals must see it as a co-worker. Let the AI do the "heavy lifting" while humans focus on decision-making and empathy.
- **From Fixed Roles to Fluid Capabilities:** Static job descriptions are out. Cross-functional knowledge, adaptability, and an open attitude toward role evolution are now in demand.
- **From Process-First to Value-First Thinking:** AI forces teams to refocus from just "following procedures" to asking, "Does this add value?" A flexible, value-centric approach is critical.
- **From Perfection to Iteration:** AI tools improve through feedback. Professionals must adopt a growth mindset, where feedback loops and experimentation are welcomed–not feared.

Use Case: Upskilling at a Managed Services Provider (MSP)

Scenario: An IT-managed services firm introduced AI-based incident categorization and chatbot systems across its global service desk.

Challenge: L1 support staff feared layoffs and lacked familiarity with AI tools. Morale dropped, and early adoption stalled.

Response: The firm launched a structured upskilling initiative:

- Phase 1: AI 101 for all staff (demystifying ML, NLP, and automation concepts).

- Phase 2: Role-specific training (for example, prompt engineering for chatbot curators, data analytics for incident managers).
- Phase 3: "AI Co-Worker Labs" where employees co-designed workflows with AI engineers.

Outcome:

- AI adoption rose by 60% within three months.
- 40% of L1 staff were promoted into AI steward, automation designer, or knowledge manager roles.
- Satisfaction scores improved significantly, both internally and for end-users.

Lesson: Upskilling with empathy and inclusion pays dividends–in performance, retention, and transformation success.

Suggested strategies for enabling upskilling and mindset shifts include:

- **Create a Culture of Curiosity:** Reward experimentation and questions about AI. Make learning visible and accessible.
- **Establish an AI Competency Framework**: Define what competencies are expected from different roles in an AI-enabled ITSM team.
- **Provide Just-In-Time Learning:** Offer modular, role-based, on-demand learning content rather than long-form training sessions.
- **Encourage Shadowing and Mentoring:** Let less-experienced team members work closely with AI champions and automation experts.
- **Make AI Visible, Not Mysterious:** Integrate AI explanations, feedback loops, and transparency into everyday tools and processes.
- **Celebrate Evolving Roles:** Recognize those who embrace change, redefine their work, and inspire others.

Few quotes from the Field

"The AI is not replacing my job–it is finally letting me do the part of my job I love."

– Incident Manager, FinTech Startup

"I thought AI would be complicated. But once I saw what it could do with my input, I realized I just needed to think differently."

– Service Desk Analyst, Global Retail Chain

As AI capabilities accelerate, the shelf-life of skills shortens–but the value of growth mindset and adaptability multiplies. The professionals who thrive in this new ITSM landscape will be those who blend technical literacy with human intelligence, and tool fluency with emotional agility.

Upskilling and mindset shifts are not one-time exercises–they are now the lifeblood of relevance and resilience in the future of service management.

The Human Side of Intelligent Service Delivery

AI is revolutionizing IT Service Management (ITSM) by improving speed, efficiency, and consistency. However, service delivery is not just about resolving tickets–it is about human experiences. Customers and employees don't just seek answers; they want to be understood, respected, and reassured. Intelligent service delivery, therefore, must be more than a blend of algorithms and automation. It must preserve the human element that builds trust, loyalty, and satisfaction.

This chapter explores how empathy, active listening, personalization, ethical communication, and emotional intelligence are essential in AI-augmented service environments. It also highlights how these qualities can be amplified–not diminished–by AI, with real-world examples and actionable recommendations.

We must understand why the human touch still matters.

AI can answer a query in seconds, predict failures before they happen, and resolve thousands of tickets simultaneously. Yet it lacks the ability to genuinely understand emotions, make nuanced ethical decisions, or establish human connection in moments of uncertainty. These are precisely the areas where ITSM professionals shine.

In high-stress scenarios–such as system outages, login failures before major presentations, or failed upgrades–users are often anxious. In these moments, AI cannot offer compassion. Only a human agent can say, "I understand this is frustrating. I'm here to help." That reassurance turns a transaction into a relationship.

Real-World Use Case: AI and Empathy in Action

Scenario: Global Service Desk of a Healthcare Firm

A senior doctor in a hospital couldn't access her diagnostic software minutes before surgery prep. She reached out to the IT service desk. The AI-powered virtual agent quickly identified a license renewal issue and provided steps to resolve it.

However, the doctor's urgency and concern were missed by the AI.

Sensing stress from the user's messages, the system escalated the call. A human support agent took over and said:

"Dr. Rajan, I completely understand how critical this is. I will stay with you until we're sure everything works perfectly."

Within minutes, the issue was resolved. The doctor thanked the agent not for the solution–but for the empathy and commitment.

Takeaway: AI solved the *problem*, but a human solved the *experience*.

Key Human Qualities That Elevate AI-Augmented Service

While AI brings speed, precision, and scalability to service management, it is the human touch that ensures empathy, creativity, and ethical decision-making remain at the core. In AI-augmented service environments, certain human qualities become not just complementary but critical. This section explores the essential traits that elevate service delivery when humans and intelligent systems work hand in hand.

- **Empathy and Emotional Intelligence (EQ)**: AI cannot yet feel, but it can be trained to detect sentiment. When a chatbot notices frustration, it can prompt escalation. However, only a human can understand context, apply empathy, and adapt to the tone of the conversation.

"I can imagine how stressful it is to deal with this just before your presentation. Let us solve this together."

Empathetic responses defuse tension and create emotional loyalty.

- **Active Listening and Human Engagement**: AI often lacks the patience or nuance to let a customer explain things in their own words. Human agents can use active listening–paraphrasing, asking clarifying questions, and reflecting emotions–to show users that they have truly been heard.

"So just to confirm, you've been trying to log in since 8 a.m., and each time the screen freezes after entering your password. Is that right?"

Such interactions build credibility and trust.

- **Personalization Through Human Insight**: While AI can access history, device information, and past tickets, humans apply discretion. For example, AI might suggest an upsell because a user meets eligibility, but a human agent will recognize that now is *not* the time–especially if the customer is already frustrated.

The human side of personalization also includes cultural awareness, tone modulation, and humor–things AI still struggles to master.

- **Trust and Transparency**: Customers are more accepting of AI when it is transparent. Telling users, "*You are chatting with an AI assistant. A human is available anytime*," fosters trust. But what happens when things go wrong?

Only human agents can take responsibility, explain failures honestly, and offer restitution.

"We are really sorry about the inconvenience. I have escalated this, and I will personally follow up until it's resolved."

Such human commitment builds confidence and satisfaction.

Human-AI Collaboration: Not Replacement, but Augmentation

AI is most powerful when it enhances human service, not replaces it. Here is how the two complement each other:

AI Strengths	Human Strengths
Fast response, 24/7 availability	Empathy, judgment, emotional connection
Pattern recognition, data processing	Understanding nuance, resolving ambiguity
Repetitive task automation	Creativity, problem-solving, personal rapport

Table 13.4: *Human AI Collaboration*

A well-designed service experience assigns AI to do the heavy lifting–classification, routing, data gathering–so humans can focus on meaningful interaction.

Service Design Thinking: Embedding Humanity in Journeys

ITSM leaders should apply service design thinking to map where automation helps and where human interaction matters most:

- Use AI to speed up low-touch interactions (for example, password resets).
- Use humans to resolve high-emotion or high-impact issues (for example, data loss, executive support).
- Embed fallback mechanisms for AI escalation.
- Let humans review and retrain AI using real feedback.

Always ask: "*What is the user feeling at this point*?" Then design the interaction to reflect that.

Practical Recommendations

Here are actionable ways to preserve the human side in AI-powered ITSM:

- Train agents in empathy and emotional intelligence. Include roleplays and feedback mechanisms.

- Use sentiment analysis to trigger human escalation. Ensure the system understands when empathy is needed.
- Make AI transparent. Inform users when they're interacting with a virtual assistant, and offer easy opt-out to a human.
- Design contextual handoffs. Ensure human agents receive full background so users don't repeat themselves.
- Balance personalization. Let AI suggest, but humans approve. Avoid over-automation that feels invasive.
- Celebrate human stories. Highlight moments where agents made a difference beyond solving tickets.

Real-Life Story: The Executive That Called Back

A Tier-1 service desk agent in a large insurance company once handled an escalated case from a senior executive. The AI assistant had offered multiple solutions, none of which worked. The executive was frustrated and late for a meeting.

The agent calmly said, "*I understand this is urgent. I'll stay with you and fast-track this myself.*"

He fixed the issue. Days later, the executive emailed the CIO—not to praise the AI, but to commend the agent's care, patience, and professionalism.

"It wasn't just that he solved my issue. It was how he made me feel—like I mattered."

Final Deduction: The Soul of Service

Technology drives scale. AI drives speed. But humanity drives connection.

The future of ITSM isn't about bots replacing people. It's about people empowered by intelligent tools to deliver smarter, faster, and more compassionate service.

When empathy, personalization, and trust remain at the heart of service delivery, organizations don't just resolve incidents—they create meaningful experiences that users remember long after the issue is closed.

Conclusion

As AI continues to reshape the foundations of IT Service Management, it is not diminishing the value of ITSM professionals—it is redefining it. This chapter has made it abundantly clear that the future of service delivery lies not in replacing humans, but in **elevating their roles** to new levels of impact, creativity, and strategic relevance.

In the AI-powered ITSM landscape, tasks that once consumed hours of manual effort–such as ticket triage, password resets, or knowledge searches–are now being seamlessly handled by intelligent systems. But these efficiencies have not rendered people obsolete. Instead, they have created room for **human strengths to shine**, empathy, ethical reasoning, relationship-building, contextual judgment, and strategic oversight.

Professionals are no longer just process executors; they are becoming **AI stewards, experienced designers, and insight translators**. They are moving from behind the scenes to the center of service transformation. Roles are evolving dynamically, and the most successful professionals are those who combine **AI literacy with emotional intelligence**, **tool fluency with cultural awareness**, and **data interpretation with human connection**.

Equally important is the **mindset shift** that underpins this evolution. From control to collaboration, from fixed roles to adaptive learning, and from rigid processes to value-driven thinking–this is the new DNA of ITSM. Organizations that foster a **culture of upskilling, experimentation, and inclusion** will not only accelerate AI adoption but will also build more resilient, engaged, and future-ready teams.

Perhaps most crucially, the chapter reaffirms the **indispensable human element** in service delivery. AI can automate resolutions, but only a human can deliver reassurance. It can detect frustration, but only a human can defuse it with empathy. It can process patterns, but only a human can translate them into trust.

The path forward is clear: **Human-AI synergy** is not just a possibility–it is a necessity. The organizations that thrive will be those that do not ask "How do we replace people with AI?" but rather "How do we empower people through AI?"

In the next chapter, **the most valuable asset is not just intelligence–but emotional intelligence. Not just speed–but sincerity. Not just automation–but authenticity.**

Multiple Choice Questions

1. What is the primary role of AI in the evolving ITSM environment?
    a. To fully replace ITSM professionals
    b. To monitor only hardware-related issues
    c. To augment and elevate human roles
    d. To eliminate the need for service desks

2. In an AI-powered ITSM environment, what new responsibility might a traditional Service Desk Agent take on?
   a. System architecture design
   b. AI algorithm development
   c. Service Experience Facilitation using AI insights
   d. Finance and budgeting
3. Which skill is becoming increasingly important for ITSM professionals in the age of AI?
   a. Memorizing incident codes
   b. Empathy and emotional intelligence
   c. Manual ticket logging
   d. Writing code in COBOL
4. Why is "prompt engineering" considered a key upskilling area in AI-enabled ITSM?
   a. It helps create ITIL incident forms.
   b. It improves server uptime.
   c. It enables more effective interactions with AI tools including virtual agents.
   d. It automates hardware provisioning.
5. What does the term "Human-AI synergy" refer to in the context of ITSM?
   a. Replacing all human input with automation
   b. The competition between human and AI roles
   c. AI and humans working together to improve service outcomes
   d. Teaching AI to behave like humans

Answers

1. c
2. c
3. b
4. c
5. c

Questions

1. How does AI augment, rather than replace, the role of ITSM professionals in a modern service environment?
2. Describe the concept of "Human-AI synergy" in ITSM. How does it impact service delivery and team dynamics?
3. In what ways have traditional ITSM roles such as Service Desk Agent or Change Manager evolved in an AI-augmented organization?
4. What is the significance of emotional intelligence and empathy in AI-powered service delivery? Provide examples.
5. Why is upskilling considered a strategic imperative for ITSM professionals in the age of AI?
6. List and explain key skill areas that ITSM professionals must develop to thrive in an AI-enabled environment.
7. What mindset shifts are necessary for professionals to successfully transition into AI-augmented ITSM roles?
8. How can organizations design upskilling programs that address both technical training and cultural readiness for AI adoption?
9. Why is it important to preserve the human element in intelligent service delivery, even as AI becomes more capable?
10. How can ITSM teams apply service design thinking to strike the right balance between automation and human interaction?

Key Terms

- **Human-AI Synergy:** In the new world of ITSM, success doesn't come from man or machine alone–it's the harmony between them. Human-AI synergy describes the collaborative partnership where AI handles scale and speed, while humans bring empathy, context, and judgment.
- **AI Augmentation:** Rather than eliminating jobs, AI augments ITSM professionals by handling repetitive tasks like triaging tickets or fetching data. This lets humans focus on higher-order thinking, customer care, and innovation.
- **Service Experience Facilitator:** As service desk agents evolve, they take on the role of experience facilitators–interpreting AI dashboards, tracking sentiment, and ensuring users feel heard, supported, and satisfied throughout the service journey.
- **AI Literacy:** AI literacy is no longer a niche skill but a foundational competency. It involves understanding the basics of how AI, machine learning, and NLP work so professionals can collaborate effectively with intelligent systems.
- **Prompt Engineering:** In an age where virtual agents are common, crafting effective prompts becomes crucial. Prompt engineering refers to designing clear and contextual instructions that help AI tools provide accurate, helpful responses.
- **Emotional Intelligence (EQ):** Even the most advanced AI cannot replicate emotional intelligence. Traits such as empathy, active listening, and understanding user frustration are uniquely human and essential in creating trust in service delivery.
- **Sentiment Analysis:** AI tools can now analyze the emotional tone of messages using sentiment analysis. While the AI detects the signal, it is still the human who responds with compassion and correct judgment when emotions run high.
- **AI Steward:** Some ITSM professionals are becoming AI stewards–those responsible for training, validating, and improving AI workflows. They ensure that automation aligns with service quality, fairness, and user needs.
- **Upskilling:** In an AI-powered ITSM environment, continuous learning becomes vital. Upskilling involves acquiring new technical and behavioral skills that prepare professionals for roles that blend human insight with machine support.
- **Service Design Thinking:** To build seamless, empathetic, and efficient services, ITSM leaders are turning to service design thinking. This approach helps map when and where to use automation versus human touch, ensuring user-centric service journeys.

CHAPTER 14
What is Next? GenAI, ChatGPT, and Beyond

Introduction

As AI continues to reshape the service management landscape, a new frontier is emerging–one where machines don't just respond to requests but anticipate needs, engage in dialogue, and co-create service experiences. This chapter looks ahead to that frontier, where **Generative AI (GenAI)**, tools like **ChatGPT**, and intelligent design thinking are pushing ITSM into uncharted but exciting territory. What began as automation of routine tasks is now evolving into **conversational workflows, adaptive knowledge systems, and empathetic AI agents** that transform how services are delivered. Generative AI brings with it the ability to craft responses, draft documentation, and even simulate service scenarios in real-time–blurring the lines between human insight and machine-generated value.

But with these advances come new questions: How do we ensure accuracy, avoid over-dependence, and preserve the human touch in increasingly AI-driven interactions? How do we design ITSM experiences that are not just functional, but fluid, intuitive, and anticipatory? This chapter explores how GenAI is redefining roles, reimagining interfaces, and revealing opportunities for deeper personalization in IT support. It also offers a forward-looking lens into how **design thinking principles**–centered on user needs, empathy, and iteration–can guide the responsible and effective integration of AI into future service strategies. As we stand on the edge of this AI-powered horizon, the goal is no longer just better service–it's **proactive, predictive, and personalized service** that feels more human, even when powered by machines.

Structure

In this chapter, we will discuss the following topics:

- The Role of Generative AI in ITSM
- AI in Service Experience, Design Thinking, and Proactive Services

- Long-Term Trends Shaping AI in Service Management

The Role of Generative AI in ITSM

Generative AI (GenAI) represents a transformative leap in how IT services are imagined, designed, and delivered. Unlike traditional AI models that classify, route, or detect, GenAI can generate new content–be it responses, summaries, workflows, knowledge articles, or even diagnostic scripts. This opens a new dimension for ITSM: where machines not only assist but co-create solutions alongside humans. The rise of tools such as ChatGPT, Google Gemini, and Claude is reshaping the expectations from virtual agents, self-service portals, and knowledge bases. In this chapter, we explore how GenAI is moving from novelty to necessity in the ITSM world.

Understanding Generative AI in the ITSM Context

Generative AI refers to AI systems capable of producing text, code, images, or other forms of content based on trained patterns. In ITSM, it's mostly used in Natural Language Generation (NLG) and Conversational AI to improve interaction, knowledge access, and resolution capabilities.

Understanding the Difference Between GenAI and Traditional AI in ITSM

While traditional AI excels at classification and prediction (for example, auto-categorizing tickets), GenAI shines in generation–drafting responses, crafting knowledge base entries, or simulating conversations. It brings creativity and fluidity to structured service environments.

Let us understand the concept further by few use cases of GenAI in ITSM:

- **Conversational Ticket Handling:** GenAI powers intelligent chatbots and virtual agents that converse naturally, ask clarifying questions, and even summarize user issues into ticket-ready formats. These bots don't just trigger workflows–they humanize them.
- **Knowledge Management Automation:** Instead of manually documenting solutions, GenAI can generate draft knowledge base articles from ticket history, resolutions, or even transcripts. It reduces knowledge fatigue and accelerates documentation turnaround.
- **Intelligent Email Summarization:** Agents often deal with long email chains. GenAI can summarize these interactions, extract key points, and highlight action items–improving efficiency and reducing resolution time.

- **Self-Healing Workflows:** By synthesizing logs and historical resolutions, GenAI can suggest or even automate corrective actions (for example, restarting a service, applying a patch), leading to autonomous remediation in low-risk scenarios.
- **User-Facing Guidance and Documentation:** GenAI can generate FAQs, SOPs, or user instructions on-the-fly based on user queries. This creates a dynamic knowledge delivery mechanism tailored to each situation.

The benefits of Generative AI in ITSM are as follows:

- **Speed:** Automates content generation, reducing the burden on agents.
- **Scalability:** Supports high-volume operations without linear increases in staffing.
- **Personalization:** Delivers tailored responses and dynamic documentation.
- **Knowledge Democratization:** Makes technical content accessible to non-technical users.
- **Proactive Experience:** Suggests next steps and preemptive measures intelligently.

Let us also understand the risks and challenges.

- **Hallucinations and Misinformation:** GenAI may generate convincing but factually incorrect responses–a phenomenon known as hallucination. This can mislead users or agents if not validated.
- **Data Privacy and IP Leakage:** When GenAI interacts with internal or sensitive data, it must be tightly governed to avoid accidental exposure of PII or proprietary information.
- **Ethical and Compliance Oversight:** As GenAI mimics human responses, it can unintentionally introduce bias or violate data residency or regulatory compliance norms.
- **Overdependence and Deskilling:** If not paired with proper training and oversight, overuse of GenAI can lead to loss of critical thinking or skill erosion among IT staff.

The following list presents governance best practices for GenAI in ITSM:

- Human-in-the-loop validation before GenAI-generated outputs go live.
- Feedback loops to improve GenAI performance over time.
- Clear tagging of AI-generated content for transparency.
- Role-based access control to ensure GenAI only accesses relevant data.
- Integration with AI governance frameworks, such as ISO 42001 and ITIL4's governance model.

To understand and understand the concept, let us look at few examples of the tool landscape and platform:

- **ChatGPT (OpenAI/Microsoft Copilot):** Widely integrated with tools such as Azure, ServiceNow, and Outlook, ChatGPT is becoming a conversational co-pilot for service desk tasks.
- **Atlassian Intelligence (Jira Service Management):** Integrates GenAI to auto-generate knowledge articles and perform inline query resolution in Jira-based environments.
- **ServiceNow Now Assist:** Aims to generate incident summaries, KB articles, and next-best actions using domain-specific GenAI models.
- **Zoho Zia (ManageEngine):** Supports GenAI features like automated replies and article generation to enhance ManageEngine's support ecosystem.

So, now the thought process is about the future outlook. Where GenAI is Headed in ITSM?

Few probable options are as follows:

- **Autonomous Agents:** Virtual engineers that not only talk but act.
- **Proactive UX:** Service bots that anticipate and fulfill needs before users raise them.
- **GenAI Co-pilots:** Embedded copilots in ITSM tools to support agents contextually.
- **Voice AI Interfaces:** Voice-driven GenAI services integrated into enterprise environments.

Final Deduction: Shaping the Future, Responsibly

The rise of Generative AI marks a new chapter in ITSM—one that moves from automation to co-creation. When guided with ethical use, strong governance, and purposeful intent, GenAI has the power to unlock new levels of efficiency, personalization, and value. But with this power comes responsibility—to ensure factual accuracy, preserve trust, and elevate the human experience rather than erode it. The role of the ITSM professional will not diminish—it will evolve. And those who embrace GenAI with a mindset of augmentation and accountability will help lead service management into a smarter, more adaptive future.

AI in Service Experience, Design Thinking, and Proactive Services

As AI matures from being a tool of automation to a catalyst of transformation, the focus in ITSM is shifting from solving problems to designing exceptional, proactive service experiences. This evolution is about more than chatbots and classification—it's about reimagining how services are conceived, delivered, and evolved with the end-user at the center. Integrating AI with design thinking empowers ITSM teams to shape experiences that are not only functional but empathetic, anticipatory, and continuously improving. This chapter explores how AI is revolutionizing the service experience, how design thinking helps shape this transformation, and how proactive services redefine ITSM from reactive support to value delivery.

Understanding Service Experience in ITSM

The service experience encompasses every touchpoint a user has with IT—from requesting support and finding knowledge to interacting with agents or systems. Traditionally reactive and fragmented, AI now enables real-time personalization, dynamic support, and contextual assistance across the user journey.

How AI Enhances Service Experience

AI-driven tools such as NLP engines, sentiment analyzers, and virtual agents offer seamless, conversational interactions. By understanding intent, emotion, and urgency, AI tailors responses and routes requests proactively, making the experience faster, more relevant, and emotionally resonant.

Applying Design Thinking to ITSM with AI

Design thinking is a human-centered, iterative approach to problem-solving that prioritizes empathy, ideation, prototyping, and testing. In ITSM, it shifts the focus from process design to experience design—ensuring that services meet real needs in intuitive ways.

It is important to find the answer for the question "Why Design Thinking Matters in AI-Driven ITSM?"

AI tools are only as effective as the experience they deliver. Design thinking helps teams avoid "tech-first" traps by grounding AI development in user pain points, emotional journeys, and feedback loops. It ensures AI amplifies empathy, not just efficiency.

Following is the list of few AI + Design Thinking in Action

- **Empathize:** Use sentiment analysis and behavioral data to identify service bottlenecks.
- **Define**: Analyze interaction patterns to define real user problems.
- **Ideate:** Collaborate with users and AI teams to brainstorm service improvements.
- **Prototype**: Build AI-driven virtual agents, predictive dashboards, or auto-responses.
- **Test:** Measure CSAT, resolution times, and AI confidence levels in real scenarios.

Now, next item in the agenda is building proactive services with AI

- From Reactive to Proactive

  Traditional ITSM responds to incidents and requests. Proactive ITSM predicts and prevents them. AI makes this possible by identifying patterns, anomalies, and leading indicators of potential issues–reducing downtime and improving user trust.

- **Examples of Proactive AI-Enabled Services**
  - **Predictive Ticketing**: Identifying issues before users report them (for example, storage threshold alerts).
  - **Dynamic Notifications**: Alerting users about service degradation before impact occurs.
  - **Usage-Based Recommendations**: Offering knowledge articles or upgrades based on behavior.
  - **Capacity Forecasting**: Using historical data to prevent performance degradation.

- **GenAI in Proactive Experience Design**

  GenAI does not just react to queries–it can create personalized touchpoints: reminding users of upcoming changes, summarizing service health, or offering onboarding guidance tailored to their role or device. This turns AI into a service concierge rather than just a problem solver.

The benefits that can be reaped from utilization of AI-Powered Experience Design are listed as follows:

- **Increased User Satisfaction:** Personalized, empathetic, and timely service builds trust.
- **Reduced Friction**: Fewer steps, less waiting, and clearer communication.
- **Stronger Adoption**: Services designed with users in mind are more readily embraced.

- **Continuous Improvement**: AI insights feed iterative improvements through user behavior and feedback.
- **Operational Efficiency**: Proactive and anticipatory services reduce volume and cost of tickets.

As we are aware, the journey so far has not been entirely smooth, we must acknowledge few prominent challenges and considerations:

- **Experience Overload:** Too many AI-generated messages or nudges can overwhelm users. Experience design must balance helpfulness with minimalism.
- **Ethical Use of Personalization**: Using user behavior and sentiment data must comply with privacy standards and avoid manipulation or bias.
- **Designing for All Personas**: Design thinking ensures AI doesn't just serve tech-savvy users but also accommodates those less familiar with digital interfaces.
- **Trust and Transparency**: When users interact with AI-driven services, clarity about what is AI-driven and what is human-supported fosters confidence and adoption.

The discussion so far prompts us to think about the role of ITSM professionals in Experience-Led AI Design.

AI doesn't replace the human; it reorients the human role. Service designers, analysts, and support leaders now serve as:

- User advocates, using AI insights to personalize services.
- Journey mappers, identifying friction points and creating smoother paths.
- Experience architects, crafting not just workflows but emotional flows.
- Feedback translators, turning sentiment and usage data into design improvements.

Final Deduction: AI with Empathy, Design with Intent

The future of ITSM is not just about intelligent systems–it is about intelligent experiences. AI, when guided by design thinking, becomes more than a technical solution; it becomes a medium for empathy, personalization, and proactivity. Service teams that blend AI innovation with human-centered design will lead the way in creating IT services that are not just efficient, but truly delightful. The goal is not just faster support, but smarter, more intuitive support that feels effortless and empowering. As ITSM continues to evolve, those who design with intention and deliver with empathy will set the new gold standard in digital service excellence.

Long-Term Trends Shaping AI in Service Management

AI is no longer a futuristic concept or a short-term tool–it is a strategic pillar shaping the future of IT Service Management (ITSM). As adoption matures, the focus shifts from isolated use cases to ecosystem-wide integration, experience-centered delivery, and governance at scale. In this final section of the chapter, we explore the long-term trends that will define how AI continues to transform ITSM–not just for the next release cycle, but for the next decade. These trends represent both the promise and the responsibility of embedding intelligence into the very fabric of digital service management.

Convergence of AI and ITSM Platforms

The convergence of AI and ITSM platforms marks a significant turning point in how services are delivered, managed, and optimized. No longer treated as separate add-ons or third-party integrations, AI capabilities are becoming natively embedded within leading ITSM tools, such as ServiceNow, Jira, and ManageEngine. This shift allows intelligent features–such as auto-triaging, generative response suggestions, sentiment-aware routing, and predictive ticketing–to function seamlessly within core workflows. As ITSM platforms evolve into intelligent service ecosystems, they empower service teams to act faster, deliver more personalized support, and uncover operational insights in real-time–without leaving the platform interface. This tight integration signals the beginning of a smarter, more unified approach to managing the digital service experience.

Embedded AI Capabilities Become Native

Leading ITSM tools–such as ServiceNow, BMC Helix, Freshservice, and Jira–are evolving from integrating AI as an add-on to embedding it as a core capability. Auto-triage, chatbot builders, AI-based routing, and generative knowledge assistants are no longer optional–they are table stakes.

Unified Data Lakes and Intelligence Layers

Future ITSM platforms will rely on shared data lakes, bringing together operations, user behavior, asset, and security data. A centralized intelligence layer will process these signals to deliver context-aware insights across incident, change, request, and problem workflows.

Rise of Autonomous ITSM

The rise of autonomous ITSM represents a bold leap from automation to intelligent self-governance in service operations. While traditional automation executes predefined scripts or workflows, autonomous ITSM systems go further—detecting anomalies, diagnosing root causes, taking corrective actions, and learning from outcomes without human intervention. Enabled by advancements in AIOps, machine learning, and policy-based engines, these systems can handle routine incidents, optimize performance, and even escalate exceptions only when necessary. For example, an autonomous ITSM platform might automatically restart a failing service, reroute user access, or generate a remediation script in real time—all while keeping stakeholders informed. This shift reduces MTTR, minimizes human error, and allows IT staff to focus on higher-value initiatives. As ITSM moves toward autonomy, the service desk of the future will be more proactive, self-healing, and resilient, fundamentally changing how we perceive support delivery.

From Automation to Autonomy

Automation handles predefined tasks. Autonomy makes decisions. The long-term trend is toward self-driving ITSM, where AI proactively initiates remediation, escalates only when necessary, and optimizes itself based on outcomes.

Event-Driven, Self-Healing Systems

AI will enable systems that listen for anomalies, correlate across domains, and act in real-time. For example, instead of logging a disk failure ticket, an autonomous system will reroute traffic, restart services, and notify impacted users—all without human intervention.

AI-Powered Experience Personalization

AI-powered experience personalization is redefining how users engage with IT services by delivering interactions that are intuitive, relevant, and context-aware. Instead of offering one-size-fits-all portals or generic responses, modern ITSM solutions infused with AI can tailor dashboards, recommendations, and workflows based on a user's role, preferences, and behavior history. Whether it's suggesting knowledge articles before a ticket is raised, customizing self-service interfaces for different departments, or proactively surfacing relevant actions, AI ensures every touchpoint feels uniquely suited to the individual. This level of personalization not only enhances user satisfaction but also reduces friction and accelerates resolution. By understanding context and anticipating needs, AI shifts ITSM from a support function to a seamless, user-centric experience that feels less like service and more like intelligent collaboration.

Role-Aware and Context-Aware Services

AI will adapt interfaces, content, and workflows based on user roles, past behavior, and preferences. A project manager will see a different self-service dashboard than a network engineer or HR associate–tailored to their context and needs.

Predictive Engagement Models

Proactive alerts will evolve into predictive nudges–suggesting password resets before expiry, offering KB articles based on behavioral signals, or auto-completing ticket forms based on usage history.

Democratization of AI in ITSM

The democratization of AI in ITSM is making intelligent capabilities accessible beyond data scientists and AI specialists–empowering service managers, process owners, and frontline agents to harness AI without deep technical expertise. With the rise of no-code and low-code AI builders, ITSM platforms are enabling users to design workflows, build chatbots, and deploy automation with intuitive drag-and-drop interfaces. At the same time, skills like prompt engineering are emerging as essential tools for interacting effectively with generative AI tools such as ChatGPT. This shift is flattening the learning curve and bringing AI innovation directly into the hands of those closest to the service experience. As a result, organizations can scale AI adoption more broadly, foster a culture of experimentation, and drive grassroots-level transformation–where every ITSM professional becomes an AI contributor, not just a consumer.

No-Code AI Builders for Service Teams

Business users and process owners–not just data scientists–will be able to design and deploy AI workflows using drag-and-drop AI builders. Platforms will offer AI-as-a-Service models that abstract model training and deployment complexities.

Prompt Engineering as a Core Skill

With GenAI, writing the right prompt becomes a form of programming. Service desk professionals will be trained in "prompt literacy" to interact more effectively with conversational agents and co-pilot tools.

Regulation, Ethics, and Trust as Pillars

As AI becomes deeply embedded in ITSM operations, regulation, ethics, and trust are no longer optional–they are foundational pillars for sustainable and responsible innovation. From data privacy to algorithmic fairness, organizations must ensure that AI decisions–such as incident prioritization, user response generation, or access control–are transparent, explainable, and auditable. Emerging frameworks such as ISO/IEC 42001 and the NIST AI Risk Management Framework are guiding the development of AI governance policies that align with enterprise risk and compliance standards. Ethical considerations, including the mitigation of bias, responsible use of user data, and clear disclosure of AI-generated outputs, are critical to maintaining user confidence. Trust is earned not just through functionality, but through accountability, consent, and fairness. As AI continues to evolve, ITSM leaders must design systems where human oversight and ethical boundaries are hardwired into every intelligent process–ensuring that technology serves people, not the other way around.

Rise of AI Governance Frameworks

Frameworks such as ISO/IEC 42001, NIST AI RMF, and COBIT AI extensions will become mandatory guides for responsible AI usage. Compliance will cover transparency, explainability, traceability, and accountability.

Transparent and Traceable AI

AI decisions in ITSM–such as risk classification or access denials–must be auditable and explainable. GenAI outputs will be tagged, logged, and subjected to validation layers to build trust.

Integration of Emotional and Conversational AI

The integration of emotional and conversational AI into ITSM is transforming service interactions from mechanical exchanges to empathetic, human-like dialogues. Emotional AI–through sentiment analysis and tone detection–can recognize user frustration, urgency, or satisfaction, enabling service systems to respond with appropriate empathy or escalate with care. Meanwhile, conversational AI, powered by advanced NLP and large language models, is evolving from scripted bots to dynamic virtual agents capable of understanding context, asking clarifying questions, and holding natural conversations. Together, these technologies allow ITSM to move beyond resolution to relationship-building, fostering trust and reducing user stress. Whether it's a chatbot detecting distress in a password reset request or a virtual assistant offering proactive reassurance during an outage, the goal is not just accuracy–it's emotional resonance and seamless communication. This fusion of intelligence and empathy marks a major leap toward more human-centric digital support experiences.

Sentiment-Aware Service Delivery

Advanced AI models will sense emotional cues from tone, keywords, and feedback–helping agents escalate compassionately or defuse tension with empathy.

Multimodal Interfaces

Voice, image, and even AR-based service interactions will become commonplace. Imagine explaining an issue by video, with AI generating a ticket, suggesting a fix, and escalating all in real time.

AI for Sustainable and Green ITSM

As environmental concerns become central to enterprise strategy, AI is emerging as a powerful enabler of sustainable and green ITSM. Intelligent monitoring and analytics can track energy consumption across data centers, end-user devices, and cloud workloads–helping organizations optimize resource usage and minimize their carbon footprint. AI-driven capacity planning ensures that infrastructure scales efficiently, avoiding both over-provisioning and energy waste. Service request automation and remote resolution further reduce travel and on-site support needs, contributing to eco-friendly operations. Additionally, future ITSM dashboards may include sustainability metrics, highlighting power savings, hardware lifecycle optimization, and emissions avoided through smarter service practices. By embedding sustainability into service management goals, AI not only enhances operational efficiency but also aligns ITSM with broader ESG (Environmental, Social, and Governance) initiatives–turning intelligent service delivery into responsible stewardship of the planet.

Energy-Aware Optimization

AI will help optimize workloads, reduce idle consumption, and promote green ITSM practices by monitoring energy-intensive processes across infrastructure.

Sustainability Dashboards

Future ITSM dashboards will not only report uptime or resolution SLAs but also carbon footprints, energy savings, and AI efficiency metrics as part of enterprise ESG reporting.

Continual Learning and Adaptive AI Models

The future of AI in ITSM lies in its ability to learn continuously and adapt dynamically. Unlike static models that degrade over time, adaptive AI systems evolve by incorporating user feedback, new data patterns, and changing business contexts–ensuring that predictions and recommendations stay relevant and effective. Whether it's refining ticket classification, improving chatbot responses, or optimizing self-healing routines, each interaction becomes an opportunity to learn and improve. Technologies such as reinforcement learning and federated learning enable AI to update itself securely and ethically across distributed environments, even where data privacy restrictions exist. This evolution creates a feedback-rich ITSM ecosystem where automation is not only intelligent but progressively smarter with experience. Continual learning bridges the gap between short-term efficiency and long-term excellence, making AI not just a tool, but a growing, adapting partner in service delivery.

Feedback-Driven Improvement

AI models will no longer be static. They will continually learn from user feedback, agent corrections, and business context–improving themselves over time.

Federated and Privacy-Preserving Learning

To balance data privacy and learning, federated AI models will train across decentralized environments–ensuring compliance while still evolving from diverse data.

Final Deduction: Designing for Tomorrow, Acting Today

The trends shaping AI in ITSM are as diverse as they are transformative–from embedded intelligence and proactive automation to personalized experiences and ethical governance. But these trends are not merely future possibilities; they are strategic imperatives for today's service leaders. By understanding these trajectories, organizations can design roadmaps that are not only future-proof but human-centered, trustworthy, and value-driven. The future of AI in ITSM will not be about machines replacing humans–it will be about AI extending human capability in ways we are only beginning to imagine. The time to prepare is now.

Conclusion

The emergence of generative AI, conversational intelligence, and design-driven service innovation is not just reshaping ITSM–it is redefining what it means to deliver value in the digital era. From automating mundane tasks to co-creating intelligent, user-centric experiences, AI has evolved into a strategic force that permeates every layer of service management. Yet, this journey is far from complete. The future of ITSM lies in how well we embrace **adaptive intelligence**, foster **responsible governance**, and maintain a **human-centered ethos** while integrating increasingly powerful AI capabilities.

This chapter offered a glimpse into the transformative possibilities ahead–from autonomous ITSM and AI-powered personalization to sustainable, ethical, and emotionally intelligent service models. These are not distant dreams–they are rapidly maturing realities. But as with any leap in capability, the path forward demands thoughtful stewardship. ITSM leaders must navigate risks such as bias, hallucinations, and trust deficits with robust frameworks and transparent practices. They must also champion skills involving **prompt engineering**, **design thinking**, and **AI literacy** to empower their teams in this new frontier.

Ultimately, the success of AI in ITSM won't be measured by how smart our systems become, but by how **seamlessly they augment human capability**, elevate user experience, and align with purpose-driven outcomes. As we design for tomorrow, the call to action is clear: **act today, responsibly and boldly**. The future of service management is not just about faster, cheaper, or smarter–it is about more **empathetic, adaptive, and intelligent partnerships between people and machines**. And that future starts now.

Multiple Choice Questions

1. What is a key distinction between generative AI and traditional AI in the context of ITSM?
    a. Traditional AI can create knowledge base articles, while GenAI cannot.
    b. Generative AI predicts future incidents, while traditional AI prevents them.
    c. Generative AI can generate content like responses or articles, while traditional AI focuses on classification and prediction.
    d. Traditional AI is better suited for emotional analysis than generative AI.
2. Which concept best describes ITSM platforms that autonomously detect, diagnose, and resolve issues without human intervention?
    a. AIOps-as-a-Service
    b. Autonomous ITSM
    c. Virtual Agent Framework
    d. Self-Service ITSM

3. What does the democratization of AI in ITSM refer to?
   a. Delegating AI decisions solely to IT leadership
   b. Replacing all human service desk agents with AI
   c. Empowering non-technical users to create and use AI workflows via low-code/no-code tools
   d. Limiting AI use to enterprise-level organizations
4. Why is sentiment analysis important in emotional and conversational AI for ITSM?
   a. It helps detect SLA violations
   b. It determines the best knowledge article to show
   c. It allows AI to detect emotional tone and respond empathetically
   d. It speeds up the escalation process through automation
5. How does AI contribute to sustainable and green ITSM practices?
   a. By promoting paperless communication only
   b. By extending the lifecycle of legacy systems
   c. By optimizing resource usage, reducing energy consumption, and enabling remote resolution
   d. By automating ITSM ticket routing only

Answers

1. c
2. b
3. c
4. c
5. c

Questions

1. Explain the role of generative AI in transforming ITSM operations. How does it differ from traditional forms of automation?
2. Discuss how AI can enhance the service experience when combined with design thinking. Provide examples to illustrate your answer.
3. What are the key characteristics of proactive service delivery in an AI-enabled ITSM environment?
4. How is the convergence of AI and ITSM platforms changing the expectations from modern service management tools?
5. Describe how autonomous ITSM works and highlight the benefits and potential risks associated with it.
6. In what ways can AI personalize the user experience in ITSM? How does personalization contribute to improved service outcomes?
7. What does democratization of AI mean in the context of ITSM, and how does it empower non-technical stakeholders?
8. Outline the ethical and governance challenges associated with AI in ITSM and suggest ways to address them effectively.
9. Describe how emotional and conversational AI can impact user satisfaction and service desk interactions.
10. Explain how AI supports sustainable ITSM practices. What role does AI play in achieving organizational ESG goals?

Key Terms

- **Generative AI:** Generative AI refers to models capable of creating original content such as text, code, or images. In ITSM, it powers intelligent responses, summaries, and knowledge base creation, adding human-like capabilities to service automation.
- **Autonomous ITSM:** Autonomous ITSM describes systems that detect, diagnose, and resolve issues without human intervention. These self-healing workflows reduce downtime and free up human resources for strategic tasks.
- **Proactive Services:** Proactive services use AI to anticipate issues and offer solutions before users even report a problem. This shifts ITSM from a reactive model to one focused on preventing disruptions and enhancing user trust.

- **Experience Personalization:** AI-driven personalization tailors the ITSM interface, suggestions, and workflows based on individual user behavior and role. It creates intuitive, context-aware service journeys that improve satisfaction and efficiency.
- **Design Thinking:** Design thinking is a user-centered methodology that emphasizes empathy, ideation, and iterative prototyping. When applied to AI in ITSM, it ensures solutions are practical, ethical, and grounded in real user needs.
- **Prompt Engineering:** Prompt engineering involves crafting precise inputs or "prompts" to extract accurate, useful outputs from generative AI systems. It is becoming a key skill for leveraging AI tools such as ChatGPT effectively in service operations.
- **Sentiment Analysis:** Sentiment analysis uses AI to assess emotional tone in user communications. This helps ITSM teams tailor responses with empathy and escalate appropriately based on detected frustration or urgency.
- **AI Governance:** AI governance involves establishing policies and controls to ensure that AI systems are ethical, explainable, and compliant. In ITSM, it safeguards against biased decisions and promotes trust in automation.
- **Sustainability Metrics:** Sustainability metrics in ITSM include data points such as energy consumption, carbon footprint, and digital efficiency. AI helps track and optimize these metrics to support environmentally responsible operations.
- **Continual Learning Models:** Continual learning models improve over time by incorporating feedback and adjusting to new data patterns. These adaptive systems ensure that AI-driven ITSM solutions remain accurate, relevant, and resilient.

Index

A

AI, architecture 62
AI, concepts
  Deep Learning (DL) 64
  Machine Learning (ML) 62
  Natural Language Processing (NLP) 65
AI, demonstrating 6-8
AI-Driven Metrics 236
AI-Driven Metrics, architecture 236
AI-Driven Metrics, categories
  Business Value 239
  Operational Efficiency 237
  Service Quality/Accuracy 238
  User Experience 238
AI-Driven Metrics, fundamentals
  Baseline/Benchmarks 240
  Continual Improvement Cycle 243, 244
  Mean Time To Resolve (MTTR) 241
  Pitfalls 242
  Power BI/Tableau 242
  Telecom Service Desk 240
AI, ensuring 2-5
AIOps 17, 108
AIOps, architecture 108, 109
AIOps, capabilities 18
  Anomaly Detection 114
  Event Correlation 113
  Root Cause Analysis (RCA) 114
AIOps, configuring 17
AIOps, ensuring 18, 19
AIOps, functions 109
AIOps, integrating 112
AIOps, scenario
  E-Commerce Platform 110
  Financial Institution 111
  Nighttime Outage 109, 110
AIOps, steps 18
AI-Powered Forecasting 153
AI-Powered Forecasting, architecture 154
AI-Powered Forecasting, configuring 154
AI-Powered Forecasting, scenarios
  Insurance Company 155
  Retail Company 155
AI-Powered Forecasting, takeaways 156
AI-Powered Forecasting, techniques 154
AI-Powered Forecasting, tips 156
AI-Powered ITSM 208
AI-Powered ITSM, concepts
  Adaptive AI Governance 211
  Cross-Border Data Processing 210
  GDPR 208
  Governance Integration 211
  ISO/IEC 42001 209
  Personally Identifiable Information (PII) 210
  User Communication 211
AI-Readiness Assessment 185

AI-Readiness Assessment, concepts
Culture 192
Data 191
Skills 190
Tooling 193
AI-Readiness Assessment, configuring 185, 186
AI-Readiness Assessment, dimensions 186
AI-Readiness Assessment, implementing 188, 189
AI-Readiness Assessment, levels 187
AI-Readiness Assessment, scenarios
Jira Service Management 188
ManageEngine 188
ServiceNow Customer 187
AI, technologies
Deep Learning (DL) 73
Machine Learning (ML) 73
Natural Language Processing (NLP) 73
Supervised Learning 73
Unsupervised Learning 74
Artificial Intelligence (AI) 2
Augments Service Professionals 250
Augments Service Professionals, ensuring 250, 251
Augments Service Professionals, illustrating 252-254
Auto-Remediation 94
Auto-Remediation, ensuring 95

C

Change Enablement 144
Change Enablement, challenges 147
Change Enablement, configuring 146
Change Enablement, illustrating 145, 146
Change Enablement, practices 147
Change Risk Analysis 144
Change Risk Analysis, components
Data Inputs 145
ML-Based Risk Scoring 145
Risk Mitigation 145
ChatGPT 84
ChatGPT, architecture 84
ChatGPT, capabilities
Conversational Ticketing 85
Drafting Response 85
Knowledge Retrieval 85
Natural Language Understanding (NLU) 84
Process/Script Guidance 85
Training/Onboarding 85
ChatGPT, challenges
Accuracy/Hallucination 86
Governance/Auditability 87
Organization-Specific Context 87
Security/Data Privacy 87
ChatGPT, integrating 87
ChatGPT, platforms
Custom GPTs 87
Jira 87
ManageEngine 87
ServiceNow 87
ChatGPT, scenarios
Agent Sidekick 86
End-User Support 85
Knowledge Base Drafting 86
Continual Improvement 33, 233
Continual Improvement, ensuring 168, 233, 234
Continual Improvement, implementing 169-171
Continual Improvement, preventing 235

D

Deep Learning (DL) 15, 64
Design Thinking 272
Design Thinking, ensuring 272-274
DL, demonstrating 64, 65
DL, ensuring 16, 17
DL, steps 16

G

GenAI, architecture 80
GenAI, implications 83
GenAI, limitations
  Auditability 82
  Bias/Relevance 82
  Data Privacy 82
  Hallucination 82
GenAI, terms
  Fine-Tuning/Context Injection 81
  Large Language Models (LLMs) 81
  Prompt Engineering 81
  Transformer Architecture 81
GenAI, use cases
  Conversational AI 81
  Knowledge Article Generation 81
  Policy Drafting 81
  Runbook/Script Generation 81
  Ticket Summarization 81
Generative AI (GenAI) 80
Governance 166
Governance, ensuring 166

I

Intelligent Service Delivery 260
Intelligent Service Delivery, ensuring 261
Intelligent Service Delivery, terms
  AI-Powered ITSM 262
  Humanity Embedding 262
Intelligent Service Delivery, use cases 260
ITIL 4 162
ITIL4 27, 115
ITIL4, case studies
  Banking Institution 135
  Government IT Agency Detects 136
  Healthcare Group Automates 134
  Insurance Firm 134
  Manufacture Firm 135
  Predictive Maintenance 136
  Retail Chain Detects 135
  Telecom Giant Cuts 133
  University IT Helpdesk 136
  User Sentiment 137
ITIL4, ensuring 27, 28
ITIL4, operations
  Event Management 116
  Incident Management 117
  Problem Management 117
ITIL 4, pillars
  Continual Improvement 167
  Governance 166
  Service Design 167
ITIL 4, principles
  Auto-Triaging 165
  Data Existing 162
  Decision-Making 164
  Focus Value 162
  Holistically View 164
  Progress Iteratively 163
  Promote Visibility 163
IT Operations 9
IT Operations, evolution 9
IT Operations, phases
  AI-Enabled Automation 10
  AIOps/Cognitive Automation 10
  Rule-Based Automation 10
IT Service Management (ITSM) 11, 25
ITSM, architecture 25
ITSM, breakdown
  AIOps 17
  Deep Learning (DL) 15
  Machine Learning (ML) 12
  Natural Language Processing (NLP) 13
ITSM, characteristics 26
ITSM, goals 26
ITSM, insights
  Automated incident 129
  Auto-Routing 128
  Root Cause Analysis (RCA) 129
  Root Cause Prediction 129
  Ticket Triaging 128

ITSM, issues
- Data Overload 46
- Decision-Making/Prioritization 47
- Delay Response 46
- Operational Intelligence 49
- Reassignment Loops 48
- Repetitive Tasks 45
- Structured Knowledge Bases 49

ITSM, pillars
- Accuracy 52
- Boost Efficiency 51
- Drive Proactivity 53

ITSM, sections
- Auto-Remediation 94
- Long-Term Transformation 55
- Phased Balancing 56
- Quick Wins 54
- Sentiment Analysis 93
- Ticket Classification 93

ITSM, tools
- Jira Service Management 90
- ManageEngine 89
- ServiceNow 88

ITSM, trends
- AI-Powered Experience Personalization 276
- Auto-Triaging 275
- Continual Learning 279
- Conversational AI 278
- Democratization 277
- Intelligent Monitoring 279
- Policy-based Engines 276
- Regulation/Ethics 277

J

Jira Service Management 90
Jira Service Management, features 90

L

Long-Term Transformation 55
Long-Term Transformation, characteristics 56
Long-Term Transformation, strategic
- AI-Augmented Asset 56
- AI-Driven Continual Improvement 56
- AIOps/Predictive Incident Management 55
- Intelligent Automation Orchestration 56

M

Machine Learning (ML) 12, 62
ManageEngine 89
ManageEngine, features 89
Maturity Models 231
Maturity Models, architecture 231
Maturity Models, ensuring 232
ML, configuring 12, 13
ML, demonstrating 62, 63
ML, types 12

N

Natural Language Processing (NLP) 13, 65
NLP, capabilities 14
NLP, demonstrating 65, 66
NLP, ensuring 14, 15
NLP, steps 14
Noise Reduction 131
Noise Reduction, integrating 131
Noise Reduction, objectives 131

O

Operational Systems 119
Operational Systems, architecture 119
Operational Systems, challenges
- Data Quality 122
- Explainability 122
- Human Oversight 122
- Security 122

Operational Systems, stages 121
Operational Systems, use cases
  Action Suggestion 120
  Conversational RCA 120
  Problem Management 121
Organizational Risk 213
Organizational Risk, frameworks
  COBIT 2019 214
  COSO ERM Framework 214
  ISO 31000 213
  NIST RMF 214
Organizational Risk, terms
  Adaptive Risk Management 220
  Controls/Mitigations, implementing 217
  ITIL4 Governance 218
  Risk Domains 215
  Roles Aligning 216
  Service Continuity 219
  Ticker Classification 216

P

Pattern Detection 132
Pattern Detection, illustrating 132

Q

Quick Wins 54
Quick Wins, characteristics 55
Quick Wins, lists
  AI-Powered Virtual Agents 55
  Auto-Categorization/Ticket Routing 55
  Knowledge Article Recommendations 55

R

Responsible AI 204
Responsible AI, architecture 204
Responsible AI, configuring 205
Responsible AI, implementing 207, 208
Responsible AI, terms
  Auto-Triage System 206
  Hallucination/ Inaccuracy 205, 206
  Robust Governance 207

S

Scale Responsibly 194
Scale Responsibly, terms
  Essential Guardrails 197
  High-Volume Tasks 195
  Natural Temptation 196
  Risk Mitigation 194
  Service Desh Team 196
  Ticket Logging 198
Sentiment Analysis 93
Sentiment Analysis, ensuring 94
Service Design 167
Service Design, enhancing 167
Service Environments, concepts
  Supervised Learning 71
  Unsupervised Learning 71
Service Experience 272
Service Experience, architecture 272
ServiceNow 88
ServiceNow, features 88, 89
Service Value Chain (SVC) 31
Service Value System (SVS) 29
SFIA 256
SFIA, concepts
  Continuous Learning 257
  Mindset 258
  Procedural Knowledge 257
  Task Execution 257
SFIA, scenarios 258, 259
Smart KBs, features 150
Smart KBs, implementing 151
Smart Knowledge Bases (KBs) 149
Strategic Adoption Model 226
Strategic Adoption Model, ensuring 226, 227
Supervised Learning 68
Supervised Learning, cons 69
Supervised Learning, pros 69
Supervised Learning, scenario 70
Supervised Learning, steps 68

Supervised/Unsupervised, comparing 69
SVC, activities
- Deliver/Support 32, 175
- Design/Transition 32, 174
- Engage 32, 173
- Improve 32, 173
- Obtain/Build 32, 174
- Plan 32, 172

SVC, concepts
- Deliver/Support 178
- Design/Transition 177
- Engage 176
- Improve 178
- Obtain/Build 177
- Plan 177

SVC, ensuring 33
SVS, configuring 29
SVS, ensuring 31
SVS, principles 30, 31

T

Tactical Adoption Model 227
Tactical Adoption Model, ensuring 227, 228
Tactical/Strategic Adoption, comparing 228, 229
Tactical/Strategic Adoption, integrating 230
Tactical/Strategic Adoption, pitfalls 229
Ticket Classification 93
Ticket Classification, configuring 93
Traditional ITSM 26
Traditional ITSM, architecture 37
Traditional ITSM, capabilities 39
Traditional ITSM, challenges 27
Traditional ITSM, ensuring 39
Traditional ITSM, issues 38
Traditional ITSM, limitations 37

U

Unsupervised Learning 68
Unsupervised Learning, cons 70
Unsupervised Learning, pros 69
Unsupervised Learning, scenario 70
Unsupervised Learning, steps 68

V

Value Streams 35
Value Streams, benefits 36
Value Streams, concepts 36
Value Streams, configuring 35
Vendor-Neutral Perspective 96
Vendor-Neutral Perspective, breakdown 97
Vendor-Neutral Perspective, checklist 98
Vendor-Neutral Perspective, configuring 97
Vendor-Neutral Perspective, practices 98
Vendor-Neutral Perspective, scenarios 99
Virtual Assistants 148
Virtual Assistants, capabilities 148
Virtual Assistants, ensuring 149
Virtual Assistants/Smart KBs, demonstating 151
Virtual Assistants/Smart KBs, takeaways 152
Virtual Assistants/Smart KBs, workflow
- Continuous Training 152
- Data Quality 152
- Governance 152
- Multi-Language 152